Jossey-Bass Teacher

Jossey-Bass Teacher provides educators with practical knowledge and tools to create a positive and lifelong impact on student learning. We offer classroom-tested and research-based teaching resources for a variety of grade levels and subject areas. Whether you are an aspiring, new, or veteran teacher, we want to help you make every teaching day your best.

From ready-to-use classroom activities to the latest teaching framework, our value-packed books provide insightful, practical, and comprehensive materials on the topics that matter most to K–12 teachers. We hope to become your trusted source for the best ideas from the most experienced and respected experts in the field.

More Praise For Celebrating Every Learner

"The collective voices and knowledge of forty-six educators with over twenty years of experience in using MI can't be wrong! An essential tool for any school or teacher that values differentiation and strives to meet the learning needs of each and every student."

—**Linda S. Nelson,** executive director, North Carolina Association of Independent Schools

"In *Celebrating Every Learner,* the teachers and staff at New City School write of their experiences using a multiple intelligences curriculum, which will strongly inform any teacher or principal looking to create powerful experiences for their own students."

—**Christine Kunkel, Ph. D.,** principal, Key Learning Community

"For over twenty years the faculty of New City School has set the standard for school-based teacher research and cutting-edge classroom practice. *Celebrating Every Learner* provides educators and leaders world-wide with inspiration and tools to create the schools that their learners need."

—**Mike Fleetham,** Learning Design Consultant, UK, www.thinkingclassroom.co.uk; author, *Multiple Intelligences in Practice* and coauthor, *Creating Extraordinary Teachers*

"*Celebrating Every Learner* is a treasure trove of practical wisdom gleaned from decades of teachers providing students with an inspired education. This book describes exemplary work that should inspire all teachers (and all principals!) around the world."

—**Branton Shearer, Ph.D.,** MI Research and Consulting, Inc., Kent State University; coauthor, *Creating Extraordinary Teachers*

Acknowledgments

Many people deserve to be acknowledged with appreciation for accompanying us on our multiple intelligences (MI) journey. What began over twenty years ago as a faculty book group reading Howard Gardner's *Frames of Mind* has evolved to become a school that values all of the ways in which children can grow and prosper.

None of our students' parents were fortunate enough to attend an MI school, and we acknowledge the confidence that they have shown in us. They are part of the educational process too; they attend intake conferences, help with dioramas, come to egg drops and student museums, attend student performances, and review the contents of portfolios.

Our board of trustees has consistently shown enthusiasm for our work with MI, our MI conferences, and our MI books. They value what we do for our students, and they support us in every way. Our school's mission statement includes the phrase "As an international leader in elementary education," and the board also appreciates our efforts to help educators around the globe grapple with the best way to use MI.

Dr. Howard Gardner, of course, deserves a special acknowledgment. He not only conceived of the theory of multiple intelligences, but he also has been a friend to New City School. He has visited us, spoken at our conferences, and cut the ribbon to open our MI library. It is so clear that Howard always has students' interests at heart! We appreciate his creativity, care, and enthusiasm.

Dedication

This book is dedicated to the students of New City School: those who have been here in the past, those who are here now, and those who will join us in the future. Their curiosity and passion for learning inspire and reward us. Through and with them, we work to make the world a better place for everyone.

Contents

CHAPTER **3**

The Bodily-Kinesthetic Intelligence

 CHAPTER **4**

The Linguistic Intelligence

CHAPTER **5**

The Logical-Mathematical Intelligence

CHAPTER **6**

The Musical Intelligence

CHAPTER **7**

The Spatial Intelligence

 CHAPTER **8**

The Naturalist Intelligence

Lesson Plans:

Part 2. Putting It All Together with the Multiple Intelligences

CHAPTER **9**

Different Intelligences Are an Aspect of Diversity *by Sheryl Reardon*

CHAPTER **10**

Learning Through Simulations
by Susie Burge

CHAPTER **11**

Assessing Through PEPs (Projects, Exhibitions, Presentations) *by Julie Stevens*

CHAPTER **12**

Assessment at New City School
by Pat Nuernberger

Foreword

I first began to think about the topic of multiple intelligences in the middle 1970s, though I did not coin the phrase "multiple intelligences" until a few years later. At the time, I thought of this line of research on the structure and development of the mind as relevant primarily to psychologists—particularly those in the specialties of cognitive psychology, developmental psychology, and neuropsychology. I was as surprised as anyone that the interest in these ideas came chiefly from the educational sector, rather than from colleagues in psychology. Yet fairly soon it became evident that, for a variety of reasons, the idea of multiple intelligences could be useful to many educators—even as, for a variety of reasons, it proved threatening or destabilizing to many psychologists.

Still, it came as a complete surprise to me when educators actually began to talk about *schools*—rather than classroom posters, nooks, or practices—that were built significantly around the idea of multiple intelligences. The first enterprise to get off the ground was the Key School (now called the Key Learning Community) in Indianapolis. Launched in 1987, it has pioneered in many infectious educational practices, ranging from video portfolios to cross-age, interest-driven pods to a "flow room." Through many ups and downs, it now consists of pre-K through 12, including a middle school and a high school. It's been visited by thousands of educators from all over the world and has influenced practices in many places.

To my knowledge, the second MI school is the New City School (NCS). Whereas Key is a public school, NCS is a private school. NCS began in the late 1960s, as a pioneering effort to provide quality education for an increasingly diverse urban population. NCS was about twenty years old when Tom Hoerr, then a relatively new head of school, first proposed that the school cast itself in an MI mode. Since then, NCS has taken MI ideas very seriously and has created a variety of innovations that, like those of the Key Learning Community, have had considerable influence beyond its walls. Further, the School has sponsored international conferences, created new entities such as an MI Library and a Centennial Garden, and issued a series of publications, including this book you are reading.

What I've written to this point is part of the educational history of our time. Donning a more personal hat, I'd like now to set down my own impressions of why the New City School occupies a very special place within that history.

From the start, the move to MI has been a cooperative enterprise. Tom Hoerr has worked closely with faculty, students, parents, and board to avoid any sense of a top-down dictate. No one has been forced to get on the MI bandwagon; proposals, criticisms, recalibrations have been encouraged and taken seriously.

Indeed, NCS strikes me as the embodiment of a learning organization. Although that term is bandied about frequently in both the business and the educational worlds, it has been honored as much in the breach as in the observance. NCS is a deeply and pervasively reflective environment. The community tries things out, seeks to learn from experiments, corrects course when necessary, and, in cases of success, seeks to understand the reasons for the success and how to build upon it. In addition to Tom Hoerr's writings over the years, Christine Wallach's chapter on how to become an MI school provides a valuable guide to the launch and maintenance of a learning organization.

Of the many facets of MI, NCS has had a particular commitment to the personal intelligences. Like any parent, I try not to play favorites among the intelligences—each is and will continue to be an important part of human nature, human experience, and human potential. Yet whenever I am asked about the intelligences that are most important to attend to at the present time, I think of, and usually cite, the personal intelligences. In an increasingly diverse and complex world, we need to be able to understand and make common cause with others, whether or not they happen to look and think the way that we do. That effort requires interpersonal intelligence. Correlatively, in the twenty-first century, each of us needs to make consequential decisions about what work to pursue, where to live, what to do when things don't work out, and, more holistically, the kind of person we want to be, and how to achieve that goal. In the absence of intrapersonal intelligence, it is not possible to function successfully. To my knowledge, the faculty of NCS has no educational peer in thinking about the cultivation of the personal intelligences.

Drawing on biological terminology, I make a sharp distinction between phenotypic and genotypic implementations of key ideas. In many schools that I visit, one sees the external, phenotypic accoutrements of MI—many MI signs displayed, corners of rooms labeled in terms of the intelligences, and youngsters bantering in the patois of MI. This embracing of MI is fine and flattering, but it can be superficial—actual practices may bear few if any enduring marks of MI ways of thinking. In contrast, at NCS the deeper ideas of MI have become part of the DNA. Teachers and staff take individual differences seriously; important lessons are conveyed in many ways. And it's significant that the lesson plans detailed here don't slavishly claim to capture a single intelligence; rather, they leave open the possibilities that lessons can be conveyed and taught in multiple ways, and that individuals may activate different intelligences as they tackle various problems, puzzles, and points. As a consequence, at the NCS the MI whole is far greater than the sum of its parts—genotype trumps phenotype.

From the start, NCS clearly sought to embody the best lessons of progressive education. Alas, within the American educational landscape, the last decades have not been kind to progressive ideas and practices. Without attempting to tease out the reasons for this rough ride, I will simply assert that progressive education—in the tradition of John Dewey, Jerome Bruner, Deborah Meier, Carmelita Hinton, and Theodore Sizer—remains the most distinctly American education in the world. Whatever the flaws and challenges of progressive education, it would be tragic if our nation were to turn its back on the brilliant ideas and practices pioneered by the progressives in the early part of the twentieth century and brought to fruition in many locales in the latter half of the century.

The New City School is a vivid example of how Progressive Education can continue to thrive even in a climate that is not hospitable. Many persons deserve credit for this commitment. But it is important and appropriate to single out Tom Hoerr, for over twenty years the courageous and thoughtful leader of the School. Tom is a progressive educator par excellence. In his leadership at NCS, and increasingly across the nation and abroad, he has embodied both the ideas and the approaches of this lively approach that truly leaves no child behind. To the extent that MI theory is part of the progressive tradition, Tom and his colleagues have found a place for its ideas within their broader educational firmament. To Tom, and to his wonderful colleagues at NCS and throughout the world, I offer my profound gratitude.

HOWARD GARDNER

Introduction

BY THOMAS R. HOERR

THE EVOLUTION OF MI

Howard Gardner spoke to human potential when he wrote *Frames of Mind* in 1983. He was a lone voice making a case that there were many different ways to be smart. To be sure, a few psychologists had speculated on multiple forms of intellect before Gardner, but none did so with his sense of definition and flair. Despite the initial resistance to MI, it has become more and more commonly accepted among educators. Psychologists and psychometricans, those who make their living (or maintain their self-concept) by relying on "g"—a single definition of intelligence—still resist MI, but educators who work in schools recognize its possibilities because they see MI in their students.

Since the publication of *Frames of Mind*, many others have argued that intelligence is more than a unidimensional quality. Robert Sternberg developed the triarchic theory of intelligence, and Daniel Goleman identified emotional intelligence. Other writers, such as Daniel Pink and Tony Wagner, have argued that success in the real world relies on more than just "school smarts." I have also written about the distributed intelligence—that is, the notion that intellect is not limited to what is inside one's skin.

Enthusiasm for MI has grown and spread. For example, *MI Around the World*, edited by Jie-Qi Chen, Seana Moran, and Howard Gardner, depicts how MI is implemented in China, Japan, the Philippines, South Korea, Australia, Norway, Denmark, England, Ireland, Scotland, Romania, Turkey, Argentina, Colombia, and the United States. Today, although there remain critics and naysayers, MI is seen as a valid and valuable tool for teaching children. The assessment mantra in the United States has made it more challenging for educators to bring MI into their schools and classrooms, but this, too, shall pass. As we see the changing and more challenging shape of the world described by Thomas Friedman (*The World Is Flat*) and Ted Fishman (*China, Inc.*), it becomes clearer and clearer that we need to capitalize on all of children's intelligences.

THIS BOOK

There has been a spate of books about MI in the past fifteen to twenty years. There are MI books that offer curriculum plans, those that suggest assessment techniques, and some that contain philosophical ruminations. To our knowledge, however, no other MI book has been written by an entire faculty, and no other MI book encompasses all of these aspects of MI. Our book is a valuable resource in several ways. First, the voices of eighteen New City School faculty members are presented in articles written about MI implementation. They speak from their experience and perspective as grade level teachers, specialist teachers, and administrators. Second, all forty-six faculty members were involved in the creation of our sixty-four lesson plans, which address purpose, procedure, assessment, and MI extensions. Finally, our book includes an administrative thrust and addresses student assessment, collegiality, and communication with parents. These factors are relevant to all teachers, whether MI is implemented in a classroom or on a school-wide basis.

We have tried to make this book as user-friendly as possible. It is organized by intelligence and by grade level group (preprimary, primary, and intermediate). Preprimary includes three-year-olds through kindergarteners. Our primary classes are grades one, two, and three. Our intermediate classes are grades four, five, and six. Graphics are used so that the reader can either peruse the pages looking at all of the lessons for a particular age or grade of child or focus on lessons designed for specific intelligences, regardless of the age of the child. Each lesson contains MI extension ideas for all of the intelligences. Of course, just as the intelligences are not totally distinct from one another, so too, despite their major focus, each of the lessons uses a variety of intelligences.

The following icons provide quick reference to the intelligence being discussed:

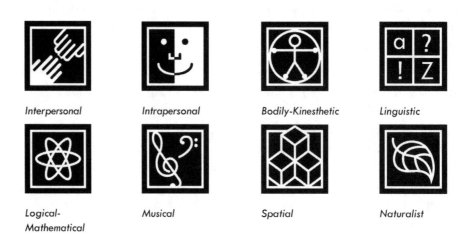

A graphic designation on each lesson plan will help you to quickly see how it fits into your curriculum. The following example signifies an interpersonal activity for the primary grades (1, 2, and 3) in the area of science.

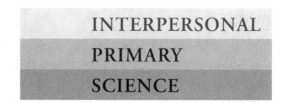

Each intelligence chapter begins with an article about that intelligence. We also include articles in Part II that explain different aspects of our MI implementation in some depth.

NEW CITY SCHOOL

The New City School is not a typical school. Prior to our discovery of MI, we were a school that valued the arts, experiential learning, and human diversity. As I noted in my book *Becoming a Multiple Intelligences School*, implementing MI seemed natural to us. Our work with MI helped us achieve what Roland Barth describes in *Improving Schools from Within* as faculty collegiality: if children are to learn and grow, their teachers must learn and grow.

We began using MI in 1988 (and were the second school to do so, after the Key School in Indianapolis). Our work with MI has evolved, and we are a different school than we were fifteen years ago when we wrote our initial MI book. We have hosted four MI conferences and are visited by hundreds of educators each year. We opened the world's first MI library in 2005. I facilitate the ASCD MI Network and distribute four on-line newsletters, "Intelligence Connections." (Send me an e-mail if you would like a free subscription.) But our work with pursuing and investigating MI is not finished. We continue to seek the best ways to bring MI into our classrooms, to work at finding the necessary balance between traditional, skill-based instruction and using MI.

New City is a unique independent school. We strive to be a diverse school in every way. This means that our students come to us from a variety of neighborhoods, representing a range of incomes (a third of our students receive need-based financial aid); 35 percent of our students are students of color, and our students represent a range of MI profiles. Some of our students excel in the scholastic intelligences (linguistic and logical-mathematical) and some do not. We like that mix! We administer a standardized achievement test each spring, and our students do very well, as they should; they come from homes where education is valued.

We hope that you find this book useful and interesting. Please feel free to send me an e-mail if you have any questions or comments. And if you can make it to St. Louis, we'd love to have you visit New City School (www.newcityschool.org).

Thomas R. Hoerr, Head of School

trhoerr@newcityschool.org

Part 1

The Multiple Intelligences

> "But an important variable in leadership seems to be the ability to sense, to be aware of, what is going on in oneself as well as what is happening in the group or organization."
>
> —JOSEPH LUFT

1

Photograph: Patti Gabriel

The Interpersonal Intelligence

Web of the Interpersonal Intelligence

Student Quotes

" Having a strong Interpersonal Intelligence is not only about interacting with others, but also thinking for and about others. "

" I'm Interpersonal because I get along with people. I share my markers with my brother and my games with my sister. "

" I'm Interpesonal because I like to work in groups and hear someone else's point of view and what they are thinking. "

" I love to be around people, and I like to figure things out by talking with others. "

Characteristics

- Enjoys cooperative games, demonstrates empathy toward others, has lots of friends, is admired by peers, displays leadership skills, prefers group problem solving, can mediate conflicts, understand and recognizes stereotypes and prejudices

Famous People

BARACK OBAMA is the forty-fourth president of the United States and the first African American to hold that office.

ELEANOR ROOSEVELT advocated for social reforms that helped the disadvantaged.

OPRAH WINFREY is the host of an internationally syndicated talk show and considered one of the most influential women in the world.

MAHATMA GANDHI was the preeminent political and spiritual leader of India during the Indian independence movement.

Adult Quotes

" The best way to cheer yourself up is to try to cheer somebody else up. "
—MARK TWAIN

" Emotional intelligence emerges as a much stronger predictor of who will be most successful, because it is how we handle ourselves in our relationships that determines how well we do once we are in a given job. "
—DANIEL GOLEMAN

The Interpersonal Intelligence

BY LAURIE FALK

In understanding the development of children, there has long been a debate of nature versus nurture. How much comes with a child on the day of birth? How much can we teach? By and large, the answer to the nature/nurture debate is that *both* matter. This is true for all of the intelligences, including the Interpersonal Intelligence—the ability to understand people and relationships. We, as educators, belong to the set of nurturers in a child's life, and the school setting offers a prime location for development of the Interpersonal Intelligence—a very important intelligence indeed!

When babies are born, they are by necessity egocentric creatures. Before long, though, they embark on interactions with parents and caregivers that begin their interpersonal journey. Throughout their development, children are constantly learning about themselves and how they are connected to the outside world. This interplay between the developing Intrapersonal and Interpersonal intelligences and relationships with self and with others continues throughout life, but its foundations are set in childhood. We are social animals, and a sense of belonging is critical to our emotional health and well-being. However, the rules, norms, and expectations of social interactions are very complex. Add innate temperament, varied family backgrounds, and cultural diversity to the mix and the task of teaching the Interpersonal Intelligence can seem almost overwhelming. But this need not be the case.

There are some important facts about the development of the Interpersonal Intelligence to keep in mind. First, much of this happens organically as human beings constantly interact with each other in many settings throughout life. This development of social learning is obvious with younger children. For example, one expects very young children to learn that verbal expression is more appropriate than physical aggression. One need only to watch a group of four year-olds and their teachers to see this skill being taught and progress being made. This kind of teaching is critical to the development of social skills. The school setting gives the adults a chance to intervene and use those teachable moments when interpersonal interactions are not going according to standards of acceptable behavior. It is imperative that we attend to child-to-child and child-to-adult interactions and use the opportunities that present themselves to teach children appropriate behaviors in real time. However, it is not just young children whose social interactions need to be observed and corrected—the fourth grade student who makes fun of another student needs adult intervention just as much as the four-year-old does.

> We, as educators, belong to the set of nurturers in a child's life, and the school setting offers a prime location for development of the Interpersonal Intelligence—a very important intelligence indeed!

It is imperative that we attend to child-to-child and child-to-adult interactions and use the opportunities that present themselves to teach children appropriate behaviors in real time.

This experiential teaching tool is invaluable; it can seem time-consuming, but it is time well spent. Regardless of a student's age, we need to intervene when the opportunity presents itself; after all, we are also teaching when we ignore inappropriate behaviors.

In addition to using teachable moments, the development of an Interpersonal Intelligence should also be taught from a planned curriculum. Specific interpersonal lessons are no different than math or linguistic lessons. If something needs to be learned, it must be consciously taught and reinforced. For example, a teamwork lesson would include instruction on the rationale for working together in groups, the specific steps to doing so successfully, and explanations of the interactive process. Then there would be a practice activity on teamwork. But this is not a one-time lesson or practice session. Teachers must give students many opportunities to practice all the skills needed for successful teamwork and acknowledge the students when they are using these skills appropriately. Additionally, they must allocate time for student reflection. If students are to learn from their experiences, it is important that they consciously think about what happened and their role in it.

If something needs to be learned, it must be consciously taught and reinforced. If students are to learn from their experiences, it is important that they consciously think about what happened and their role in it.

Just as in teaching mathematics or history, reflection is best if it is done in different ways. Certainly there are times when a group discussion provides students with the chance to process the lesson together and to engage in a group activity where insights can be shared. At other times, however, individual reflection can take place by writing in journals or by reflecting on a few questions during quiet time allocated for thinking about what the lesson means to them. Reflection should happen often so that it becomes automatic and so that students develop the habit of evaluating their feelings, behavior, motivation, and performance. This process gives students the means to internalize their experiences and connect their Interpersonal and Intrapersonal intelligences.

The combination of specifically teaching the Interpersonal Intelligence through lessons that address interpersonal skills and using teachable moments to educate in real time is powerful and effective.

The number and variety of interpersonal skills to be mastered are significant and complex. Respect, cooperation, empathy, compromise, caring, assertiveness, negotiation—these are but of few of the interpersonal skills we need to teach. And if they are to be internalized and learned, they cannot be taught and practiced just once. There is a critical need to teach the skills multiple times with increasing complexity as children develop. The combination of specifically teaching the Interpersonal Intelligence through lessons that address interpersonal skills and using teachable moments to educate in real time is powerful and effective. We must continuously recognize and reinforce these skills. Often, this is a simple statement said privately to a student—"I noticed you were willing to compromise when the group wanted to go with someone else's idea." These observations and comments can be tailored to a student's temperament, strengths, and challenges. A shy student can be noticed being more assertive and an argumentative student can be reinforced for efforts to get along with others. Reinforcing positive behavior helps to build the Interpersonal skills that don't come as easily to some individuals as they do to others. Of course, these teachable moments also need to be used when the behavior does not meet with expectations, but the same kind of simple, private statement can be used—"I see that your group can't decide on a plan and you're the only one who wants it your way. Do you think you can compromise?" A key component of this technique is to keep the teacher language nonjudgmental and unemotional. The student should be self-motivated to do the right thing because it's the right thing to do, not because it pleases others. This requires teachers to observe constantly and comment often, but it will solidify the development of Interpersonal skills in a meaningful and permanent way.

Success is measured in many ways in school and in life. Real success, though, comes with a sense of happiness and satisfaction. Human beings need human interaction and relationships. The goal in all schools should be to recognize the value of the Interpersonal Intelligence and to teach and encourage its development in every student.

The goal in all schools should be to recognize the value of the Interpersonal Intelligence and to teach and encourage its development in every student.

Picture This!

INTERPERSONAL

PRIMARY

SOCIAL STUDIES

PURPOSE:

Cooperation, compromise, and communication are directly taught as small groups work together to draw pictures. Over the course of four days, the groups are required to make more decisions to complete the pictures.

MATERIALS:

Four large sheets of paper per group, markers, task sheet, chart paper, rating sheet

PROCEDURE:

1. Children work in the same group of three or four children throughout the activity. Each day, as a warm-up, the groups are given a question upon which they must reach consensus:

   If you could change one thing about our class, what would it be?

   What is a chore at home you dislike doing?

   If you had to eat one food for lunch for a week, what would it be?

   What is a book you all like?

   If you could learn a new musical instrument, what would it be?

   After the groups reach consensus, have a brief check-in and ask questions, such as "Who had to compromise?" "What was hard?" and "What made it easy?"

2. Explain that each group works together to draw a picture. Discuss what problems might arise. Tell the class you will be circulating and jotting down notes of things you see and hear that indicate people are working cooperatively. Ask the children to give examples of what you might hear and see.

3. Give each group the first task sheet. Before they begin to draw, encourage the groups to make a plan and talk about how they will divide the tasks.

4. Walk around and record things you hear, such as "OK," "What do you think?" "That is a good idea!" "Is it OK if I . . . ," and "How about . . . ?"

5. When the pictures are completed, gather the class and share some of the things you heard and saw, recording them on a chart to display.

6. Ask the class how things went in their groups. Children should offer comments without mentioning specific names. Ask questions such as "What might you do differently the next day?" "Is everyone having the chance to offer ideas?" "Is anyone taking over?" "Did anyone have to compromise?"

7. Each child privately fills out a rating sheet showing how their group cooperated and then gives a one to five rating, with one being uncooperative and five being very cooperative, to each member of the group including him or herself.

8. Follow the same procedure on each of the next three days with tasks 2, 3, and 4. Start each day with a consensus-building question, then go over the charts and talk about what behaviors they want to improve. On the last day, children reflect and share the ways they improved their ability to cooperate, compromise, and communicate during the process.

9. Create a permanent chart based on what cooperation looks and sounds like. Children sign the chart to show they will use the ideas on the chart. Hang the chart up for future reference.

ASSESSMENT/REFLECTION:

Using a class checklist, record whether the children were able to decide what to draw the last day in an appropriate amount of time and with thought and consideration for everyone in the group. Specific behaviors to note include details from the class chart that show cooperation, communication, and the ability to compromise.

MI EXTENSIONS:

The Spatial Intelligence was also used in this lesson.

Linguistic: Under the headings Cooperative Words and Uncooperative Words, children sort phrases, such as "Good idea," "I should go first," and "Give it to me!"

Bodily-Kinesthetic: Children pantomime situations of cooperation for other children to guess. For example, they might pantomime sharing materials. These ideas could be generated by the children or the teacher. The children share what would be heard in this situation.

Logical-Mathematical: Wearing badges that say "Cooperation Detectives," the class stands quietly in the back of various classrooms and jots down examples of people working cooperatively. Note words heard, body language, and things seen. Poll results and make a graph to show cooperation at various grade levels.

Intrapersonal: In their journals, students formulate and write about a goal they would like to reach to improve their ability to cooperate, compromise, or communicate.

Teamwork Task Sheet—Day 1

Work with your team to draw a picture of a house. Your picture must include:

1 house with

4 windows

1 door

1 chimney

3 trees

grass

2 clouds

1 sun

Teamwork Task Sheet—Day 2

Work with your team to draw a picture of a pond. Your picture must include:

pond

boats

fish

lily pads

grass

turtles

log

Teamwork Task Sheet—Day 3

Work with your team to draw a picture of a playground.

Teamwork Task Sheet—Day 4

Work with your team to draw a picture.

The House We Built

PURPOSE:
Students will develop the teaming skills of cooperation, compromise, and communication while discovering the architectural principle of structural strength of the triangle in geodesic domes and bridges.

INTERPERSONAL

PRIMARY

SCIENCE

MATERIALS:
Newspaper, masking tape, images of various structures: geodesic domes, bridges, columns, towers, and skyscrapers

PROCEDURE:
1. Show several pictures of structures while students discuss what they see in the images and what gives the structures their strength.
2. Divide the class into small groups. Each student makes a minimum of six newspaper rolls by rolling a section of newspaper into a tubular shape and securing the ends with masking tape.
3. Before groups begin working, review the expectations and skills important for working collaboratively so that students remember to listen, share ideas, compromise, and stay on task.
4. Instruct students to build a free-standing structure large enough for all members of the group to get inside, using only the rolled tubes and tape. Groups draw a plan for their structure and have it approved before building.

ASSESSMENT/REFLECTION:
Each student shares something he or she did that helped the group as they planned and built. Someone in each group tells the class what someone else in that group did that was helpful.

Each group devises a way to test the strength of their structure and demonstrates their method of proof.

MI EXTENSIONS:
Other intelligences used in this lesson are Spatial and Logical-Mathematical.

Bodily-Kinesthetic: Read *What It Feels Like to Be a Building* by Forrest Wilson, which uses human figures to replicate architectural structures. Students experiment with duplicating one of the human configurations shown in the book.

Logical-Mathematical: Using various building blocks, construct geometric models of buildings.

Naturalist: Find examples of animal homes and discuss what gives each one its strength.

Making Museums

INTERPERSONAL

PRIMARY

SOCIAL STUDIES

PURPOSE:

Students work together to create a museum at the end of a unit of study; for example, Plant, Body, or Westward Expansion museums. The focus is the process of working together and using the interpersonal skills of cooperation, perseverance, tenacity, compromise, communication, and problem solving. The galleries contain exhibits the students have created that show the knowledge and understandings they have gained during their studies.

MATERIALS:

Various art and craft materials children use to create exhibits for the museum and gifts for the gift shop, writing materials, poster board, samples of plaques that go with exhibits, *Katie's Picture Show* by James Mayhew, *Visiting the Art Museum* by Brown and Brown

PROCEDURE:

After talking about, reading about, and visiting museums, students create an interactive museum with exhibits pertaining to a particular area of study. The children serve as docents, security guards, clerks at the gift shop, and curators while the museum is open.

1. Discuss museums with the class and ask the following questions:

    What is a museum?

    Why do you think museums were created?

    Who has ever been to a museum?

    What types of museums are there?

    Who works in museums and what do they do there?

    What exhibits might be found in a museum?

2. Read *Katie's Picture Show,* a story about a young girl visiting a museum, and *Visiting the Art Museum.*

3. With the students, make a list of tasks necessary to create and run a museum. The list might include the following: make the exhibits, make plaques to display with the exhibits, create posters to advertise the museum, arrange the exhibits, make maps, and write invitations or fliers for visitors. Assign tasks from the list.

4. With the children, brainstorm ideas for exhibits, encouraging them to think about exhibits they have seen or read about that were memorable, fun, or interactive. Students may need help adapting their ideas for exhibits to connect with the theme of their museum. When displays are completed, the class decides how they should be organized and displayed.

5. Continue to assign jobs from the job chart, keeping in mind the strengths of the students. For those working on the plaques, show

examples and discuss what they include: title, directions, explanation of what to do and what is learned. Some children can create posters advertising the opening, while others can create brochures or maps for visitors. Price and display merchandise for the Gift Shop. Interested children practice role-playing being a docent in the museum. Consider how the interaction would change when showing around a child as opposed to an adult.

6. Just as all the students had a task setting up the museum, they should have some responsibility when the museum opens. As a class, decide what each child's role will be.

ASSESSMENT/REFLECTION:

To assess the cooperative part of working on the museum, children talk or write in journals about the parts of the project that were easy, difficult, enjoyable, or unpleasant. Children comment on how they contributed to the museum, worked in a group, shared ideas, listened, compromised, and solved problems.

When reflecting on the exhibit or product they created, children ask themselves whether their exhibit appealed to visitors or taught something, and how it might be improved.

MI EXTENSIONS:

There is an opportunity for all the intelligences to be used in this project, depending on what exhibits are made.

Linguistic: Create an audio tour of the museum by having each child write a script explaining his or her exhibit. It is recorded and then played when people go through the museum.

Intrapersonal: Make a form for visitors to complete before they leave the museum that rates their visit. It could include comments about the exhibits, gift shop, the workers, the educational value, their enjoyment, as well as a place to offer suggestions.

Logical-Mathematical: Devise a way to organize the data from the rating forms visitors filled out after their visit to the museum and discuss the results.

Musical: Make a CD of music that would be appropriate for background at the museum.

Getting to Know You

PURPOSE:

Students build community by learning about their classmates' interests through the interview process. They develop their ability to listen actively.

MATERIALS:

Teacher-created graphic organizer, class list worksheet

PROCEDURE:

1. Brainstorm a list of questions that tell what the students would like to know about each other. Use this list to create a graphic organizer.
2. Students are given a partner they do not know very well. They interview their partners, asking questions to get the information needed to fill in the organizer.
3. Students use the graphic organizer to tell the class what they have learned about his/her partner.

ASSESSMENT/REFLECTION:

After all the presentations are completed, students fill in a worksheet that has every student's name, telling something new they have learned about each of their classmates.

MI EXTENSIONS:

This lesson also uses the Linguistic Intelligence.

Logical-Mathematical: Students create a graph that shares the information collected in the interviews.

Spatial: Students draw a portrait of their partners, including symbols that represent their partners' interests.

Linguistic: Students write a paragraph that tells about the classmate they interviewed.

Bodily-Kinesthetic: After the presentations have been shared, each student pantomimes one of the interests shared by his or her partner. Having listened carefully, the class determines what that interest is.

Musical: Create a class playlist based on the favorite songs of each student. As they listen, students match the song with the person who preferred the song.

Masai Jewelry

PURPOSE:

Children create aesthetic works while learning how to organize and share materials as they work in cooperative groups. The economic concepts of scarcity and supply and demand are reinforced. Adaptations could involve the study of other cultures, works of art, or other materials. For example, the pottery or weavings of certain Native American tribes could be used as the focus. The materials will need to fit the topic explored.

MATERIALS:

Head pins; round-nosed pliers; monofilament; wires; bags containing beads, buttons, shells, and other materials; examples or pictures of Masai jewelry; teacher-created sample; scissors; inventory list worksheet and trading worksheet; a map of Africa

PROCEDURE:

1. Show the children pictures or examples of Masai jewelry and locate on a map where the Masai live. Make a list of the materials that the students see in the pictures.

2. Show the students the available materials and demonstrate how to make a necklace using the beads, wires, pliers, monofilament, and head pins.

3. Cooperative learning groups are formed, and each child is given a bag of *some* of the necessary materials (beads and pliers, or shells, wire, and scissors, and so on), an inventory list, and a trade sheet.

4. The children record what is in their bag on the inventory sheet, and then are told to begin making a necklace. It does not take them long to figure out they need to trade to get all of the necessary materials to complete a necklace. Call the students together to demonstrate how trades are recorded on the trade worksheet, then send them back to work.

5. As needed, call the students together to discuss trading strategies, to determine what is working and what is not working.

6. The students practice problem-solving strategies while recording their trades.

7. Finished necklaces are photographed and displayed.

ASSESSMENT/REFLECTION:

Observe how students interact in groups.

- Did students verbally communicate needs?
- Were students assertive in appropriate ways?

Students will use the principles of supply and demand to determine the value of the work they have created.

- Each student ranks the pictures of the group's necklaces in order, from least valuable to most valuable. They explain the reasoning they used to determine the order (for example, the group had two shells and ten glass beads; therefore a necklace with a shell is more valuable than a necklace with glass beads).
- Their rationale demonstrates their understanding of the economic principles.

MI EXTENSIONS:

During this lesson, students also used their Bodily-Kinesthetic (fine motor) and Spatial intelligences.

Intrapersonal: Students identify their reactions and feelings about this experience. Questions might include:

- How did you feel when everyone was trading materials?
- What are your feelings about the necklace you created?
- How will you solve problems in the future based on what you have learned?

Linguistic: Students create a list of rules that serve as trading agreements, based on problems they encountered and issues they confronted.

Logical-Mathematical: Based on the level of the students, the least-valuable bead or tool is given a monetary value. The students then use the trading sheets to determine the value of all the materials, creating a classroom price chart. They then determine the value of their necklace.

Musical: Instead of creating jewelry, use the same procedure to create Boombahs, a stick with various kinds of noise makers attached. It can be shaken or hit on the ground to generate a sound. For this, the materials might include anything that can make a noise—jingle bells, washers, buttons, small pie plates—and a dowel rod, stick, or small branch from a tree.

Rainforest Simulation

PURPOSE:

Students become citizens of an imaginary island country covered with rainforest. They assume roles and work to achieve goals related to their group identities. Students work to resolve conflicts while experiencing varying perspectives of diverse groups of people.

INTERPERSONAL

INTERMEDIATE

SOCIAL STUDIES

MATERIALS:

Large floor map, divided into grids, of the imaginary country of Forestia; fake money; posters to record any laws passed; and a folder for each of the five interest groups, containing a small map, goals for their group, and directions

PROCEDURE:

1. Discuss the following questions with the students:

   Why are the rainforests important?

   Should the rainforests be cut down or protected?

   What are the advantages and disadvantages of each approach?

   Should the animals and plants be protected? Why or why not?

   Are there problems with the rainforests? What are they?

   Why are the rainforests being destroyed?

2. Tell the students that different groups of people in the rainforest have different points of view. This simulation will help them understand these various perspectives. Before the simulation begins, use the following discussion questions to facilitate conflict resolution before problems arise:

   Do you think everyone in your group will agree on everything?

   How might you settle disagreements in your group?

   How might you control your attitude if your choice isn't selected?

3. Place the map on the floor and tell the students they are now citizens of Forestia. Explain that their country is an island covered mostly by rainforest, with two large cities, a mountain chain, and several rivers. It is a very poor country with few schools, hospitals, or roads. As citizens of the country, the students will decide what improvements need to be made.

4. Divide the class into five small groups, each representing a group of people in the country: the government, villagers, industrialists, environmentalists, and bankers. If you have a small number of students, you could play the role of the banker. Each group receives a folder containing a map, goals for that group, money, and directions. The

following money allocation is recommended, although other values could be assigned:

>Villagers: $10,000
>
>Environmentalists: $10,000
>
>Industrialists: $50,000
>
>Bankers: $100,000
>
>Government: $100,000

5. At the beginning of the game, no one owns land. As groups acquire land, they cover that space on the map grid using color-coded squares. Hospitals, roads, ports, railroads, and cities are added to the map as they are built. Clear-cut forest squares are colored black.

6. Each folder contains the goals for that group.

   Government Goals: You have been elected to office by the voters. Your goal is to make the best possible decisions about your country to improve it in every way possible.

   Industrialist Goals: Your goal is to establish industry, which will bring jobs, money, electricity, and badly needed goods into the country. You also want to make some profit for your investors.

   Villager Goals: You live in very crowded villages and are very poor. You do not have enough food, hospitals, schools, or roads. Your goal is to improve your lives.

   Environmentalist Goals: There are endangered species of plants and animals to be protected. Your goal is to protect and save as much of the rainforest as possible.

   Banker Goals: You are in charge of the money and land. You collect money when land is sold and mark off on the map who owns each area.

7. For each group to work efficiently, members will each have a specific role to play: a president or leader, a secretary, a treasurer, and a spokesperson. The class will define the duties of each role; for example, the job of the leader is not to be bossy, but to see that the group gets the job done, works together, and stays on task. All decisions in each group are made by majority vote.

8. The actual game can be organized in a number of ways. One way is to have two main Decision cards for each group (see the final page). As the group members discuss, vote, and choose a course of action, you can make Consequence cards. For example, if the government decided on choice #3, "Set land aside for animal preserves," they would go to a card file and pull consequence card #3. It could read, "Stop! If you have not decided on a budget, pull consequence card #1 before you proceed. Once you have a budget, you may purchase land from the bankers. The price of one square mile is $10,000." Another way is to organize a flow chart, outlining possible decisions and consequences.

9. The members of the groups must work together to resolve conflicts. Emphasize that there are no "bad guys" in this game. Every group wants what is best for the group and, to a certain extent, for the country. For example, the industrialists will bring jobs, needed goods, and money into the country. The students in any group must decide what they can do if they don't like the actions of another group. Methods of protest could include Bad Press Release cards,

which result in penalties, or Good Press Release cards, which accumulate points. Red cards could indicate emergencies, such as picketing or protestors blocking logging trucks.

10. Over the course of several days, students play the game by voting on decisions for their groups, taking action, and working to resolve conflicts with other groups.

11. The game is scored by giving one point for each goal that is attained. Talk about the various perspectives people have about the rainforest. A hungry villager with children to feed and inadequate education might not be interested in preserving birds. The students begin to realize that there are no easy answers, although some solutions are definitely better than others.

12. Take a few minutes at the end of each class period to discuss what went well, what problems arose, how conflicts were resolved, and what strategies individuals used to help promote cooperation.

ASSESSMENT/REFLECTION:

Discuss whether each group had the same point of view when they looked at the country. How were the goals of each group different? How well did each group meet its goals? What made it easy or hard to meet the goals?

What were the effects on the country? Look at who owns each section on the map and what was done with the section. What situations are similar in the real world? Students reflect on how well they played the game individually, how well their group members worked together, and how well their group compromised and worked with other groups.

MI EXTENSIONS:

During this lesson, students also used their Logical-Mathematical Intelligence.

Naturalist: Apply this simulation to a natural ecosystem in your local community, such as a river, wetlands, desert, prairie, woodlands.

Logical-Mathematical: Define a continuum in the room, one end representing 100-percent agreement, the other 100-percent disagreement. Make a number of statements about the rainforest, then have the students move to a place on the continuum that demonstrates the student's beliefs as a group member or represents the student's own personal beliefs.

Intrapersonal: Ask the students whether their own personal beliefs are the same as the group they were in. How did that feel? Did their beliefs affect how they tried to influence the group's decisions? Discuss what happens when an individual's beliefs do not match the group's beliefs.

The decision cards are used to lead players through the game. Each decision that a group makes leads them to other choices. As the game begins, each group draws their color-coded Decision Card I. They discuss, vote, and make a decision, then go to the box and draw the card for their numbered choice.

Government Decision
Card I—Choices:

1. Decide on a budget.

2. Build schools, roads, hospitals.

3. Set land aside for animal preserves.

4. Set land aside for industries to use.

5. Set land aside for villagers to farm.

Government Decision
Card II—Choices:

6. Tax the villagers.

7. Tax the industries.

8. Tax zoos and preserves.

9. Ask other countries for financial aid.

Industry Decision
Card I—Choices:

1. Try to buy land from bankers.

2. Offer jobs to the villagers.

3. Print books and papers about how Industry will help Forestia.

4. Try to buy land from villagers.

Industry Decision
Card II—Choices:

5. Cut the trees and sell the wood.

6. Start mining for gold and minerals.

7. Ask environmentalists for advice.

8. Let hunters and zoo keepers capture animals.

Villagers Decision
Card I—Choices

1. Ask government or bankers for financial support.

2. Ask government for schools and hospitals.

3. Start to cut and burn forest to plant food.

4. Look for jobs with industrialists.

Villagers Decision
Card II—Choices:

5. Start to cut and burn forest to plant land for farming food.

6. Let hunters and zoo keepers catch animals before cutting trees.

7. Cut wood and sell to industrialists.

8. Ask environmentalists for advice.

Environmentalists
Card I—Choices:

1. Try to get information on endan-gered species.
2. Try to raise money.
3. Ask government to make laws.
4. Organize a protest.
5. Print books and posters.

Environmentalists
Card II—Choices:

6. To buy land for animal preserves.
7. To print books to inform people.
8. To pay scientists to do research.
9. To set up a zoo where animals can be kept and bred.

Bankers
Card I—Choices:

1. Buy some land as an investment.
2. Ask another group to buy land.
3. Invest some money in another group.
4. Ask government to raise price of land.

Bankers
Card II—Choices:

5. Build ports for shipping.
6. Ask environmentalists for advice.
7. Build large cities; attract tourists.
8. Build roads or railroads.

Rainforest Simulation Map

The country is a small island of twenty thousand square miles surrounded by ocean. It is nearly covered with tropical rainforest; there is a river and a mountain chain in the west.

200 miles

100 miles

Gold Rush Inventions

PURPOSE:

As part of a unit on Westward Expansion, children collaborate with classmates to design a poster advertising an original and unique invention that would enable the 49ers to strike it rich during the California Gold Rush. Working cooperatively, students share ideas, brainstorm, come to consensus, and reflect on their participation and the completed project. Students learn to communicate their ideas through the spatial concepts used to design a poster.

MATERIALS:

Gold Fever! Tales from the California Gold Rush by Rosalyn Schanzer and/or *Gold Fever!* by Catherine McMorrow, poster board, art materials, gold glitter, gold pens, markers, examples of advertisement posters

PROCEDURE:

1. Read one of the books and discuss the entrepreneurial spirit of the Gold Rush. Emphasize how outlandish inventions could be sold to those who were desperate enough to believe the ridiculous claims about such inventions. Discuss whether or not these inventions could have worked and what might have motivated people to buy them.

2. Show the students' advertisement posters and identify the design components, such as title/heading, illustrations, slogans, and text. Talk about layout and space and discuss what makes them aesthetically pleasing. Draw attention to the graphic design elements of space, proximity, size, and color.

3. Small groups of students work together to design an advertisement poster. Explain the elements that each poster must include: a catchy title (invention name, such as The Goldinator or The Goldblaster), a slogan, a drawing or diagram of the invention, how the invention is used (could include a short description or labeling), and selling points such as a money-back guarantee or being safety tested. The posters must have a pleasing three-color palette, one of which is gold.

4. In their groups, students brainstorm, plan, and sketch ideas for a new Gold Rush invention. Each student is expected to contribute at least one idea that will be incorporated into the final design. Circulate during this time to observe and take notes on how students are interacting, communicating, and compromising.

5. Once each group reaches consensus, consult with each team about their plan. They then begin work on the final poster.

6. While the students are working together, notice how they interact, share space, and problem-solve issues pertinent to group work. Does anyone emerge as a leader? Is someone doing more or less than his or her fair share? How are conflicts resolved? Does the group keep the aesthetic elements in mind as they work?

7. Each group presents their poster to the class.

ASSESSMENT/REFLECTION:

Is someone dominating the discussion? Does everyone have a chance to contribute? Is anyone a passive member? Is there someone who is organizing and leading the group or keeping them on task? Is there anyone impeding the work of the group? How is the group solving problems if any arise? Does anyone seem to have more thoughtful, original, or creative ideas than others?

Children reflect on how they worked in a group by completing the following sentence starters:

I was a good group member because I _____.

I _____ was a good group member because _____.

One challenge we faced was _____.

What I like most about our idea is _____.

Next time I want to try to _____.

Children reflect on their group's poster by completing the following checklist:

- ❑ Title or heading
- ❑ Slogan
- ❑ Drawing or diagram
- ❑ How invention is used
- ❑ Selling point
- ❑ Pleasing three-color palette
- ❑ Elements of graphic design
- ❑ The invention and design fits the time period
- ❑ The invention would be useful to a 49er
- ❑ The idea is original

MI EXTENSIONS:

During this lesson, students also used their Intrapersonal, Spatial, and Linguistic intelligences.

Bodily-Kinesthetic: Act out an infomercial for the group's product.

Linguistic: Write a testimonial for one of the inventions. Write a product review that would appear in a consumer magazine. Write a letter of complaint pertaining to one invention.

Musical: Write a jingle to accompany the advertisement. Use instruments to perform it.

Unfairness on Purpose: A Problem-Solving Mind-Set

PURPOSE:

Students experience unfairness in a controlled setting and problem-solve a solution to meet the needs of the group members. Through a guided discussion following the experience, students understand that there are a variety of ways to solve the problem of what is fair and equal to take care of individual needs and wants. This concept of "unfairness on purpose" can be adapted to any situation in which goods, labor, or access need to be determined.

INTERPERSONAL

INTERMEDIATE

SOCIAL STUDIES

MATERIALS:

Variety of popcorn (cheese, caramel, and plain); other materials could be substituted, such as colored paper or different colored and sized pencil boxes

PROCEDURE:

1. Divide the class into groups of four to six.
2. When the students are out of the room, distribute the popcorn unfairly. Give some students in each group lots of cheese and caramel corn; give other students in the group only one kind; give some students one kernel. When students return, tell them you have prepared a surprise popcorn party. They are to go to their seats with their group and the party may begin.
3. Students notice that the popcorn has been distributed unfairly. The teacher explains that it is the group's responsibility to find a solution upon which they all agree.
4. Have each small group share with the class how they solved the popcorn problem. Record the solutions and facilitate a discussion on the various ways the problem was solved.

ASSESSMENT/REFLECTION:

Given a real-life scenario in which goods or resources are distributed unequally among groups of people, students take a position to debate with another student or have a discussion as a panel showing opposing views. A consensus must be met that everyone agrees on.

MI EXTENSIONS:

During this lesson, students also used their Intrapersonal Intelligence.

Linguistic: Students compose a reference sheet of vocabulary terms with their own definitions that would be helpful when solving problems. These might include *compromise, consensus,* and *equitable.*

Intrapersonal: Repeat this activity with a different variable and with different group configurations. Students reflect on their ability to solve problems and notice how they can persuade, give suggestions appropriately, compromise, and reach conclusions.

Activities to Support the Interpersonal Intelligence

INTRAPERSONAL

- Murphy-Meisgeier Type Indicator for Children
- Trust and team-building activities
- Partnering and Big Buddy activities with other grades
- Appreciation statements
- Developing rubrics or rating sheets for activities

BODILY-KINESTHETIC

- Role-playing, creative dramatics
- Recess
- Provide a service to another group of people
- Send, receive, and interpret messages through gestures, Morse code, flags, or sign language

LINGUISTIC

- Debate or panel discussions
- Person of the Week interviews
- Partner poems, group story writing
- Peer support groups
- Reciprocal teaching or jigsawing

LOGICAL-MATHEMATICAL

- Develop a flow chart to show classroom or playground rules the class has developed.
- Chart or graph interactions during television shows.
- Play strategy games, competitive and noncompetitive.
- Describe a pattern you have made while someone else tries to copy it.
- Sort by favorite activities or personality attributes.

MUSICAL

- Play instruments with others.
- Sing with a group.
- Compose a round from a familiar song that reinforces a skill.
- Create group rhythmic patterns.
- Match music to moods.

SPATIAL

- Create a group mural.
- Do partner drawings.
- Create a group quilt.
- Describe a picture you have drawn while your partner tries to recreate it.
- Redesign book covers for the same book or story to show different perspectives or points of view.

NATURALIST

- Eco-action service projects
- Group or neighborhood garden
- Outdoor team building activities
- Group care of classroom pets
- Nature scavenger hunts

Identifying the Interpersonal Intelligence in Your Students

Children function at many different levels within the intelligences. Through observation of everyday activities, one can create a profile showing the level of functioning within a particular intelligence and the intelligences in relation to each other. The levels described show increasing engagement and proficiency.

YES NO **APPRECIATES:**

❏ ❏ Demonstrates interest in others, enjoys social interaction, and is able to differentiate the moods, feelings, and intentions of others

❏ ❏ Verbally communicates needs

❏ ❏ Participates in group activities and discussions

❏ ❏ Can identify and label emotions and feelings of other people

❏ ❏ Understands stereotypes and prejudices

❏ ❏ Seeks out social interactions and situations

❏ ❏ Initiates friendships and relationships

YES NO **PERFORMS:**

❏ ❏ Is able to apply the intelligence to problem-solve a given social situation and respond to the mood, feelings, and intentions of others

❏ ❏ Cooperates with others and works at conflict resolution

❏ ❏ Reads, understands, and empathizes with others

❏ ❏ Is able to confront and be assertive in appropriate situations

❏ ❏ Interrupts put-downs, stereotyping, and ethnic and gender jokes

❏ ❏ Accepts constructive feedback and acts on it

❏ ❏ Is able to compromise and negotiate

❏ ❏ Volunteers help when others need it

❏ ❏ Knows when to seek assistance

❏ ❏ Solves social problems independent of assistance

❏ ❏ Invites someone to join a group

❏ ❏ Organizes a group interaction and is able to influence others

CREATES:

☐ ☐ Is able to apply the intelligence to generate appropriate and varied social outcomes

☐ ☐ Can generate a positive atmosphere to help focus a group's efforts

☐ ☐ Exhibits leadership that enables others to work at a higher level

☐ ☐ Can anticipate and change the course of a conversation or comment

☐ ☐ Can generate solutions or find words to help others with conflict resolution

☐ ☐ Organizes and carries through on a large-scale class project

Group: _____   Date: _____

How Are We Doing?

Give two examples for each statement.

1. We each contributed ideas:

Often_____   Sometimes_____   Not very much_____

2. We listened to each other:

Often_____   Sometimes_____   Not very much_____

3. We encouraged each other:

Often_____   Sometimes_____   Not very much_____

4. We built on each other's ideas:

Often_____   Sometimes_____   Not very much_____

Name: _____ Date: _____

Self-Assessment: Groupwork

1. I shared in my group today.

2. I encouraged others in my group to share.

3. I listened to others.

4. Others talked with me.

5. I felt supported by people in my group.

6. We worked on the task cooperatively.

Children's Resources

Books and Recordings

Alexander, Lloyd. *The Big Book for Peace*. Dutton Books, 1990.

Aliki. *We are Best Friends*. Greenwillow Books, 1982.

Baehr, Patricia. *School Isn't Fair*. Four Winds Press, 1989.

Buekrens, Adam. *Hi, I'm Adam: A Child's Story of Tourette Syndrome*. Hope Press, 1991.

Burnett, Karen. *Simon's Hook*. GR Pub., 1999.

Carl, Eric. *House for Hermit Crab*. Picture Book Studio, 1987.

Delton, Judy. *Two Good Friends*. Crown, 1986.

dePaola, Tomie. *First One Foot, Now the Other*. Putnam, 1980.

Ets, Marie Hall. *Play with Me*. Viking Penguin, 1976.

Forest, Heather. *Feathers*. August House Publishers, Inc., 2005.

Friedman, Laurie. *Angel Girl*. Carolrhoda Books, 2008.

Grahame, Kenneth. *The Wind in the Willows*. David and Charles, 1992.

Grimes, Nikki. *Danitra Brown, Class Clown*. HarperCollins Publishers, 2005.

Havill, Juanita. *Jamaica's Find*. Houghton Mifflin, 1986.

Hurwitz, Johanna. *Hot and Cold Summer*. Morrow, 1984.

Jacobson, Jennifer. *Andy Shane and the Very Bossy Dolores Starbuckle*. Candlewick, 2006.

Johnson, Angela. *Do Like Kyla*. Orchard Books, 1990.

Jones, Rebecca C. *Matthew and Tilly*. Dutton Children's Books, 1991.

Klamath County YMCA Family Preschool. *The Land of Many Colors*. Scholastic, 1993.

Korschunow, Irina. *The Foundling Fox*. HarperCollins, 1984.

Krementz, Jill. *How It Feels to Live with a Physical Disability*. Simon & Schuster, 1992.

Leuy, Virginia. *Let's Go to the Art Museum*. Harry Abrams, Inc., 1983.

Lionni, Leo. *Swimmy*. Pantheon, 1968.

Lobel, Arnold. *Frog and Toad Are Friends*. HarperCollins, 1970.

Ludwig, Trudy. *Just Kidding*. Tricycle Press, 2005.

Mayhew, James. *Kate's Picture Show*. Bantam Little Rooster, 1989.

McLerran, Alice. *Roxaboxen*. Lothrop, 1990.

McLuhan, T. C. *Touch the Earth*. E. P. Dutton, 1971.

Miles, Miska. *Annie and the Old One*. Little, Brown, 1971.

Munson, Derek. *Enemy Pie*. Raincoast Books, 2000.

Pinkney, Gloria. *Back Home*. Dial, 1992.

Pinkwater, Daniel. *The Big Orange Splot*. Scholastic, 1977.

Polacco, Patricia. *Chicken Sunday*. Philomel Books, 1992.

Polacco, Patricia. *Mrs Katz and Tush*. Bantam, 1992.

Polacco, Patricia. *The Bee Tree*. Philomel Books, 1993.

Rodman, Mary Ann. *My Best Friend*. Puffin Books, 2007.

Rosenthal, Amy. *Cookies: Bite-Size Life Lessons*. HarperCollins Children's Books, 2006.

Rostand, Edmond. *Cyrano de Bergerac*. Vintage Books, 1990.

Rylant, Cynthia. *Missing May*. Orchard Books, 1992.

Smith, Doris Buchanan. *Taste of Blackberries*. Scholastic, 1973.

Spier, Peter. *People*. Doubleday, 1980.

Spinelli, Eileen. *Somebody Loves You, Mr. Hatch*. First Aladdin Paperbacks, 1996.

Spinelli, Jerry. *Maniac Magee*. Harper Trophy, 1992.

Stevens, Janet. *The Great Fuzz Frenzy*. Harcourt Books, 2005.

Stevenson, James. *Monty*. Greenwillow Books, 1992.

Stewart, Sarah. *The Friend*. Farrar, Straus & Giroux, 2004.

Taylor, Mildred D. *Mississippi Bridge*. Bantam Books, 1992.

Weeks, Sarah. *Two Eggs, Please*. Aladdin Paperbacks, 2007.

Weninger, Brigette. *A Ball for All*. Penguin Young Readers, 2006.

Wilhelm, Hans. *Tyrone The Double Dirty Rotten Cheater*. Scholastic Inc., 1991.

Willems, Mo. *I Love My New Toy*. Hyperion Books, 2008.

Williams, Vera. *Amber Was Brave, Essie Was Smart*. HarperCollins, 2001.

Wilson, Forrest. *What It Feels Like to Be a Building*. Landmark Preservation Press, 1988.

Winthrop, Elizabeth. *Katherine's Doll*. Dutton Children's Books, 1983.

Woodson, Jacqueline. *The Other Side*. G. P. Putnam's Sons, 2001.

Yashima, Taro. *Crow Boy*. Puffin Books, 1976.

Zimmer, Tracie. *Sketches for a Spy Tree.* Houghton Mifflin Company, 2005.

Zolotow, Charlotte. *The Hating Book.* HarperCollins, 1969.

Zolotow, Charlotte. *The Quarreling Book.* HarperCollins, 1982.

Games

Friends Around the World: A Game of World Peace. Angland, Walsh. Aristoplay Ltd., 1989.

Hidden Talents: Learn About Your Friends. Pressman, 1994.

Max. Family Pastimes.

Secret Diary: The Game of Sharing Secrets and Surprises. Golden-Western Pub. Co.

The Princess Game. Family Pastimes.

The Sleeping Grump. Family Pastimes.

The Ungame: Kids Version. Talicor Incorporated, 2002.

Toot & Puddle Game. Gamewright Inc., 1999.

Totika. Open Spaces, 2005.

Whoonu. Cranium, 2005.

Teachers' Resources

Burke, Kay. *Authentic Learning*. Corwin, 2009.

Chen, Jie-Qi, ed. *Project Spectrum: Early Learning Activities*. Teachers College Press, 1999. (This is volume 2 of Project Zero Frameworks for Early Childhood Education.)

Cherry, Clare. *Think of Something Quiet*. David S. Lake, 1981.

Cohen, Cathi. *Raise Your Child's Social IQ*. Advantage Books, 2000.

Drew, Naomi. *Learning the Skills of Peacemaking*. Jalmar Press, 1987.

Elman, Natalie Madorsky and Kennedy-Moore, Eileen. *The Unwritten Rules of Friendship*. Little, Brown and Company, 2003.

Gibbs, Jeanne. *Tribes*. Center Source Publications, 1987.

Greene, Ross. *The Explosive Child*. HarperCollins, 2005.

Helm, Judy Harris, and Katz, Lilian. *Young Investigators: The Project Approach in the Early Years*. Teachers College Press, 2001.

Jones, Alanna. *104 Activities That Build: Self-Esteem, Teamwork, Communication, Anger Management, Self-Discovery, and Coping Skills*. Rec Room Publishing, 1998.

Lewis, Barbara. *The Kids' Guide to Social Action*. Free Spirit Pub., 1991.

McCarthy, Marietta. *Little Big Minds*. Penguin Group, 2006.

Miller, Jamie. *10-Minute Life Lessons for Kids*. Harper Perennial, 1998.

Palmer, Hap. *Hap Palmer Favorites*. Alfred Publishing, 1981.

Pincus, Debbie. *Interactions*. Good Apple, 1988.

Sax, Leonard. *Why Gender Matters*. Broadway Books, 2005.

Schwartz, Linda. *Think on Your Feet*. The Learning Works, 1987.

Silver, Gail. *Ahn's Anger*. Plum Blossom Books, 2009.

Thomson, Barbara. *Words Can Hurt You*. Addison-Wesley, 1993.

Wormeli, Rick. *Summarization in Any Subject: 50 Techniques to Improve Student Learning*. ASCD, 2005.

"When one is a stranger to oneself, then one is estranged from others too."

—*ANNE MORROW LINDBERGH*

Photograph: Patti Gabriel

The Intrapersonal Intelligence

Web of the Intrapersonal Intelligence

Student Quotes

" Knowing yourself helps you understand your friends and people around you. "

" I lie awake at night and think about the day, whether I'm just reliving a moment or thinking how I could have done something differently. "

" I can see myself on the *inside*. "

" Often those people who don't seem very intra are actually the most of us all. "

Characteristics

- Pursue personal interests, set realistic goals, identify and label feelings, sense their own strengths and weaknesses, are confident in their abilities, daydream, are insightful and reflective, are intuitive, follow their instincts, are comfortable with themselves, express a sense of justice and fairness

Famous People

MARVA COLLINS knew she could teach at-risk children, using her own methods.

SIGMUND FREUD created a new area of psychotherapy based on three forms of self.

ARNOLD ADOFF, author of *All the Colors of the Race*, wrote poetry describing his feelings and experiences.

CONFUCIUS was a Chinese thinker and social philosopher whose teachings have deeply influenced many.

MOTHER TERESA was an internationally famed humanitarian and advocate for the poor and helpless.

Adult Quotes

" Intrapersonal people are successful because they know who they are, not because of being in the right place at the right time. "
—*THOMAS R. HOERR*

" Our ultimate freedom is the right and power to decide how anybody or anything outside ourselves will affect us. "
—*STEPHEN R. COVEY*

Intrapersonal Is the Key to Success

BY THOMAS R. HOERR

At New City School we take a very pragmatic approach to education. Our goal is to prepare students to succeed in the real world, not just to excel in school. They need to perform well in school, but that is just the beginning. Consequently, although we value all of the intelligences—we are an MI school!—we believe that the personal intelligences are more important and that the Intrapersonal is the most important intelligence. Possessing a high degree of Intrapersonal Intelligence enables an individual to capitalize on his or her strengths in the other intelligences. A strong Intrapersonal Intelligence enables an individual to reflect on performance, to compensate for his or her weaknesses, and to chart a path for growth.

Prior to the publication of *Frames of Mind*, educators did not think that being skilled in working with others or that knowing oneself extremely well were forms of intelligence. Although we may have heard someone say that Paul has "good people skills" or Betty has "a good sense of herself," we did not equate these characteristics with intelligence. But Gardner's pragmatic definition of intelligence—the ability to solve a problem or create a product that is valued in a society—and his theory of multiple intelligences changed all that. This was reinforced a decade or so later by Daniel Goleman in his book *Emotional Intelligence*. Today Goleman's "EQ" (for Emotional Quotient, in contrast with IQ for Intelligence Quotient) is a commonly used term.

> A strong Intrapersonal Intelligence enables an individual to reflect on performance, to compensate for his or her weaknesses, and to chart a path for growth.

Daniel Goleman says, "Much evidence testifies that people who are emotionally adept—who know and manage their own feelings well, and who read and deal effectively with other people's feelings—are at an advantage in any domain of life, whether romance and intimate relationships or picking up the unspoken rules that govern success in organizational politics." He describes four areas of EQ:

1. *Knowing one's emotions.* Self-awareness—recognizing a feeling as it happens—is a keystone of emotional intelligence. Self-awareness is being aware of both our mood and our thoughts about that mood.

2. *Managing emotions.* Handling feelings so that they are appropriate is an ability that builds on self-awareness.

3. *Recognizing emotions in others.* Empathy, another ability that builds on emotional self-awareness, is the fundamental "people skill."

4. *Handling relationships.* The art of relationships is, in large part, skill in managing emotions in others.

Of course, Goleman's first two EQ areas are the Intrapersonal Intelligence, and his last two are the Interpersonal Intelligence.

A NEW WAY OF LOOKING AT SUCCESS

As educators, our job is to prepare kids so that they can flourish in the real world. Unfortunately, most people mistakenly believe that what is required to be successful in school is the same as what is required to be successful in life. In fact, however, success in these two arenas requires very different sets of skills (see *The Unschooled Mind*, Gardner, 1991, and *The Triarchic Mind*, Sternberg, 1988). It is true that the ability to read, write, and compute well is important; however, in general, those who get ahead in the world—whatever your criteria—do not do so simply because they read or write or compute better than others. The people who flourish in real life do perform well in traditional academic areas, but they excel because of their ability to understand and work with others and their ability to capitalize on their strengths and compensate for their weaknesses. They excel because of their strength in the personal intelligences.

Many of the difficulties that we encounter in everyday life are the result of problems we have in working with others or from problems they have in working with us. The ability to get along and work well with others has always been an essential quality for success; with our ever-shrinking world, it will be even more important in the future. Whatever the question, future technological advances will make the answers easier to find; the ability to work collaboratively with others in finding those answers will be what determines whether or not one is successful.

A high degree of Interpersonal Intelligence—being sensitive to the needs and moods of others, understanding them, and being able to work with them—is surely a very important component of this kind of success. Yet we believe that Intrapersonal Intelligence—knowledge of one's own strengths and weaknesses—is the key, the starting point, the most important intelligence. Possessing a strong Intrapersonal Intelligence means that we know our strengths and weaknesses and how we are perceived by others.

ACTING AS A RESULT OF INTRAPERSONAL INTELLIGENCE

If we are successful, it is because we are able to find a context in which our strengths come to the fore and our weaknesses are minimized. It is also because we recognize our weaknesses and know how to accommodate them. Perhaps we delegate the things we don't do well to others, or we choose our tasks so that we can succeed without mastering our weaknesses, or perhaps we seek assistance from others. Either an individual is aware of his or her weaknesses and compensates for them, or the weaknesses remain unrecognized and unaddressed, hindering growth and success.

This means that just as it is important that our students learn to read and write and compute, it is also important that they learn about

> The people who flourish in real life do perform well in traditional academic areas, but they excel because of their ability to understand and work with others and their ability to capitalize on their strengths and compensate for their weaknesses.

> The ability to get along and work well with others has always been an essential quality for success; with our ever-shrinking world, it will be even more important in the future. Possessing a strong Intrapersonal Intelligence means that we know our strengths and weaknesses and how we are perceived by others.

> If we are successful, it is because we are able to find a context in which our strengths come to the fore and our weaknesses are minimized. It is also because we recognize our weaknesses and know how to accommodate them.

themselves, their strengths and weaknesses, along with how they are perceived by others. It is incumbent upon us to help our students improve their Intrapersonal Intelligence.

IMPROVING INTRAPERSONAL INTELLIGENCE IN THE CLASSROOM

How do we do this at New City? First, we consciously teach the MI model and the intelligences, as developmentally appropriate, to all of our students. Understanding MI is a good way to teach each child to begin to look at his or her intelligence profile. Children learn that there are different kinds of intelligences, not better and worse kinds. Just as some of us are African American, some Asian, and some Caucasian, some of us are talented linguistically, some spatially, and some musically. All of us have strengths and weaknesses, and all of us need to learn what we do well and what requires more attention.

For many students, understanding their own array of strengths and weaknesses is very empowering. One example comes to mind: A fourth grade student who was skilled in logical-mathematical tasks had always felt inferior to his linguistically gifted older sister. He struggled with reading, whereas she read book after book after book. One day, however, after learning about the different intelligences and reflecting on his own intelligence profile, he told his teacher with delight, "I've got it: she's talented linguistically, but I'm strong logically-mathematically!" This awareness helped him understand the difference between himself and his sister and legitimized his strength for him.

For these reasons the personal intelligences have been given a great deal of attention by our faculty in our curriculum development and teaching. Because who you are is more important than what you know, we felt that it was important to begin each child's report card (and parent-teacher conference) by focusing on development in the personal intelligences. The first page of our progress report (report card) is entirely devoted to reporting student progress in the personal intelligences. A child's growth in attributes such as "motivation," "confidence," "appreciation for diversity," and "teamwork" is shared with parents using symbols (AC = area of concern, DA = developing appropriately, ED = exceptional development) and narrative comments.

> For many students, understanding their own array of strengths and weaknesses is very empowering.

Teachers everywhere work to help students understand each other and work together. We are no different. "Tell her how you feel," "Use your words," and "What would you do differently?" are typical comments made to children who are having difficulties interacting with others. Similarly, we have been using the Responsive Classroom model throughout our grades, beginning each day with a Morning Meeting, and using a portion of that time to help our students reflect on their interactions with others.

Although Morning Meeting is the most recent setting for this kind of reflection, it is simply another strategy. Throughout our school, in all grades, students are asked to reflect on the role that they played in learning, in the classroom, and at lunch or recess. "Think to yourself," a teacher will ask, "what is the best way for you to learn this information?" or "Take a moment and think, what did you do to make this activity a success?" After a moment she might continue, "Were you a good team member? What specific thing did you do to be helpful? What could you have done that you didn't? And what were three things you did that were not helpful?" Although the exact format—the kinds of questions, their specificity, and whether or not the answers are shared with others— varies, the thrust of helping children reflect on their behaviors and the roles that they played is present at all grade levels. In the primary and intermediate grades, journaling is often assigned to facilitate children's reflection.

Teachers provide activities and structures for children to assess their own performance and work on areas that need strengthening. Not only do many activities conclude with children being given time to reflect and self-assess, but in some classes students also are given spaces on their papers or worksheets to write about how they have contributed to the group's efforts and what they might do differently in the future. Some teachers use quotes from the children's reflection in their progress reports or notes to their parents. Occasionally, in some classes, children are brought together to work with others who are trying to improve simi- lar areas. For example, one teacher created PEP (Personal Effectiveness Performance) Groups after having her students identify the behaviors on which they wanted to work. One group worked on reducing the times that they would interrupt others; another group met to plan how they could be more assertive in speaking out in class; and others came to- gether to share ideas and support one another in their quest to be more organized. Teachers facilitate children giving developmentally appropri- ate feedback to one another. Older students, in particular, learn to give one another both positive and negative feedback about their work and play performances.

As another step in the quest to improve our students' Intrapersonal Intelligence, in the past decade or so we have been including them in parent-teacher conferences. Students in grades two through six join their teacher and parents at our second parent-teacher conference in November of each year. Prior to that meeting, the teacher and student have worked to develop the student's two goals—one scholastic and one personal. The student is present for a portion of the conference and shares those goals. This is a good way to help students set goals and monitor progress; it brings the home and school together, and also helps students develop their presentation skills and Interpersonal Intelligence. The student's progress is reflected on subsequent report cards and in later parent-teacher conferences.

Finally, our focus on the Intrapersonal Intelligence has affected us by helping our faculty members become more aware of how we work with and interact with one another. It has helped us improve our own Intrap- ersonal Intelligence. If we expect our students to constantly grow and develop, we can expect no less from ourselves. Faculty and committee meetings often have periods in which the leader asks the individuals to pause for a moment and think about what they, personally, did to move the group forward. And each August, during our week-long in-service prior to the start of school, we devote time to "being a good teammate." Part of that time is spent reflecting and part is spent sharing and giving feedback to others. By working to improve our own Intrapersonal Intelligence, we know that not only will we be better educators and better people, but our students will benefit too.

If we expect our students to constantly grow and develop, we can expect no less from ourselves.

Me Bags

INTRAPERSONAL

PRIMARY

SOCIAL STUDIES

PURPOSE:

Students develop and practice oral presentation skills as they share information about themselves using items brought from home. Through reflection, they notice strengths and areas that need improvement for both the delivery and the content of the presentation.

MATERIALS:

Brown paper grocery bags, teacher-completed Me Bag, video equipment, digital camera, journals, teacher-made reflection sheets, teacher-made assessment rubric

PROCEDURE:

1. Demonstrate a Me Bag presentation. Explain that everything in the bag has a "what" and "why" component. Share "what" items you have chosen and "why" they tell something about you.

2. To reinforce the what and why components, the students discuss the items in the bag and how they relate to you. Students discuss and share something they learned about you. The children suggest items that would never be found in your bag and why.

3. Use your presentation as an example of what makes a good presentation. Create a list that will serve as a rubric for student presentations. The list should include introduction, proper posture, good volume, clear speaking voice, and eye contact with the audience.

4. Tell the students they will put together a Me Bag at home. In their journals, students record a list of things they might include in their bags. Remind them about the "what" and "why" components and that everything must fit in their bags.

5. Children write their names on the bags they are given. A letter is attached to the bag, informing parents about the activity and giving a deadline for having bags back to school for the student presentations. Stress a five- to six-minute time limit for the child's presentation.

6. Record the presentations and take photographs for the students' reflections. Children reflect on the content and their presentation skills.

ASSESSMENT/REFLECTION:

Use a rubric created from the student-generated list to rate the presentation skills of the students. After students view their recordings, they reflect on their presentation strengths and what they need to change to improve.

MI EXTENSIONS:

This lesson also uses the Interpersonal and Linguistic intelligences.

Linguistic: Students write a Me Poem based on the items they included in their bags.

Interpersonal: Create "Who Am I?" riddles with lists or drawings of the items on the top flap, and the student's name underneath.

Logical-Mathematical: Use hula hoops on the floor to form a Venn diagram, each circle representing one child. Working in pairs, children place one item at a time from their bags on the diagram.

I Am . . .

PURPOSE:

The students use the book *Quick as a Cricket* by Audrey Wood as a writing prompt to create similes showing their unique qualities.

MATERIALS:

Quick as a Cricket by Audrey Wood, large paper, markers, scissors, crayons, other art supplies

PROCEDURE:

1. Read the story *Quick as a Cricket* by Audrey Wood.
2. Students act out the comparisons within the story, thinking about how they are like and different from the animals.
3. The children draw self-portraits in the middle of a large piece of paper. Around the self-portraits, they draw pictures of animals that share components of who they are, such as a horse because we run fast or a bee because we work hard.
4. Children add words to their posters as they complete their drawings. Each sentence should state the simile; for example, *I am as fast as a horse.*

ASSESSMENT/REFLECTION:

Note whether the similes were accurate and the pictures reflect the child as others see him or her.

MI EXTENSIONS:

This lesson also uses the Spatial and Linguistic intelligences.

Logical-Mathematical: Collect and graph the data to show how many students identified with the same animals.

Bodily-Kinesthetic: Act like me! Have each child read the words from his or her poster as the rest of the class acts out the movements of the animals.

Linguistic: Assemble the pictures to make a big book for others to read.

Naturalist: Sort a list of all the animals the children used to create their similes. Students determine the categories for the sort, such as fast, loud, or strong animals.

Interpersonal: Conduct a group sorting activity in which children move to different areas of the classroom based on animals and their characteristics. Are you more like a monkey or a snake? Once in groups, children share why they felt they belonged in that area. Repeat with other animals from their simile list.

Content of Their Character

PURPOSE:

Children identify the strengths of character in a notable figure discussed or read about in class; for example, Dr. Martin Luther King Jr., and identify his or her personal strengths. Children notice similarities between themselves and the person being studied.

MATERIALS:

Happy Birthday, Martin Luther King by Jean Marzollo, a copy of the "I Have a Dream" speech by Dr. Martin Luther King Jr., two paper doll outlines for each student, an outline of Dr. King, a blank silhouette of the same picture.

PROCEDURE:

1. Students share their prior knowledge of Dr. Martin Luther King.

2. Read *Happy Birthday, Martin Luther King* by Jean Marzollo.

3. Introduce the phrase "Content of their character" and read excerpts from Dr. King's "I Have a Dream" speech.

4. Ask the students to describe the kind of person Dr. King was, listing their ideas. Help the students make a connection between these ideas and the phrase "Content of their character."

5. Show the students the cutout picture of Dr. King. Beneath this picture attach a blank, cutout silhouette of the same picture so that the one on top makes a flap.

6. Each student chooses words or phrases from the class list to write on the blank silhouette under the picture of Dr. King.

7. The next day, ask the students to think about the content of their characters, again listing ideas. Distribute two outlined paper dolls to each child. On one, they create a picture of themselves. This becomes the top flap. On the other, they write words to describe themselves, using the list as a reference.

8. Children highlight any characteristics they share with Dr. King. Students share the contents of their characters.

ASSESSMENT/REFLECTION:

Through sharing and observation, and during group discussions, note whether the children have accurately identified their strengths and the similarities between themselves and Dr. King. During literature circle or when reading a book about another notable figure, children recognize the strengths of that person and notice similarities between themselves and the notable figure.

MI EXTENSIONS:

During this lesson, students also used their Spatial and Linguistic intelligences.

Interpersonal: Children use their "content of character" paper doll to compare with a classmate's. They could then highlight similarities using a different color.

Logical-Mathematical: Children create Venn diagrams comparing themselves to Dr. King or other notable figures.

Goal Setting

PURPOSE:
This lesson is used to help children become aware of behaviors that create a learning environment, to help them set boundaries and to help them focus their attention on specific behavioral or academic areas that support the learning community. Students will gain increasing self-awareness and self-control and develop the ability to be self-directed.

INTRAPERSONAL

PRIMARY

SOCIAL STUDIES

MATERIALS:
Chart paper, journals or reflection sheets

PROCEDURE:
1. Ask children what a goal is and together come to a meaningful working definition.
2. Ask the students to think of something about themselves upon which they wish to focus. This will undoubtedly be difficult at first. Have the children limit goals to the school environment; for example, "I will not interrupt" or "I will keep my hands to myself in line." You may need to give suggestions; for example, some goals that students had set in other years.
3. Stress that they are all here to help support one another, and everyone has room for improvement. As the children share their goals, record them on a piece of chart paper next to each child's name.
4. Students come up with a plan to help them reach the goals they have set. They also share how classmates can support them and help them reach their goals. Students need to determine how they will know when they have reached their goals.
5. Allow time each week for children to reflect on individual progress using their journals or reflection sheets. Ask students to share ways other children have supported their progress.
6. As the earlier goals are reached, new goals are set.

ASSESSMENT/REFLECTION:
Students reflect on their progress and their willingness to work toward reaching their stated goals. Classmates meet to share journals or reflection sheets and to discuss whether they feel their goals have been reached, giving examples and discussing strategies. Teacher observations determine whether the purpose of the lesson has been met.

MI EXTENSIONS:
This lesson also uses the Interpersonal and Linguistic intelligences.

Logical-Mathematical: Periodically, on a scale of one to five, students rate their progress toward reaching their goals. Connect the points to form a line graph, or create a bar graph. This could be graphing for individuals or a whole group.

Bodily-Kinesthetic: Students share strategies that worked toward achieving their goals by doing a role-play for the class.

Interpersonal: Interview students in an older grade. What advice can an older student give that will help younger students see the value of life-long goal setting? The older student becomes a mentor for the younger student.

Autobiography: My Story

PURPOSE:

Students reflect on their personal life experiences and represent these using various intelligences. These are collected each year during the student's tenure at the school and show learning and growth over time.

MATERIALS:

Paper (skin-colored for second grade; be sure to provide an assortment of shades for all students), magazines, photographs, writing and drawing utensils, various art supplies, *I Like Me* by Nancy Carlson, *All I Am* by Eileen Row, and *Hands* by Lois Ehlert.

Kindergarten: Students listen to a read-aloud of the books *I Like Me* and *All I Am*. With the class, brainstorm a list of words that complete the following prompts, which serve as the starting place for the poems the students write: "I have . . . I like . . . I am good at . . . I am learning to . . . I love . . ." Students write their own Me Poem using words from the brainstormed list. Some students may need to draw pictures and dictate the words to the teacher. When the poems are finished, the students can read the poems to the class, or the teacher can read the poem and have the students guess who each poem is about.

First Grade: The students read *Hands* by Lois Ehlert. The book tells how the author used her hands growing up. Ehlert's book features cut paper illustrations. Using the book *Hands* as a model, students create an autobiographical flip book. Student first fill in a graphic organizer that is divided into four sections: past (when you were born, special childhood memory), present (favorite intelligence, a school year memory), changing and learning (something that has changed about the student since the beginning of the year, and something the student has learned during this school year), and future (what the student hopes to do in the future). They use the organizer to write sentences for each of the four parts of their life story on a six-by-four-inch piece of paper. These pieces are glued to a six-by-eighteen-inch strip of construction paper in chronological order. There will be a two-inch space left for the title. On separate six by four inch pieces of construction paper, students create construction paper collaged images for each of the four parts of their personal narrative. These become flaps that are taped over the different parts of the autobiography.

Second Grade: Students read and explore autobiographical poetry. They use a graphic organizer to list things they do with their hands using each intelligence. The Spatial and the Intrapersonal intelligences are not included because the lesson already uses these. They trace their hands lightly in pencil on skin-colored paper and write the words from their organizer along the outline, letting each digit stand for one of the intelligences. The words that describe how the last intelligence is used are written on the palm. They go over the writing with a fine tip marker or a pen, erasing the pencil marks when this step is completed. They cut out the hand and glue it to a contrasting color of paper.

Third Grade: Students study the various ways people have recorded their life events throughout history; for example, journals, timelines, and photo albums. Students brainstorm a list of major events in their lives and record them on a timeline with years equally spaced apart. Students illustrate the events they place on the timeline using drawings or photographs.

Fourth Grade: Students begin by brainstorming a list of their major accomplishments and projects from the school year. They create a spatial collage representing items from the list. The materials for the collage might include photographs, magazines, drawings, natural materials, or found items.

Fifth Grade: Students use the structure of a traditional five-paragraph essay to communicate their personal improvements over the course of the school year. Each paragraph in the body addresses a different area of improvement and growth.

Sixth Grade: Students design an autobiographical graph using significant events in their lives. With the help of other family members, they brainstorm a list of events from their lives. After narrowing the list by selecting two significant events from each year, students create an illustration to accompany each event. Students caption each picture with a title and sentences that tell who, what, when, and where. Each event is rated on a scale from positive five to negative five showing emotions tied to the event or the significance of the event. Students draw a timeline lengthwise on a piece of twelve by eighteen inch construction paper. Students glue each of their illustrations with captions on the graph, using the rating as a guide to determine placement above or below the line. Events with positive values are placed above the timeline and those with negative values appear below the line. Positive events might include playing on a team or going on a trip. A negative events might be the loss of a pet or having a best friend move out of town.

ASSESSMENT:

Did the students follow instructions and guidelines to create their autobiographies? Observe students' interpretations of their personal life experiences. Were the students able to communicate their life experiences in a developmentally appropriate way? Did students communicate life events through their autobiographies? When it applies, were students aware of the connections between their emotions and life events? Were students able to portray their intelligences in their autobiographies?

Letter to Myself

PURPOSE:

Students develop and evaluate study skills and test-taking strategies. By writing letters to themselves, they use the self-talk strategy to remember the approaches they found most helpful.

MATERIALS:

Journals, paper, envelopes

PROCEDURE:

1. Prior to the first spelling test, students are asked to interview their parents or older siblings on ways to study for a spelling test.

2. The next day, on chart paper, list the strategies the children collected during their interviews. These may include such things as practicing quizzes, writing the words out, turning the words into pictures, tapping or drumming the words out, recording or listening to the words on tape, drawing the words in dirt, or painting the words on the sidewalk with a wet brush.

3. Have each child pick one strategy to use to study for the test and record this in the child's journal telling where and when the child will use this strategy. After the test, students evaluate and record how that particular strategy worked. Refer to the original chart to pick a new strategy for each upcoming test. Repeat the reflective process after each test.

4. After three tests, students compose a short letter to themselves evaluating what has worked and what has not. File letters for later reflection.

5. In preparation for a different test format, such as a multiple-choice vocabulary test, repeat the interview process to gather new strategies. Use the same lesson format to test and reflect on the effectiveness of the new set of test-taking strategies.

6. Review all the letters to prepare for the standardized tests. Conduct more interviews to gather tips and strategies for this type of test.

7. After finishing the standardized tests, students write themselves a letter stating the test-taking strategies they have learned, used, and felt were successful. For this last letter, have each student self-address an envelope.

8. Save the letters and give them to the students before the standardized tests the following year.

ASSESSMENT/REFLECTION:

Did students' confidence and test-taking attitudes improve? Are they able to articulate different strategies and articulate the value of using a strategy? Did test scores improve?

MI EXTENSIONS:

During this lesson, students might use their Interpersonal, Linguistic, Musical, Bodily-Kinesthetic, and Spatial intelligences.

Interpersonal: Students who want to work on the same strategy to prepare for a test meet and study together.

Logical-Mathematical: Students collect data on whether or not students used any strategies to prepare for the test and the scores earned. Students graph the information and share implications.

Spatial: Introduce a new format to help children learn and remember their strategies; for example, making a mind map or a poster illustrating good test-taking tips.

What I Believe

PURPOSE:
Students identify, categorize, and define concepts or things as needs, values, or resources on a Venn diagram based on their individual beliefs. Students expand their appreciation for diversity as they listen to the choices of others. They may face challenges when explaining and defending the placements that reflect personal beliefs.

INTRAPERSONAL

INTERMEDIATE

SOCIAL STUDIES

MATERIALS:
Dictionaries, vocabulary list, blank Venn diagrams, chart paper, markers

PROCEDURE:
1. Define the terms *needs*, *values*, and *resources*. Discuss how these words are similar and different so that everyone is working with the same definitions.

2. Provide each student with a list of the same terms and phrases: *independence, music, education, free time, house/apartment, religion, trust, privacy, communication, computer, routines, car, time alone, money, books, family, honesty, exercise, choices, friends, vacation, health care, TV, clothes, rules*

3. Each student categorizes each term as a need, value, or resource and writes them on a Venn diagram.

4. In small groups, students use the same vocabulary list and reach consensus about the placement of the terms on a large Venn diagram. Students compromise on the placement of the words, and all students in the group must be able to rationalize the placement of any word.

5. On the large diagrams displayed around the room, students note similarities and differences among the groups' Venn diagrams. Invite each group to defend or explain its thinking on the placement of the terms. Group members explain how they reached consensus on some of the terms.

6. Display the individual diagrams around the larger group diagrams. Lead a discussion using the following questions:

    What was one word that was easy for you to place on your diagram and why?

    What was one word that was more difficult to place and why?

    What general observations can you make about the Venn diagrams?

    What are some things you learned about yourself and about the people in your group?

ASSESSMENT/REFLECTION:
During the groups' explanations, take notes on how well the students are able to defend and explain their placement of words. After the discussions, students write for fifteen minutes about the activity and the discussion.

MI EXTENSIONS:

During this lesson, students also used their Interpersonal and Linguistic intelligences.

Interpersonal: Each student creates a list of five words that reflect their own needs, wants, and resources. In small groups, students compare similarities and differences in their lists and discuss how peer conflicts can result from differences in the way things are categorized. How equal were the lengths of the lists? What conclusions can be drawn?

Linguistic: This lesson could be adapted to connect to any conflict studied. In a study of the Civil War, terms could include *autonomy, capital, independence, cotton, religion, power, recognition, land, unification, labor, freedom, identity, equality, food, shelter, segregation,* and *slavery.* Students in each of the small groups would be divided so that half represented those from Southern states and half represented those from Northern states. Conflict would be a major factor in discussions, and the need for compromise would present itself. As students from each group explained their placement of terms on the Venn diagram, connections could be made to actual events from history.

Musical: Find, sing, and discuss songs that express needs, values, or resources. Reach consensus on what the songs' lyrics represent.

Spatial: Use magazines and newspapers to create a collage organized to reflect wants, values, or resources.

Simile for Me

PURPOSE:

The students find common characteristics between themselves and other entities. They look for similarities between themselves and such things as the country, a city, a river, a lake, or a screened-in porch. Students discover the ways they are similar to and different from their peers.

MATERIALS:

Worksheet, chart paper, index cards, markers, art supplies

PROCEDURE:

1. Give each student the worksheet "Which Are You More Like?" and explain that they will be analyzing their personalities by comparing themselves to the things on the sheet. They are not to choose items they like best; instead, they must determine which items have characteristics similar to their personalities. The students should not discuss the questions or their responses with each other. Students circle their responses to the questions and turn their papers over when they have finished.

2. When everyone has finished, spend a few minutes debriefing the exercise as a large group by asking the following questions: "What was the most difficult question to answer?" "What was the easiest question to answer?"

3. Select a question for the students to examine in greater depth. On the back of their papers, students list reasons why they are like the item in the question. For example, if a student selected river, she might write "aggressive, impatient, strong, adventurous, rushing, risk-taker." A student who selected lake might write "quiet, open-minded, big-hearted, patient, welcoming, laid back, dependable."

4. After the students have recorded their reasons, put them into the two groups; send the rivers to one part of the room and the lakes to another part of the room. On chart paper, students decide how to represent the ways they are like the item. They might create a mind-map, a list, or a mural. Each student must share at least one idea from the back of his or her worksheet.

5. The group discusses the ways its members are like the item. Not everyone will agree because children look at themselves differently.

6. Display the charts and allow the children to share, clarify, question, and comment on the charts.

7. Assign another question to analyze, following the same procedure. After charting several of the questions, discussions of the charts might include an analysis of who was in your group each time, what you learned about yourself, what you learned about your classmates, and whether your peers saw you the way you saw yourself.

8. Prior to one of the final analyses, students list the people they think will be in their group on an index card, which they give to the teacher. During the discussion, share how accurate the students were with their predictions.

ASSESSMENT/REFLECTION:

Your observations during the activity will reveal each student's ability to think figuratively. The index cards provide information on the students' knowledge of their peers.

MI EXTENSIONS:

This lesson also uses the Spatial and Linguistic intelligences.

Linguistic: Students write a metaphorical poem using one of the items from their list.

Logical-Mathematical: Each student makes a frequency chart to display with whom they were grouped and the number of times they were grouped with each person.

Musical: Strings, percussion, brass, and wind instruments are used to create the choices for the worksheet.

Naturalist: Use objects from nature to create the similes.

Which Are You More Like?

1. The country or the city?

2. The present or the future?

3. Physical or mental?

4. An arguer or an agree-er?

5. A turtle or a rabbit?

6. Likely to walk on thin ice or to tiptoe through the flowers?

7. Leather or suede?

8. A computer or a quill pen?

9. A rock band or an orchestra?

10. A "No Trespassing" sign or a "Public Swimming" sign?

11. A rollerblade or a pogo stick?

12. A motorcycle or a tandem bicycle?

13. A gourmet or a fast-food fan?

14. A river or a lake?

15. A screened porch or a bay window?

16. A mountain or a valley?

Activities to Support the Intrapersonal Intelligence

INTERPERSONAL

- Use "Magic Circle" (Human Development Corporation) as a community building tool with your class.
- Analyze your role in a group.
- Request feedback and react to it.
- Describe yourself, have a classmate describe you, then compare.
- Role-play the ending to an open-ended story or situation.

BODILY-KINESTHETIC

- Visualize through movement a part of the story and create a story from that point of view.
- Listen to a made-up situation; use body movement to react.
- Assume the role of a character using voice and body language.
- Do needlework that expresses a belief or feeling.
- Construct own personal space using LEGO bricks or other materials.

LINGUISTIC

- Write "Dear Abby" letters asking for advice.
- Administer an interest or personality inventory.
- Write in journals or create diary entries as a character in a story.
- Record "How I feel" statements on a tape.
- Act like objects that describe you.

LOGICAL-MATHEMATICAL

- Create charts and graphs of interests.
- Construct Venn diagrams to show how students are similar or different.
- Construct a feelings map.
- Make a personal timeline.
- Use a clock to record how you spend your day.

MUSICAL

- Bring in music that reminds you of a special time in your life.
- Listen to a song and describe how it makes you feel.
- Create body music (pantomime) that shows your feelings.
- Share your favorite song with the class.
- Construct a melody.

SPATIAL

- Use magazine pictures to create a personal collage.
- Put together a mobile that shows who you are.
- Create a mind map of your likes and dislikes or interests.
- Draw or paint self-portraits.
- Develop a slide show or photo display to show who you are.
- Design your dream room.

NATURALIST

- Observe in nature while being quiet, still, and alone.
- On a map, explain what kind of climate you prefer and why.
- Reflect after envisioning yourself in a different ecosystem.
- Play games in which you share your nature preferences.
- Sit in a garden and record your thoughts.

Identifying the Intrapersonal Intelligence in Your Students

Children function at many different levels within the intelligences. Through observation of everyday activities, one can create a profile showing the level of functioning within a particular intelligence and the intelligences in relation to each other. The levels described show increased engagement and proficiency.

YES NO **APPRECIATES:**

☐ ☐ Is consistently aware of feelings and abilities and is able to differentiate among them

☐ ☐ Recognizes that different feelings and abilities exist and gives them labels

☐ ☐ When reading a story, can identify a given character's feelings

☐ ☐ Can recognize his or her own strengths and weaknesses

☐ ☐ Knows when to ask for help and when not to ask

☐ ☐ Values and enjoys time to oneself

YES NO **PERFORMS:**

☐ ☐ Is able to self-assess, understand feelings and abilities, and use them to problem-solve in a social situation

☐ ☐ Accurately recognizes a character in a story who thinks, acts, and feels similar to the way the student does

☐ ☐ Through knowing strengths and weaknesses, determines what situations to avoid and those in which to become involved

☐ ☐ Is able to reflect on his or her own feelings

☐ ☐ Is willing to try something in an area in which the student knows he or she is weak and not become frustrated by a lack of success

☐ ☐ Accepts limits but is willing to take risks

☐ ☐ Accepts responsibility for his or her own actions

☐ ☐ Actively solicits feedback from others

☐ ☐ Accurately self-assesses

YES NO **CREATES:**

☐ ☐ Generates original solutions and outcomes to problems

☐ ☐ Expands personal horizons and limits

☐ ☐ Rather than avoiding weaknesses, tackles the situation in an original way

☐ ☐ Although weak in one area, can align him- or herself with those who are strong and use them as mentors

Intrapersonal Assessment

Name: _____ Date: _____

	Yes	Usually	No
1. I was comfortable being a leader.			
2. I was comfortable being a follower.			
3. I stayed focused on the job.			
4. I helped solve problems.			
5. I accepted responsibility for my own actions.			
6. I was an active listener.			

My intrapersonal goal is _____

_____

Children's Resources

Books and Recordings

Adero, Malaika. *Up South: Stories, Studies, and Letters of This Century's African-American Migrations.* The New Press, 1993.

Adler, David A. *The Number on My Grandfather's Arm.* UAHC Press, 1987.

Adoff, Arnold. *Black Is Brown Is Tan.* HarperCollins, 1973.

Aliki. *Feelings.* Greenwillow Books, 1984.

Allington, Richard, and Cowles, Kathleen. *Feelings.* Raintree, 1991.

Aneona, George. *Helping Out.* Clarion Books, 1985.

Bang, Molly. *When Sophie Gets Angry—Really, Really Angry . . .* Scholastic, 1999.

Bertrand, Cecile. *Mr. and Mrs. Smith Have Only One Child, But What a Child.* Lothrop, Lee and Shepard, 1992.

Boegehold, Betty. *You Are Much Too Small.* Bantam, 1990.

Caines, Jeannette. *Abby.* Harper Trophy, 1984.

Carle, Eric. *The Grouchy Ladybug.* Scholastic, 1977.

_____. *The Mixed-Up Chameleon.* HarperCollins, 1984.

Carlson, Nancy. *Arnie and the Stolen Markers.* Viking, 1988.

_____. *Like Me.* Viking Penguin, 1988.

Cheltenham Elementary School. *We Are All Alike, We Are All Different.* Scholastic, 1991.

Choi, Nyul Sook. *Year of the Impossible Goodbyes.* Houghton, 1991.

Christiansen, C. B. *My Mother's House, My Father's House.* Atheneum, 1989.

Clements, Andrew. *Big Al.* Scholastic, 1991.

Cohen, Barbara. *Molly's Pilgrim.* Lothrop, 1983.

Cooney, Nancy. *The Blanket That Had to Go.* Putnam, 1981.

Curtis, Jamie Lee. *When I Was Little.* HarperCollins, 1993.

dePaola, Tomie. *Nana Upstairs, Nana Downstairs.* Putnam, 1973.

Dubanevich, Arlene. *Pig William.* Bradbury, 1985.

Dwight, Laura. *We Can Do It!* Checkerboard Press, 1992.

Eisenberg, Lisa. *Sitting Bull: Great Sioux Chief.* Dell, 1991.

Farber, Norma. *How Does It Feel to Be Old?* Dutton, 1979.

Filipovic, Zlata. *Zlata's Diary: A Child's Life in Sarajevo.* Viking, 1994.

Fluek, Knoble Toby. *Memories of My Life in a Polish Village.* Knopf, 1990.

Frandsen, Karen. *Michael's New Haircut.* Children's Press, 1986.

Frank, Anne. *Anne Frank: The Diary of a Young Girl.* Pocket Books, 1952.

Gackenbach, Dick. *Harry and the Terrible Whatzit.* Clarion, 1979.

Gehret, Jeanne. *Eagle Eyes: A Child's Guide to Paying Attention.* Verbal Images, 1991.

Geonnel, Heidi. *Sometimes I Like to Be Alone.* Little, Brown, 1989.

George, Jean Craighead. *Julie of the Wolves.* Hall, 1972.

———. *The Talking Earth.* Harper Trophy, 1983.

Hamilton, Virginia. *Many Thousand Gone—African Americans from Slavery to Freedom.* Knopf, 1993.

Harris, Robie. *The Day That Leo Said, "I Hate You."* Little Brown, 2008.

Henkes, Kevin. *Chrysanthemum.* Greenwillow Books, 1991.

———. *Sheila Rae the Brave.* Greenwillow Books, 1987.

Holman, Felice. *Slake's Limbo.* Scribner, 1974.

Hudson, Nade. *I Love My Family.* Scholastic, 1993.

Kahn, Victoria. *Purpilicious.* HarperCollins Publishers, 2007.

Keller, Holly. *Horace.* Greenwillow, 1991.

Khan, Rukhsana. *Ruler of the Courtyard.* Viking, 2003.

Kherdian, David. *By Myself.* Henry Holt Co., 1993.

Krasilovsky, Phyllis. *The Shy Little Girl.* Scholastic, 1992.

Kraus, Robert. *Leo the Late Bloomer.* Simon & Schuster, 1971.

Leaf, Munro. *The Story of Ferdinand.* Scholastic, 1964.

Leighton, Maxinne R. *An Ellis Island Christmas.* Viking, 1992.

Lester, Helen. *Pookins Gets Her Way.* Houghton Mifflin, 1987.

Liao, Jimmy. *The Sounds of Colors.* Little, Brown, 2006.

MacLachlan, Patricia. *All the Places to Love.* HarperCollins, 1994.

Mandelbaun, Pili. *You Be Me, I'll Be You.* Kane/Miller Book Pub., 1990.

Martin, Bill Jr. *Knots on a Counting Rope.* Holt, 1987 .

Marzolla, Jean. *Happy Birthday, Martin Luther King.* Scholastic, 1993.

Mayer, Mercer. *All By Myself.* Western Publishing, 1983.

McKissack, Patricia. *Stitchin' and Pullin': A Gee's Bend Quilt.* Random House, 2008.

Michelson, Maureen R. *Women and Work—Photographs and Personal Writings.* New Sage Press, 1986.

Munsch, Robert. *The Paper Bag Princess.* Annick, 1980.

Muth, Jon J. *Zen Shorts.* Scholastic, 2005.

Napoli, Donna Jo. *Albert.* Silver Whistle, 2001.

Naylor, Phyllis. *Shiloh.* Atheneum, 1991.

O'Dell, Scott. *Island of the Blue Dolphins.* Houghton Mifflin, 1960.

Petrillo, Genevieve. *Keep Your Ear on the Ball.* Tilbury House, 2007.

Pfister, Marcus. *The Rainbow Fish.* North-South Books, 1992.

Philips, Barbara. *Don't Call Me Fatso.* Steck Vaughn, 1991.

Polacco, Patricia. *Thank You, Mr. Falker.* Philomel Books, 1998.

Reynolds, Peter. *So Few of Me.* Candlewick Press, 2006.

Ripken, Cal, Jr. *The Longest Season.* Philomel Books, 2007.

Roe, Eileen. *All I Am.* Bradbury Press, 1990.

Rus, Jacob. *How the Other Half Lives.* Dover, 1971.

Rylant, Cynthia. *Missing May.* Orchard, 1992.

Say, Allen. *Grandfather's Journey.* Houghton, 1993.

Scholes, Katherine. *Peace Begins with You.* Little, Brown, 1990.

Sharmat, Marjorie. *I'm Terrific.* Holiday House, 1977.

_____. *Say Hello, Vanessa.* Holiday House, 1979.

Shyer, Marlene. *Here I Am an Only Child.* Aladdin, 1985.

Simon, Norma. *All Kinds of Families.* A. Whitman, 1976.

_____. *I Am Not a Crybaby.* Puffin Books, 1989.

_____. *I Was Too Mad!* Whitman, 1974.

Speare, Elizabeth George. *The Sign of the Beaver.* Dell, 1983.

Steig, William. *Sylvester and the Magic Pebble.* Simon & Schuster Books for Young Readers, 1969.

Taylor, Mildred. *Roll of Thunder, Hear My Cry.* Dial, 1976.

Taylor, Theodore. *The Cay.* Doubleday, 1969.

Udry, Janice. *What Mary Jo Shared.* Hale, 1969.

Volvavkova, Hana. *I Never Saw Another Butterfly . . .* Schocken Books, 1993.

Waddell, Martin. *The Owl Babies.* Candlewick Press, 1992.

Watts, Melanie. *Scaredy Squirrel.* Kids Can Press, 2006.

Wells, Rosemary. *Shy Charles.* Dial, 1988; Viking, 2001.

Williams, Vera B. *Cherries and Cherry Pits.* Greenwillow Books, 1986.

Wong, Janet. *Alex and the Wednesday Chess Club.* Margaret K. McElderry Books, 2004.

_____. *Apple Pie 4th of July.* Harcourt, 2002.

Wood, Audrey. *Quick as a Cricket.* Child's Play, 1982.

Yep, Laurence. *Child of the Owl.* HarperCollins, 1977.

Zolotow, Charlotte. *William's Doll.* HarperCollins, 1972.

Games

Face It! A Fun Game to Learn About Feelings. Childswork-Childsplay, The Center for Applied Psychology, 1991.

Feelings and Faces Game. Lakeshore, 1993.

Mindtrap. Mindtrap Games, 1991.

Not So Scary Things. Iron Mountain Game Company, 1989.

Personality Probe, Kids' Edition. N. L. Associates, 1987.

The Ungame: Kids Version. Talicor Incorporated, 2002.

Toot & Puddle Game. Gamewright Inc., 1999.

Totika. Open Spaces, 2005.

Whoonu. Cranium, 2005.

Teachers' Resources

Bissell, Harold, Ph.D. *Human Development Program: Activity Guide III.* Palomares and Associates, 1972.

Burke, Kay. *Authentic Learning.* Corwin, 2009.

Capacchione, Lucia. *The Creative Journal: The Art of Finding Yourself.* Swallow Press, 1979.

Chen, Jie-Qi, ed. *Project Spectrum: Early Learning Activities.* Teachers College Press, 1999. (This is volume 2 of Project Zero Frameworks for Early Childhood Education.)

Cohen, Cathi. *Raise Your Child's Social IQ.* Advantage Books, 2000.

Drew, Naomi. *Learning the Skills of Peacemaking.* Jalmar Press, 1987.

Elman, Natalie Madorsky, and Kennedy-Moore, Eileen. *The Unwritten Rules of Friendship.* Little, Brown and Company, 2003.

Forte, Imogene. *The Me I'm Learning to Be.* Incentive, 1991.

Gardner, Howard. *Frames of Mind.* Basic Books, 1983.

———. *The Unschooled Mind.* Basic Books, 1991.

Graves, Donald H., and Sunstein, Bonnie S. *Portfolio Portraits.* Heinemann, 1992.

Greene, Ross. *The Explosive Child.* HarperCollins, 2005.

Hart, Leslie A. *Human Brain and Human Learning.* Books for Educators, 1983.

Helm, Judy Harris, and Katz, Lilian. *Young Investigators: The Project Approach in the Early Years.* Teachers College Press, 2001.

Jones, Alanna. *104 Activities That Build: Self-Esteem, Teamwork, Communication, Anger Management, Self-Discovery, and Coping Skills.* Rec Room Publishing, 1998.

Kincher, Jonni. *Psychology for Kids.* Free Spirit, 1990.

The Magic Circle Human Development Program. Palomares and Associates, 1974.

McCarthy, Marietta. *Little Big Minds.* Penguin Group, 2006.

Meisgeier, Charles, Ed.D., and Murphy, Elizabeth. "Murphy Meisgeier Type Indicator for Children." Consulting Psychologists Press, 1987.

Miller, Jamie. *10-Minute Life Lessons for Kids.* Harper Perennial, 1998.

Palmer, Hap. *"Sammy," Hap Palmer Favorites: Songs for Learning Through Music and Movement.* Alfred, 1981.

Pergola, Beth. "Wonderful Me," Sing It Instead. Instrumental Only, 1989.

Sax, Leonard. *Why Gender Matters*. Broadway Books, 2005.

Silver, Gail. *Ahn's Anger*. Plum Blossom Books, 2009.

Sternberg, Robert. *The Triarchic Mind*. Viking, 1988.

Stock, Gregory, Ph.D. *The Kids' Book of Questions*. Workman, 1988.

Wormeli, Rick. *Summarization in Any Subject: 50 Techniques to Improve Student Learning*. ASCD, 2005.

"If anything is sacred, the
human body is sacred."

—*WALT WHITMAN*

3

Photograph: Patti Gabriel

The Bodily-Kinesthetic Intelligence

Web of the Bodily-Kinesthetic Intelligence

Student Quotes

" I eat, breathe, drink and dream BK. Use it every day or you can lose it. BK rocks! "

" It isn't just if you are fast or strong, you have to have skill and agility. "

" You don't have to be good at all sports; you just have to play and have fun. "

" I'm not the most skilled person, but I still do BK every day, and that's what matters. "

" BK isn't just about sports; it's also about movement such as dancing, running and other stuff. "

Characteristics

- Dexterous, agile, enduring physical energy, quick, well-defined body control, takes in information through bodily sensations, hands-on learner, well-coordinated motor skills, athletic, likes to figure out how things work, performer, demonstrates skill in crafts, uses body language, enjoys exhilarating experiences

Famous People

JIM CARREY uses his body to communicate emotions and humor in the many comedies in which he stars.

LEBRON JAMES displays talent and teamwork on the basketball court.

KATHERINE DUNHAM was an accomplished modern dancer and choreographer who founded her own dance company and school.

DAVID COPPERFIELD entertains fans around the world with his sleight-of-hand magical illusions.

DR. CHRISTIAAN BARNARD performed the first successful human-to-human heart transplant.

Adult Quotes

" Interest and proficiency in almost any one activity—swimming, boating, fishing skiing, skating—breed interest in many more. Once someone discovers the delight of mastering one skill, however slightly, he is likely to try out not just one more, but a whole ensemble. "

—MARGARET MEAD

" Lack of activity destroys the good condition of every human being, while movement and methodical physical exercise save it and preserve it. "

—PLATO

The B-K Everyday

BY PAT NUERNBERGER, TOMMI ROGERS, AND LAUREN McKENNA

Elena is moving down the field, weaving back and forth with the soccer ball on an invisible string, causing defenders to stumble. Paul balances his body on the beam, seeming to defy gravity as he jumps and lands on a tiny bar of wood. Dana makes the playing cards appear from her sleeve and your ear, moving her hands and fingers more quickly and subtly than the eye can perceive. Marcus jumps with glee, skipping every other circle and landing on only the even or only the odd numbers as he learns to count by two. Maria finds rhythm in everything she hears and constantly moves her body to the beat and melody.

Large muscles, small muscles, coordination, legerdemain, and rhythm all fall within the Bodily-Kinesthetic (B-K) Intelligence.

The B-K Intelligence involves the ability to control body movements and handle objects skillfully. It encompasses everyone who demonstrates a tendency to use the body to communicate, respond, or understand in a given situation. Individuals who are strong in the B-K Intelligence generally have exceptional coordination, balance, and dexterity; an almost elastic-like flexibility; and powerful muscle strength, quick speed, and a marked sensitivity of touch. B-K students tend to have a keen sense of body awareness; they like physical movement, dancing, making and inventing things with their hands, and expressive role-playing. Some students exhibit their B-K Intelligence by communicating well through body language and other physical gestures. They can often perform a task much better after seeing someone else do it first and then mimicking their actions. They tend to enjoy physical games of all kinds and prefer to demonstrate to someone else how to do something rather than tell them how to do it. B-K students often find it difficult to sit still for long periods of time and may become distracted by their need to be actively involved in what is going on.

> Individuals who are strong in the B-K Intelligence generally have exceptional coordination, balance, and dexterity; an almost elastic-like flexibility; and powerful muscle strength, quick speed, and a marked sensitivity of touch.

For children whose strength lies in the B-K Intelligence, physical education class is the highlight of the school day. It is a place where learning is active rather than passive, where learning by doing is the norm, and where movement is encouraged. Their B-K Intelligence doesn't shut off when they leave PE class or recess. By interacting with the space around them, B-K students are able to remember and process information; they learn best through a hands-on approach, actively exploring the physical world around them. But all students, not just those who are strong in B-K, will benefit from active experiences in the classroom; physical activities help focus many students' attention and improve their memory function. It should be just as natural for a math teacher to use movement in the classroom as for a PE teacher to have students skip-count. The more drama, creative movement, dance, manipulatives, games, and exercising

All students, not just those who are strong in B-K, will benefit from active experiences in the classroom; physical activities help focus many students' attention and improve their memory function.

Most of the activities done in physical education cross the midline and require coordination of body systems. Thus it becomes clear that daily quality physical education is essential for optimal learning.

Movement is important at all ages, but stimulating the B-K Intelligence as early as possible will help students in later grades.

Learning should *not* be a spectator sport!

that can be brought into the classroom, the more that learning will be exciting and memorable for everyone.

We must provide children with plenty of whole body experiences, both to develop vestibular (balance sense) and proprioceptive (awareness of body in space) skills. Jumping, crash landing, and running are all movements through which children "feel" their joints and that aid in developing their senses. Arm and leg crossover exercises requiring students to cross the midline enable the brain to organize itself and forces both hemispheres of the brain to "talk" to each other, important skills necessary for reading and writing. Most of the activities done in physical education cross the midline and require coordination of body systems. Thus it becomes clear that daily quality physical education is essential for optimal learning.

Movement is important at all ages, but stimulating the B-K Intelligence as early as possible will help students in later grades. Tossing and catching balls, balloons, and scarves helps with visual tracking, which aids in copying or reading text from left to right; large movements that come from the shoulder, such as working with a parachute, help with handwriting.

The President's Council on Fitness and Sports suggests thirty minutes of physical activity a day to stimulate the brain. How does movement have an impact on learning? Vigorous activity triggers the release of brain-derived neurotrophic factor (BDNF), which enables one neuron to communicate with another. Physical breaks with quick movement exercises replenish the brain's focus, so teachers should try to build them in throughout the school day as much as possible. *Brain Gym* is one way in which this is accomplished at New City. Our students in grades three through six do not have multiple recess times, so they are scheduled for B-K class every day for thirty minutes. Each class is divided in half, and while one group is with our B-K/PE teacher, the other group is participating in Reading/Writing Workshop. This benefits everyone.

The B-K Intelligence seems to be the most underappreciated intelligence in our schools, and, as Howard Gardner notes, it is not widely developed in our culture. Outside of sports it is not well regarded, especially as a form of expression. Unfortunately, many teachers also overlook the value of physical responses, which are innate to most children. Learning should *not* be a spectator sport! Students need opportunities to actively process information.

The B-K Intelligence has many permutations: large and small muscles, building and assembling, pantomime and mime, dance and performance. Here are some examples of how using the B-K Intelligence can help students learn their scholastic content:

- Kindergarten students learn the importance of periods, question marks, and exclamation points by using their bodies to create the symbols and then show how and when they should be used. They also build a life-size, functioning human body using pasta, popsicle sticks, and yarn.

- First graders learn about pollination by reenacting the sequence of pollen gathering by bees, and they create a small group presentation depicting the various stages of growth. They then are enmeshed in construction paper as they *become* a plant so that they can demonstrate the functions of roots, stems, and leaves. Their feet are roots, firmly planted in the soil; their legs and arms are stems, their hands are leaves, and their heads become flowers.
- Second graders use poster-sized words to visualize sentences, then move themselves (and their words) to create new sentences while learning about sentence fluency and interesting beginnings and transitions. They also create dioramas to depict monuments that should have been built but were not. These dioramas require creativity and small-muscle dexterity.
- Third graders also create dioramas that capture what they have learned about the Native American tribe they have researched, depicting the environment, housing, food, and rituals. Building the diorama requires coordination, manipulation of tiny objects, and use of small muscles, another aspect of the B-K Intelligence. (We need to remember that the B-K Intelligence is more than kicking, swimming, dancing, and throwing.) They learn the concept of ratios by physically putting themselves into the shape of a full-sized buffalo that has been created on the floor with masking tape. They scrunch together, compare, and measure, feeling the size of the buffalo's appendages in contrast to theirs.
- Fourth grade students use the fundamentals of charades and mime to simulate a mirror plane, a rotation axis, and an inversion center. They also create a wooden musical instrument—a psaltery—by measuring, sawing, and filing. (At New City, they played their instruments at a school assembly.)
- Fifth graders design and present a play that depicts the history of our country, relying on movement, dance, singing, and pantomime to tell their story. The Fifth Grade Egg Drop is a tradition: each student designs and builds a container that will cushion their raw egg as it is thrown from a second floor window. The entire school stands outside and cheers on the egg drops! (Recently we have also added an optional Spatial task by allowing students to make their egg-protector as aesthetically pleasing as possible. Students voted on the best designs.)
- Sixth graders simulate the journey of Pacific salmon during the spawning season by creating an obstacle course through which they pass—jumping, running, and simulating swimming—in science class. They also begin their year with a two-night overnight that emphasizes the B-K, Naturalist, and personal intelligences.

Dance is also an excellent movement tool. Exposing students to other cultures through dance deepens their awareness of a world in which differences should be celebrated. Our fifth graders incorporated hip-hop dance into their class play and used it to depict the emotions that African Americans experienced during slavery. Using dance to physically represent the emotions of the main character in a story or to interpret the meaning behind a piece of poetry offers an excellent avenue for strengthening the connection between reader and author.

The PE teacher can also be an invaluable resource to classroom teachers by communicating the roles that students play in PE class: Are students followers or leaders? What roles do they play? Team leadership is a very important quality, and sometimes it is shown most clearly during PE or recess times.

What can classroom teachers do? Take a closer look at your plan book:

- Revise just one lesson this week by incorporating one B-K activity.
- Talk with your PE teacher. Ask her what she might be able to do during her class to reinforce one concept or topic you plan on covering this coming month.
- Ask your PE teacher to suggest something that you can do in your room to reinforce one of her activities or borrow a piece of equipment that you can use for one of your lessons.

What about your classroom? Take a look around:

- Can students move around in your room and not have to be at their desks for the entire period?
- Are there materials that allow students to build or design, to explore a new concept physically, to have hands-on experiences and learn by doing?
- Are there spaces for students to practice plays, dance, or other movement activities?

Students don't need to be shown how to move; they just need to be allowed to do so.

Some teachers are uncomfortable incorporating B-K into their lessons because they don't see themselves as physical people or they fear looking foolish in front of their students. That's the beauty of B-K enhanced lessons. You are not the one being asked to move (although it's never a bad thing to do so). Students don't need to be shown how to move; they just need to be allowed to do so. They need you to give them the opportunities, perhaps a little guidance, and a sincere affirmation of their efforts—they'll do the rest. It's that simple!

Everybody's Moving

PURPOSE:

Students identify and confront stereotypes while exploring the various activities enjoyed by the main character of *Oliver Button Is a Sissy* by Tomie dePaola. They recognize that any form of exercise is valuable for both boys and girls.

BODILY-KINESTHETIC
PRIMARY
LANGUAGE ARTS

MATERIALS:

Oliver Button Is a Sissy by Tomie dePaola, jump ropes, balance beam, shower puffs, baskets, assorted balls and/or bean bags, targets for aiming, juice can lids, thick rubber bands, various dress-up items, equal amounts of like articles, in bags (enough for three or four children)

PROCEDURE:

1. Read *Oliver Button Is a Sissy* by Tomie dePaola.

2. Discuss the things Oliver did that were considered unusual for a boy, such as not liking ball games, walking alone, jumping rope. Introduce the word *stereotype*. Brainstorm a list of activities that both girls and boys enjoy.

3. The following activities could be set up as centers for the children to rotate through:

    Jumping rope: Provide different ropes and let the children practice different types of jumping rope.

    Picking Flowers: Have balance beam set up for children to cross, bend, pick flowers or shower puffs, put in basket.

    Playing ball: Children practice throwing balls or bean bags at various targets.

    Tap dancing: Children attach juice can lids to the bottom of their shoes to produce a tapping sound and practice tap dancing.

    Dress-up: Children race against a partner or within a small group to be the first to put on all the dress-up items in their bag.

4. During a class discussion students consider which centers were most often visited by boys and girls, which activities felt comfortable to perform, which made students feel uncomfortable, and why the students made the choices they made.

ASSESSMENT/REFLECTION:

Create a checklist to note the behaviors of the students. As the students visited each center, did they make decisions about participation in the activities based on appropriate information rather than on stereotypes? Were they sensitive to the choices of others? Did they show concern and empathy for others?

MI EXTENSIONS:

This lesson also uses the Linguistic, Intrapersonal, and Interpersonal intelligences.

Linguistic: Have children write or draw a reflection about the activities they felt most comfortable doing and explain their choices.

Interpersonal: Have the students sort a pile of toys into traditional "boy" toys and "girl" toys. Use the groupings to question the faulty assumptions that people can make about gender and interests. Although some boys or girls will prefer certain toys and activities, there is much more overlap than might be assumed. Students must resolve the disagreements that arise.

Intrapersonal: Ask students if they have ever been teased about their interests in a certain activity. Role-play a situation in which one student is teased for his or her choices. How does the student react to being teased? Discuss how a student might be assertive when confronting stereotypes.

Logical-Mathematical: Place toys or a list of games on a Venn diagram labeled as "boy activities" and "girl activities." As with the preceding Interpersonal activity, use these groupings to elicit a dialogue about false assumptions.

Musical: Listen to the song *I'm Me and You're You* by Laurie Berkner. Use Laurie's verse pattern to create a new verse with a partner.

Express Yourself

PURPOSE:
Children notice, identify, and show feelings through facial expressions and body language.

MATERIALS:
King Bidgood's in the Bathtub by Don Wood and Audrey Wood (a literature set or big book so children can most easily see the facial expressions of characters), chart paper, camera, mirrors, dress-up clothes, clip art picture frame, bucket, large cutout tub (or a chalked outline of a bathtub on the floor), numbered sheet for reflection

PROCEDURE:
1. Read the book *King Bidgood's in the Bathtub*, for enjoyment.
2. Ask your students to think of ways in which people communicate. How do people communicate without words? When reading the book a second time, pay close attention to the facial expressions (eyes, eyebrows, mouths) and body language of the characters. Stop periodically to let the children practice making the same expressions while looking in a mirror. As you read, create a chart of adjectives to label the expressions seen in the book.
3. Children dress up as a king or queen and strike a pose showing one of the expressions from the class chart. Take a photograph of each child to crop and glue in a clip art frame. They title their work to include an adjective, the word *queen* or *king*, and their name (*A Proud Queen Sophie* or *The Surprised King Ben*).
4. During the third reading, children act out the story using the tub prop that has been cut out of paper or marked in chalk on the floor. Students take turns depicting the page carrying the bucket of water, King Bidgood sitting in the bathtub, and the various people who join him in the tub. As the teacher reads the story, the actors pay careful attention to body language and expressions that help communicate the story.
5. After acting out the story, a group discussion follows that includes questions such as: Which feelings were easiest or most difficult to portray? Which expressions do you use most or least often?

ASSESSMENT/REFLECTION:
Number each of the children's royal portraits and cover the title. Children will examine the portraits and on individual numbered sheets write the expression from the class adjective chart that they think best describes each portrait. Were the students able to accurately name most of the emotions expressed?

MI EXTENSIONS:

During this lesson, children also use their Interpersonal and Intrapersonal intelligences.

Spatial: Children study their photographs and draw a royal self-portrait to place in a matching clip art frame, paying close attention to the expression shown in their photograph.

Musical: Teach children to waltz, then have a King Bidgood masquerade ball. Children need to be aware of their partner's body language. Masks can be made by cutting a paper plate in half, cutting two eye holes, decorating it, and attaching a craft stick handle.

Logical-Mathematical: Choose four or five expressions from the class chart. Visit another classroom, the lunchroom, or playground to tally and graph the number of times each expression is observed.

Continental Twister

PURPOSE:
Students locate and identify the seven continents on a map. This activity could also be used to help students learn to identify countries, states, land forms, or landmarks.

MATERIALS:
Large laminated world floor map for each team, game cards for each team, small world maps of continent outlines for each child

PROCEDURE:
1. Write the word *continent* on the board and elicit a working definition from the class.

2. Form groups of four or five students. Give each group a large laminated map of the world for the floor and ask them to locate the seven continents.

3. Review the concepts of right and left. Provide each group with two stacks of game cards. One stack of cards shows pictures and the names of the continents. The other stack has cards that say "right hand," "left hand," "right foot," "left foot."

4. One child in each group is the caller. The players follow the directions of the caller as he or she draws a card from each stack. When someone falls, the game is over and one of the standing players becomes the new caller.

ASSESSMENT/REFLECTION:
Students will label the continents on the blank maps of the world without using other resources.

MI EXTENSIONS:
In this lesson, students also use the Interpersonal and Spatial intelligences.

Linguistic: Put clues for the continents in the form of riddles. For example, "Which continent name contains the most syllables?" and "Which continent name contains an A, but not an N?" The students locate the continents on the map using the riddles.

Logical-Mathematical: Using string, groups outline each continent to find perimeters. Use nonstandard units of measurement (hands, feet, fingers) to determine the area of each continent. Order and compare this data.

Musical: Create a song about the seven continents and perform it for the class, using a familiar tune like "He's Got the Whole World in His Hands" or "What a Wonderful World." As the song is sung, students locate the continents on a map.

Spatial: Tear pieces of construction paper into the shapes of the continents. Glue them on large paper to create a map of the world.

Sensing Our Bodies

BODILY-KINESTHETIC

PRIMARY

PHYSICAL EDUCATION

PURPOSE:

Through a variety of activities, children develop balance, coordination, strength, speed, flexibility, and endurance. Visual and motor planning skills are reinforced.

MATERIALS:

Trikes that are propelled by placing feet on the handle bars, buddy walkers, scooter boards, jump ropes, hula hoops, scoops, balloons, scarves, balls, roller skates, balance board, labyrinth, zoom ball, bean bags, spinners, mini trampoline

Smart Moves by Carla Hannaford, *Brain Gym* by Paul E. Dennison and Gayle E. Dennison, *The Out-of-Sync Child* by Carol Stock Kranowitz, *The Out-of-Sync Child Has Fun* by Carol Stock Kranowitz, *Yoga for Youngsters* by Kat Randall, *The Morning Meeting Book* by Roxann Kriete

PROCEDURE:

1. Over the course of the year, the materials listed are put into the Bodily-Kinesthetic center. The activities are set up in a location that provides sufficient space for the children and materials. When a piece of equipment is put in the center, students brainstorm a list of ways that the equipment should be used safely.

2. The following is a list of possible activities to help you get started. Many more ideas can be generated by the children or found in the books listed in the materials section.

   Balloons: With a partner, hit the balloon back and forth across a line marked on the floor. Use a pair of pantyhose stretched over a wire hanger as a racket. Working alone, see how many times you can hit the balloon, keeping it in the air.

   Hula hoops: Line them up in a pattern on the floor and let the children move through them placing one foot in each hoop. How many different ways can they move down the hula hoop path?

   Scarves: Juggle with two, three, or four scarves. Create an interpretive dance. Make parachutes by adding a weight.

   Mini-trampoline: Jump while spelling new words or practicing math facts. Jump with one foot or with one hand behind your back. Create jumping patterns like jump, clap, jump, clap. Count by twos, fives, or tens.

   Balance board: Invite a buddy to join you on the board and maintain your balance.

3. At the completion of a center, students check in with the teacher.

ASSESSMENT/REFLECTION:

During check-in at the completion of the center, students do a demonstration of how they used the material. Observing them will provide information on each child's gross motor development and skills. You may choose to keep a checklist of desired motor development benchmarks.

MI EXTENSIONS:

During this lesson, students also use the Interpersonal Intelligence.

Musical: Play music and let the students dance while wearing paper plates on their feet or move like different kinds of creatures, animals, fairies, or giants.

Spatial: Manipulate Play-Doh or modeling clay to create a sculpture. Create a collage by using tweezers or chopsticks to pick up found or collected objects and glue them to another surface.

Linguistic: Recite poetry or nursery rhymes while doing the center activities.

Literature Live

BODILY-KINESTHETIC
INTERMEDIATE
MUSIC

PURPOSE:

Students create a performance art piece that involves the elements of movement (energy, intensity, direction, dimension, and level) to illustrate story elements such as character, plot, setting, conflict, theme, or mood.

MATERIALS:

A variety of musical selections, multimedia device, books

PROCEDURE:

1. Explain to the students that creative movement, when organized, is another way to tell a story.

2. Explain the elements of movement, one at a time, as students take on the characteristics of animate or inanimate objects.

   Energy is the force that initiates, controls, and stops movements (think of a vehicle as it accelerates and stops).

   Intensity describes the movement in terms of strength and weakness (think of clouds on a windless, a breezy, or a stormy day).

   Direction is going from one place to another (think of flowing water).

   Dimension refers to how the movement looks and feels different based on the size of the movement (think of a rabbit grazing for food versus escaping a predator).

   Level is the position—high, medium, low, or in between—of the movement (think of various garden flowers).

3. As a class, choose a character from a story that has been studied. Choose the elements of movement that reflect the character and write them on the board.

4. Choose music that fits the mood of the story. With music in the background, have students work in small groups to plan a performance art piece that interprets the character from the story. Have each group share what they have created with the class. Discuss the variety of movements that were used to interpret the same character.

5. Now that the class has practiced how to create a performance art piece that uses the elements of movement, assign specific story elements that small groups will interpret. This could include additional characters, plot, setting, climax, or conflict and resolution. Each group takes a different element and plans the story details to convey to the audience.

6. Allow time for the students to plan their interpretation. Have them select three or four elements of movement that they want to use and begin to explore and improvise. They need to determine the dimension, level, direction, intensity, and energy of each movement.

After there has been ample time for practice, have the students perform for the class.

ASSESSMENT/REFLECTION:

With the students, create a rubric that reflects the characteristics students display to show their understanding of the elements of movement. Students defend their interpretation of the story elements in an artist's statement.

MI EXTENSIONS:

This lesson also uses the Interpersonal, Linguistic, and Musical intelligences.

Intrapersonal: After the students have planned their interpretation, give them a checklist that will help them assess the following:

- Do the movements express your ideas?
- Is the movement interesting?
- Are the required elements included?
- Are you satisfied with the order of the movements?
- Should the order or actual movements be changed?

Linguistic: Students collect movement words (jargon) that describe movements related to other activities: various sports, cooking, acting, or sewing.

Musical: The students can use various pieces of recorded music or instruments to interpret the elements of movement.

Prepositional Charades

PURPOSE:

Students identify prepositional phrases as a part of speech. Students will use their interpersonal skills to communicate with their peers and work cooperatively. This lesson could also be used to teach other parts of speech, such as nouns, verbs, adjectives, adverbs, interjections, or conjunctions.

BODILY-KINESTHETIC

INTERMEDIATE

LANGUAGE ARTS

MATERIALS:

Phrase strips and a basket from which the players can pull the strips

PROCEDURES:

1. Prepare strips of paper for the charades by writing a prepositional phrase on each (such as "through the window," "on the carpet," "under the sun"). Be sure there is at least one for each student in the class.

2. The class is divided into teams of three or four students. Each group decides on their playing order within the group. The groups decide on the playing order of the groups.

3. Review the rules for charades and provide the following tips for play:

   - Hold up fingers to show the number of words in the phrase.
   - When a word is guessed correctly, point to your nose with one hand and to the correct guesser with the other hand.
   - Cup one hand behind an ear to show that you want a word that sounds like another word.
   - No team may talk, comment, or consult while it is another team's turn. By doing so, that team loses a point.

4. The first player from the starting team draws a strip and has one minute to act it out for his or her team. If a team member guesses correctly, the team receives two points.

5. If the minute elapses and no team member has guessed correctly, the next team in the rotation gets ten seconds to consult and then may make a guess. If they guess incorrectly, the opportunity to guess goes to the next team. The team that does guess correctly earns one point.

6. If no team succeeds in guessing correctly, the phrase strip is returned to the basket.

7. Continue play until all students have had a chance to act out a phrase. Total up team points.

ASSESSMENT/REFLECTION:

Students are asked to highlight prepositional phrases on a written assessment. On a checklist, note the students' use of eye contact, body language, facial expressions, and responses to audience feedback.

MI EXTENSIONS:

This lesson also uses the Linguistic and Interpersonal intelligences.

Intrapersonal: In prepositional phrases, students list all the activities they do in one day, such as "out of bed," "down the stairs," "in the car," "in my backpack."

Linguistic: In teams, students think of commonly used phrases that start with a preposition. Share the lists and score by either the longest list or giving a point for each phrase that no other team has on their list.

Musical: Have students think of song titles that contain prepositional phrases, such as "Tiptoe Through the Tulips," and "Somewhere over the Rainbow." Have the students use the song titles in a game of charades.

Spatial: Rather than act out the prepositional phrases, students draw them on the board for the team to guess, in a manner similar to the game *Pictionary*.

Disabilities Simulation

PURPOSE:

The students become sensitive to and aware of the differences in daily life faced by individuals who are differently abled. These simulations allow the students to experience life as a physically disabled, a hearing impaired, and a visually impaired student.

MATERIALS:

Blindfolds or scarves, earplugs, donated or loaned wheelchairs, elastic bandages, sports tape, yardsticks, notepads, teacher-created parent letter, teacher-created Braille cards, *How It Feels to Live with a Physical Disability* by Jill Krementz

PROCEDURE:

1. Before this lesson begins, contact medical supply stores or parents to explain the simulation and ask for the loan of wheelchairs that can be used during the simulation.

2. Send a letter to parents explaining the three simulations along with a permission slip that must be signed. The letter specifies the days of each simulation and provides details about each one. Alert non-classroom personnel (resource teachers and other support staff) of the simulations so that they can adapt their curriculum as well.

3. Students are partnered with a same-gender partner throughout the simulations. The work begins with community- and trust-building activities, such as trust falls or team-building games. The first two simulations, physically disabled and visually impaired, each take two days. During these, one person takes on the role of helper while the other experiences the disability. The second day, they switch roles. The hearing impaired simulation takes place in one day.

4. Work begins with the physically disabled simulation. The students must confront two problems during different parts of the day. One is being wheelchair bound; the other is losing the use of their dominant arm while the thumb of their other hand is taped down. Problem-solve to determine the order in which the pairs of students will experience these situations.

5. Ideally, the experience lasts for the entire day. However, it is important that at least thirty minutes be budgeted into the schedule for introductions and debriefing at the end of the day. During the introduction, students make predictions about what they will experience and the emotions they will feel.

6. Once some students are settled into wheelchairs and others have their arms and thumbs taped, look at the configuration of the room. Discuss what accommodations need to be made so students can move around in their wheelchairs. Take the students to the hallway and see if any barriers exist there. Can students use the drinking fountain, get over the threshold, maneuver the wheelchair into the bathroom stall, and reach the soap dispenser?

7. Students proceed through their regular day. The role of the partner is to help only when asked, because although people who are differently abled may need some accommodations, they can still do many things for themselves. Before lunch and recess, discuss accommodations that need to be made.

8. In a discussion, note what accommodations the students with their arms and thumbs taped need to complete their daily routine. For instance, what do they use to keep their paper from sliding around? How do the students' experiences differ based on being differently abled? Keep a list of problems and the ways in which students solved them. How much help was needed from the partners?

9. To help students understand the differences between empathy and sympathy, read *How It Feels to Live with a Physical Disability* by Jill Krementz.

10. Ongoing discussions during the day are vital, as well as time at the end of the day for reflection. What surprised the students? What was easier or harder than anticipated? What feelings did the students experience? Talk about how the first group's experiences can help students the next day when they switch roles.

11. The most difficult simulation is being blindfolded. Before the simulation begins, teach the guides how to safely lead their partners. Do *not* use a blindfold during the practice. To lead properly, the sighted partner stands on the left of the person who is simulating being visually impaired, puts her right hand on her right hip, and offers her arm to the blindfolded person, who grasps her upper arm but does not link arms. This technique will keep the guide just a half step in front of the blindfolded person, allowing that person to receive information from the slight arm and shoulder movements of the sighted person. The guide walks at a normal pace and is constantly whispering information to her partner; for example, "We just passed the drinking fountain. We are approaching the library, and you are doing great." Before putting actual blindfolds on, partners practice this in the classroom, hallway, and on the stairs. Stairs are a dangerous obstacle. Be sure students maintain several yards between each set of partners. Sighted partners guide the blindfolded partner by whispering, "Step, step, step, last step." Always have the person who is blindfolded on the railing side. Guides must always stay with their partners except in the restroom stall. If a sighted partner does not follow the established procedures, she will not be allowed to continue in the simulation. Partners must stay together even at recess.

12. After being blindfolded, students are given a task they can easily accomplish, such as "Get out your spelling folder" or "Find your math book." Familiarize blindfolded students with their environment by having partners find common objects from around the

room for them to hold and identify. Discuss how student manage lunch and recess routines.

13. Teach students the six-dot Braille cell. Using an index card, make a Braille cell numbering the descending dots on the left, one, two, and three, and the descending dots on the right, four, five, and six. So each dot can be felt, punch a hole with a pencil.

14. In addition to completing regular classroom activities, students could go through an obstacle course of wastebaskets, using a yard-stick as a cane, while their sighted partners give oral directions. Continue reading from Jill Krementz's book.

15. During the debriefing session and ongoing discussions, students offer feedback for the sighted partner and share strategies for the second day, when the roles are reversed. These insights and problems are added to the class list under a heading for this impairment.

16. The last simulation, of hearing impairment, is the hardest to stage, as earplugs do not fully block out sound. To compensate, the teacher mouths words instead of speaking them out loud and also wears earplugs. The entire class does this simulation together. Provide notepads so partners can communicate by writing notes to each other and introduce some basic sign language.

17. During the first discussion of the day, children read each other's lips as they decide on the signal to be used to get everyone's attention. Flipping the lights off and on works well.

18. During discussions, students share the difficulties, feelings, and successes they experienced while being hearing impaired. These are added to the class list under the Hearing Impaired heading.

ASSESSMENT/REFLECTION:

Students show their awareness of the difficulties in daily life faced by individuals who are differently abled by finding commonalities on the lists. Students choose an area of the building that could be changed to be made more accessible to those who are differently abled, then develop a plan for those changes.

MI EXTENSIONS:

This lesson also uses the Interpersonal and Intrapersonal intelligences.

Linguistic: Watch a TV show or a DVD with the sound turned off. Discuss the difficulty someone with a hearing impairment might encounter as she tries to follow the story line and the need to rely on the action and body language of the actors. Watch another program using closed captions. The need to concentrate on the written words causes the viewers to miss the action and body language. Discuss the advantages and disadvantages of both.

Interpersonal: Invite differently abled members of the community to come talk about their life experiences, one before the simulation activity and one after. Students submit to the teacher, ahead of time, two questions they would like to have answered. To assess the sensitivity and growth they have acquired by undergoing the simulations, note the changes in their questions. Display the questions, without names, and discuss their appropriateness and what students will learn by asking that question.

Intrapersonal: Choose one area of the building that needs to be changed to make it more accommodating for those who are differently abled. Create and act on a plan to bring this awareness to others. Find ways to initiate change.

Living Museum

PURPOSE:

Students demonstrate an understanding of how to conduct research within the genre of biography and share accurate information in a two- to three-minute dramatic presentation. Students discern the significant events in an individual's life and must be prepared to answer questions about their subject's life.

MATERIALS:

Age-appropriate biographies, costumes, props, milk crates, construction paper, card stock, markers, device for recording presentations

PROCEDURE:

1. Organize age-appropriate biographies by intelligences. Ask students to peruse the selections and to identify three individuals that they are interested in studying further. Students select one of the three choices and set up a reading schedule based on the number of pages in the book and the number of days available for research.

2. Model how to take notes on a biography. The notes focus on stages of life: childhood, education, young adulthood, professional life, major accomplishments, and the contribution the individual made. Possible methods for note-taking include mind maps, T-charts, summary paragraphs, sticky notes, and notecards.

3. As students independently read the biographies, they take notes using a chosen method.

4. After the biography is read and notes are compiled, students organize and construct a two- to three-minute monologue from the perspective of the individual. The monologue should include highlights from the individual's life.

5. Students construct an outline on a note card to remind them of the important events to share during their presentations.

6. Practice, practice, practice. Use a timer to ensure that the monologue fits within the two- to three-minute requirement. Students gather props and costume materials. Practice the monologue, using props and acting techniques, standing on a crate, problem-solving, and projecting.

7. Use card stock to make a nameplate with name and years of birth and death. Use construction paper and markers to make "push here" buttons and affix to upside-down milk crates.

8. Scatter milk crates throughout the designated performance space. The day of the presentations, students choose a crate. Students place the nameplate on the floor in front of them. They will stand on the crate in a frozen position and will "come to life" when the "push here" button is pushed. Upon finishing the monologue, students will state that they have time for two questions.

9. Invite families and the school community to come discover the citizens who have made a difference at the Living Museum.

ASSESSMENT/REFLECTION:

Videotape students and observe how well students followed the outlined criteria. Did they stay within the two- to three-minute timeframe? Did the monologue contain accurate information? Was it easy to follow? Was the student captivating? Did he or she engage the audience? Did the student maintain focus? How was the student's delivery (eye contact, projection, enunciation)? Did the props detract from or enhance the presentation?

MI EXTENSIONS:

During this lesson, students also used their Linguistic and Interpersonal intelligences.

Intrapersonal: Have students take home their recording and view their performance. Students reflect on the established criteria and rate their performance. What worked? What could be improved?

Logical-Mathematical: Students construct a timeline for their chosen individual. As a class, compile a timeline of all the individuals researched. What do you notice? Do dates overlap? What do they have in common? Each student creates a Venn diagram comparing his or her own life to that of the person researched.

Musical: Gather music from the periods in which the students' individuals lived. Compare and contrast the pieces. What is the mood like? What instruments were used? What is the tempo? How do the choices of composers or musicians reflect the attitude of the time?

Spatial: Have students create a portrait of their individual in an appropriate setting. Research the art form of portraiture. What do you learn about them from the clothing, setting, props, style, and color choice in the portrait?

Name: _____ Date: _____

Living Museum Video Viewing Reflection

Rate yourself on a scale of 0 to 10 (0 lowest, 10 highest) on the following:

Loudness: _____

Eye contact: _____

Costume and props: _____

Content of speech: _____

Estimate of average score: _____ Actual: _____

I included in my speech how my person made a difference. Yes _____ No _____

My speech was between two and three minutes. (Please time accurately.) _____

My favorite part of this project was

_____

_____

_____

If I were going to do this project again, I would _____

_____

_____

Activities to Support the Bodily-Kinesthetic Intelligence

INTERPERSONAL

- Role-play
- Drama, mime, and charades
- Athletics or sports
- People as game pieces during floor games like chess or checkers
- Use of facial expressions

INTRAPERSONAL

- Acting techniques that require the artist to become a character
- Individual sports
- Meditation and yoga
- Hobbies like gardening or cooking
- Use of an activity to avert anger or frustration; for example, hitting pillows, tearing paper, or squishing Play-Doh

LINGUISTIC

- Playing a game to practice content; for example, catching the ball and answering a question or juggling while spelling words
- Sign language
- Demonstrations
- Handwriting or forming letters with the body
- Practicing spelling words by writing them with a paintbrush and water or drawing them in the sand or on someone's back

LOGICAL-MATHEMATICAL

- Problem-solving using manipulatives
- Creating floor graphs using bodies
- Solving story problems by acting them out
- Chisanbop (Korean finger math) and other finger counting systems
- Body math to reinforce patterning, estimating, shapes, and counting

MUSICAL

- Dancing
- Playing a musical instrument
- Jogging, jumping rope, and exercising to music
- Musical story-telling performances
- Creating rhythms using your body

SPATIAL

- Using tools while cutting or taking apart machines
- Creating Play-Doh and clay sculptures
- Building
- Hair braiding
- Craft activities like sewing, quilting, and weaving

NATURALIST

- Nature walks
- Gardening
- Simulations
- Sensory awareness activities
- Creating art similar to that of Andy Goldsworthy

Identifying the Bodily-Kinesthetic Intelligence in Your Students

Children function at many different levels within the intelligences. Through observation of everyday activities, one can create a profile showing the level of functioning within a particular intelligence and the intelligences in relation to each other. The levels described show increased engagement and proficiency.

YES NO **APPRECIATES:**

☐ ☐ Consistently demonstrates interest, respect, and enjoyment within the intelligence

☐ ☐ Enjoys movement activities as an observer or participant

☐ ☐ Enjoys fine motor activities as an observer or participant

☐ ☐ Collects sports cards

☐ ☐ Enjoys tactile experiences like clay, sand, and water

☐ ☐ Talks about, attends, writes, or reads about sporting events

YES NO **PERFORMS:**

☐ ☐ Is able to apply the intelligence to re-create an exhibit or demonstration or problem-solve within a given situation

☐ ☐ Demonstrates skill in fine motor (such as knitting, sewing, origami) or gross motor activities

☐ ☐ Participates in plays, puppet shows, sports, and dance

☐ ☐ Enthusiastically uses playground equipment

☐ ☐ Is skillful in taking apart and putting objects together (such as LEGO bricks, toasters, models)

☐ ☐ Is able to use tools effectively to solve a problem, make an object

☐ ☐ Plays jacks, pickup sticks, and string games; handclaps rhythms

☐ ☐ Voluntarily moves body (that is, does work standing up, wiggles, taps, prefers movement to sitting still)

☐ ☐ Has inner sense of where one is in space, kinesthesia

☐ ☐ Forms letters and numbers well

YES NO **CREATES:**

☐ ☐ Is able to apply the intelligence to generate original work, to develop unique solutions to problems or create prototypes

☐ ☐ Choreographs a dance or invents a new game

☐ ☐ Demonstrates new dramatic style

☐ ☐ Designs and constructs with a distinctive, recognizable style, as in jewelry, dance

Children's Resources

Books and Recordings

Adoff, Arnold. *Sports Pages.* HarperCollins, 1990.

Allard, Harry. *Miss Nelson Has a Field Day.* Houghton Mifflin, 1985.

Asch, Frank. *Bear Shadow.* Prentice, 1985.

Barber, Tiki and Ronde. *By My Brother's Side.* Simon & Schuster, 2004.

Bildnes, Phil. *Shoeless Joe and Black Betsy.* Simon & Schuster, 2002.

Christopher, Matt. *The Dog That Pitched a No-Hitter.* Trumpet Club, 1988.

Cunxin, Li. *Dancing to Freedom: The True Story of Mao's Last Dancer.* Walker, 2008.

Deans, Karen. *Playing to Win: The Story of Althea Gibson.* Holiday Books, 2007.

dePaola, Tomie. *Oliver Buttons a Sissy.* Harcourt Brace, 1979.

Dodds, Dayle Ann. *Wheel Away.* HarperCollins, 1989.

Eriksson, Eva. *Crash Course for Molly.* R. & S., 2005.

Fleischman, Paul. *Lost: A Story in String.* Holt, 2000.

Galdone, Paul. *The Three Little Pigs.* Clarion, 1970.

Glenbock, Peter. *Teammates.* Harcourt Brace, 1990.

Isadora, Rachel. *Max.* MacMillan, 1976.

Jay, Allen. *The Bicycle Man.* Houghton Mifflin, 1982.

Kalon, Kalan. *Jump, Frog, Jump!* Greenwillow, 1981.

Krementz, Jill. *How It Feels to Live with a Physical Disability.* Simon & Schuster, 1992.

———. *A Very Young Dancer.* Knopf, 1976.

Lasky, Kathryn. *Tumble Bunnies.* Candlewick Press, 2005.

Long, Loren. *Barnstormers: Game 1: Porkopolis.* Simon & Schuster, 2007.

Marzollo, Jean. *Pretend You're a Cat.* Dial Books for Young Readers, 1990.

Mcauly, Emily. *Mirette on the High Wire.* Putnam, 1992.

Mochizuki, Ken. *Be Water My Friend: The Early Years of Bruce Lee.* Lee and Low Books, 2006.

Ormerod, Jan. *Ballet Sisters: The Duckling and the Swan.* Scholastic, 2007.

Parker, Kristi. *My Dad the Magnificent.* Dutton Children's Books, 1990.

Petrillo, Genevieve. *Keep Your Ear on the Ball.* Tilbury House, 2007.

Pinkney, Andrea Davis. *Alvin Ailey.* Hyperion, 1993.

Rabe, Bernice. *The Balancing Girl.* Dutton, 1981.

Rappaport, Doreen. *Dirt on Their Skirts: The Story of the Young Women Who Won the World Championship.* Dial Books for Young Readers, 2000.

Richards, Beah. *Keep Climbing, Girls.* Simon & Schuster, 2006.

Rockwell, Lizzy. *The Busy Body Book.* Crown Publishers, 2004.

Sachs, Marilyn. *Matt's Mitt and Fleet-Footed Florence.* Avon Books, 1991.

Schaefer, Carole. *Dragon Dancing.* Viking, 2007.

———. *Someone Says.* Viking, 2003.

Smith, Charles Jr. *Diamond Life.* Orchard Books, 2004.

———. *Winning Words.* Candlewick Press, 2008.

Ungerer, Tomi. *Crictor.* Ediciones Alfaguara, 1986.

Weatherford, Carole. *Champions on the Bench.* Dial Books for Young Readers, 2007.

Winter, Jonah. *You Never Heard of Sandy Koufax?!* Schwartz & Wade Books, 2009.

Games

Azuma: The Game of Reckless Abandon. Parker Brothers, 1992.

Bowling Set. Fisher-Price, 1990.

Guesstures. Milton Bradley, 1990.

Hammer and Nails. Creative Toys, 1991.

Jumpin' Monkies. Pressman Toy, 1991.

Kids on Stage: The Charades Game for Kids. University Games, 1988.

Looney Tunes: Smash 'em. Tyco, 1994.

Nerf Table Hockey. Parker Brothers, 1987.

Spoon and Egg Coordination Game. Lakeshore, 1991.

Tricky Fingers: A Skill Game for the Whole Family. Reger Games, 1990.

Twister. Milton Bradley, 1986.

Unimax: Moveable Mazes. Inimax Toys, 1990.

Teachers' Resources

Beall, Pamela, and Hagon, Susan. "Head, Shoulders, Knees, and Toes." In *Wee Sing and Play*. Price, Stern, Sloan, 1981.

Burke, Kay. *Authentic Learning*. Corwin, 2009.

Caney, Steve. *Steven Caney's Invention Book*. Workman, 1985.

Cassidy, Nancy and John. "Whole World in His Hands." In *Kids Songs*. Klutz Press, 1988.

Chen, Jie-Qi, ed. *Project Spectrum: Early Learning Activities*. Teachers College Press, 1999. (This is volume 2 of Project Zero Frameworks for Early Childhood Education.)

Cole, Joanna, and Calmerson, Stephanie. *The Eentsy, Weensty Spider*. Morrow Junior Books, 1991.

Cole, Joanna. *Anna Banana, 101 Jump Rope Rhymes*. Scholastic, 1989.

Flaghouse Special Populations (catalog) www.flaghouse.com.

Fluegelman, Andrew. *New Games Book*. Dolphin Books/ Doubleday, 1981.

Gregson, Bob. *The Incredible Indoor Games Book*. Fearon, 1982.

Hannaford, Carla. *Smart Moves*. Great River Books, 2008.

Helm, Judy Harris, and Katz, Lilian. *Young Investigators: The Project Approach in the Early Years*. Teachers College Press, 2001.

Kranowitz, Carol Stock. *The Out-of-Sync Child*. Perigee Trade, 1998.

———. *The Out-of-Sync Child Has Fun*. Perigee Trade, 2003.

Kriete, Roxann. *The Morning Meeting Book*. Northeast Foundation for Children, 2002.

Macaulay, David. *The Way Things Work*. Houghton Mifflin, 1988.

Macfarlan, Allan and Paulette. *Handbook of American Indian Games*. Association Press, 1958.

Patterson, Marilyn. *Every Body Can Learn: Engaging the Bodily-Kinesthetic Intelligence in the Everyday Classroom*. Zephyr Press, 1997.

Randall, Kat. *Yoga for Youngsters*. Kat's Kid Kreation, 2003.

Stewart, Ciccione Georgiana. *Aerobics for Kids*. Lakeshore, 1980 tape #KM7043.

Weissman, Julie. *Kids in Motion*. Alfred, 1993.

Wirth, Marian Jenks. *Teacher's Handbook of Children's Games*. Parker, 1976.

Wormeli, Rick. *Summarization in Any Subject: 50 Techniques to Improve Student Learning*. ASCD, 2005.

"Language is magic: it makes things appear and disappear."

—NICOLE BROSSARD

4

Photograph: Patti Gabriel

The Linguistic Intelligence

Web of the Linguistic Intelligence

Student Quotes

" My greatest intelligence is Linguistic because I read a whole lot, write a whole lot, and make my own books."

" It is fun to tell stories that you make up or to think up your own endings to someone else's story."

" I'm Linguistic because I like to play word games."

" I know I am Linguistic because I'm a good writer, love to read and rhyme, and speak a different language."

Characteristics

- Good at reading and writing, spells easily, enjoys word games, understands puns, jokes, riddles, tongue-twisters, has well-developed auditory skills, readily incorporates descriptive language, easily remembers written and spoken information, good story teller, uses complex sentence structure, appreciates the subtleties of grammar and meaning, often enjoys the sounds and rhythms of language, loves to debate issues or give persuasive speeches, able to explain things well

Famous People

E. E. CUMMINGS will be remembered as one of the most popular poets of the twenty-first century.

MARTIN LUTHER KING wrote and delivered speeches that still inspire today.

BRUCE SPRINGSTEEN, "the Boss," is an American singer-songwriter.

BOBBY NORFOLK is a nationally acclaimed storyteller.

J. K. ROWLING, LEMONY SNICKET, and ROALD DAHL are favorite authors of New City third graders.

Adult Quotes

" The limits of my language stand for the limit of my world."
—LUDWIG WITTGENSTEIN

" Language shapes the way we think and determines what we can think about."
—BENJAMIN LEE WHORF

The Multiple Intelligences Library

BY JOE CORBETT AND JESSICA BROD-MILLNER

New City School opened the world's first multiple intelligences library in December 2005. We began the planning a few years earlier when we determined that the room we were using to house our library was too small. Our MI library of 4,400 square feet fills a former gymnasium and has two levels. We wanted this space to be more than just a traditional repository of books; we wanted it to be a place where students and teachers alike could stretch their thinking and employ their creativity. To this end, MI was a guiding principle in the design of the space.

We spent three years thinking about, researching, and designing our library. We held focus groups with students, faculty, and parents, and each time we asked, "What should be in an MI library?" Our head of school, Tom Hoerr, also posed this question to thousands of educators at conferences and through his MI newsletter. A committee composed of parents, faculty members, and board members visited local school and municipal libraries. All of this information was used to create a request for proposal that listed the expectations for our MI library. It was sent to a number of architecture firms, and after many discussions and interviews, we chose Kevin Kerwin (of HKW Architects, St. Louis, Missouri) as our architect. It was clear that he was receptive to seeing how incorporating all of the intelligences in the design of the library could make it a more interesting and educational setting for everyone. And it has! As a result, although it is still a Linguistic setting that is rife with books, our MI library supports all of the intelligences.

> We wanted this space to be more than just a traditional repository of books; we wanted it to be a place where students and teachers alike could stretch their thinking and employ their creativity.

There are multiple places where children can use their Interpersonal Intelligence, notably the second floor amphitheatre and the large first floor gathering area, as well as two conference rooms for meetings or quiet work, and a number of larger tables for group interaction. There are many nooks and crannies that were designed to allow children opportunities for quiet, Intrapersonal exploration. We have a "wet" room that invites students to explore activities that may involve paints, glue, and other experiences that traditional libraries cannot accommodate. The walls of this room are both dry erase board and magnetic, allowing children opportunities to exercise their Spatial Intelligence.

We have an extensive, updated collection of over thirteen thousand titles, which are accessible throughout the building through our networked electronic catalog. Because we value diversity, we seek to find culturally diverse books. Our librarian conducts regular Book Chats with the students and often shares titles of new and/or must-read titles at faculty meetings. Our librarian's goal is to integrate the library collection, as well as the library space, with classroom curriculum and support the development of all students' multiple intelligences.

TRADITIONAL LIBRARY AND INFORMATION INQUIRY

There are, of course, traditional components to the library. Our full-time librarian sees students from the preschool through the sixth grade on a regular basis. Classes come once or twice a week. During this time the librarian teaches traditional library skills, conducts Book Talks, and, on most visits, reads aloud to the classes.

We think that there is much to be gained from students learning and enjoying nonelectronic board games, so our librarian coordinates school-wide tournaments for checkers, *Boggle, Othello,* and chess. These games give students the chance to exercise their Logical-Mathematical and Linguistic intelligences. A strong emphasis on sportsmanship lets students stretch their Interpersonal and Intrapersonal intelligences as well. Each grade's boy and girl winners play a faculty member in an afternoon tournament (and because ten students simultaneously play against one adult, the chances of student victories increase—much to the adult's chagrin!). As another way of supporting MI, there is also a competition—students vote for the winner—to create a T-shirt design for each of these contests. This allows us to also highlight students' Spatial Intelligence.

CLASSROOM CURRICULUM SUPPORT AND INTEGRATION

> There are many opportunities for the library space to be used to further students' understanding of a topic or concept that is addressed in the regular classroom. This might be done by using library books or conducting research, or the library might be used as a venue for other kinds of activities or experiences.

There are many opportunities for the library space to be used to further students' understanding of a topic or concept that is addressed in the regular classroom. This might be done by using library books or conducting research, or the library might be used as a venue for other kinds of activities or experiences. There are many different cross-grade meetings that happen in the library. For example, the fifth graders meet with their preschool buddies to read, play games, or draw together. Sixth grade students assist their kindergarten pals on a science project that involves tracing the younger children's bodies and drawing their bones. Fourth grade classes use the library to present their Living Museum biographies. Classes will often have speakers present to an entire grade in one of the more intimate spaces in the library or use the space as a forum for sing-along gatherings. We are continually searching for nontraditional ways to use this wonderful space.

PURE MI

We also use our MI library as a setting to help children explore and develop the various intelligences.

Collection Display: To address the Naturalist Intelligence, there are huge fresh water and salt water fish tanks and a bird house on the outside of a window. In addition, the library houses a large display case that exhibits literature, art objects, and collections. Because the Naturalist Intelligence is based on classifying, categorizing, and sorting, students, parents, and teachers are invited to share their personal collections at particular times during the school year. They are also asked to answer a number of questions about their collection, such as: How did you begin collecting? What inspired you to begin your collection? Which intelligences are you using as you explore this collection?

Musical Area: A musical area, with headphones and many tapes and CDs, is on the second floor of our library. Materials are organized so that students can listen to music of specific cultures and time periods.

Small Motor Puzzles: As a way to address the B-K Intelligence, we offer many puzzles and games that rely on children's small motor muscles and dexterity.

MI Centers: These centers grew from a desire on the part of the teachers to provide opportunities for their students to explore MI for the sake of MI. They are designed to give students a chance to explore and choose areas of their intelligences in which they are most interested. Children from preschool through sixth grade attend MI centers each month with their class, but are also invited to come to centers during their recess time, and many students do so.

During the school year our MI centers highlighted our teacher specialists and their areas of teaching (such as art/spatial, performing arts, B-K, science). Students were invited to learn about the specialist teacher through a center called "Specialist Investigator," where they could explore a display of photographs and artifacts about that individual. The Bodily-Kinesthetic center included games like tinikling (a popular Philippine dance with bamboo poles), juggling, hacky sack, Double Dutch jump rope, jacks, marbles, designing rules, yoga, rhythm (juggling) sticks, stilts (yes, in the library!), Body Dice, and Rhythm Flags.

MEETINGS AND LEARNING

Because of its focus on and support of all of the intelligences, our library also offers other kinds of experiences and learning opportunities.

Art Gallery and Displays: The Evan Delano Gallery (adjacent to and a part of the library) provides students and families with opportunities to experience and display art. We have hosted exhibits that feature art by friends, students, or staff members. Exhibits have included paintings, photographs, drawings, ceramics, glass sculptures, woven baskets, jewelry, and more. Students have learned about cultural diversity through art. They have been given opportunities to respond to and challenge the artwork through questions and conversation. Students have also been invited to participate in a number of New City School art exhibitions to experience the artistic process first hand. They have created art work, written artists statements, and attended art openings in their honor. Gallery exhibitions in 2008–2009 included *The Red Earth: A Native American Collection*, a student exhibit called *Change*, and an alumni art exhibit.

MI Resources for Teachers: The library houses a number of resources to support grade level curriculums in dynamic ways. We have art posters and prints available for checkout, as well as art resource kits created by the St. Louis Art Museum. Videos and DVDs are available as well. The newest addition to our collection is a set of forty art images from the *Picturing America* series, created by the National Endowment for the Humanities, which is on display in the art gallery space, as well as in individual classrooms to support grade level themes.

The Personal Intelligences: Our library is designed to enhance both the Interpersonal and Intrapersonal intelligences. As a parent once said, "It's a place where you can get lost and also a place where you can find yourself." There are many tables designed for students to work collaboratively, and there are also many spaces that enable students to be by themselves. It is not uncommon to see a group of youngsters working collaboratively while ten feet away another student is lost in a book.

Saturday Story Time: One Saturday morning each month, our library doors are opened to the neighborhood and community for a story time experience. One of our teachers comes in to read stories, sing, and lead the children in activities.

Our library is the meeting location at New City School. Faculty and parent meetings are held here, as are meetings with educators who come to visit us and presentations by guest speakers. The library is also a great place for student exhibits and displays, from the Living Museum to the Spatial display of Egg-Drop Containers. As you can see, our MI library is the heart of our school.

Word Work

PURPOSE:

Students use a variety of intelligences to practice and master conventional spellings, strengthen their decoding skills, and build their sight word vocabularies by focusing on common blends, word families, short and long vowel patterns, and sight words.

LINGUISTIC

PRIMARY

LANGUAGE ARTS

PROCEDURE:

Interpersonal

In teams, students write all the words they can think of from different categories, such as animals, clothing, or food. Each word must begin with the same letter. Teams share lists. Points are given for words that no other group has found.

Set a timer for five minutes. Children work in teams to write down as many words as they can think of that fit into a specific spelling pattern, such as the *sh* digraph or the long /a/ *ai* pattern. After five minutes, groups share their words. Points are awarded for correctly spelled words that the other teams did not record.

Spatial

Students are assigned a letter sound that is found in words on the Word Wall. Students cut pictures of objects from magazines that have the sound and make a collage of the pictures.

Students draw a picture of a given word, without using numbers, letters, or words. Other students must guess and correctly spell the word being illustrated to earn points.

Bodily-Kinesthtic

Students are placed on teams. When the teams are given a word, one student from each team races to the board to write the first letter. The student returns to the team and passes the chalk to the next person, who races to add the next letter. This continues until the word is complete and correct. Points are awarded for speed, accuracy, and legibility.

Students act out Word Wall words for the rest of the class to guess and spell correctly.

Word family endings are taped to the floor in the style of a hopscotch game. Children hop from box to box, saying a word that would be a member of each word family.

Musical

A word family is chosen for students to play on a xylophone. Letters that could be used to make a word in that family are taped to the bars of the xylophone. The word family letters are taped to the last two bars. Students say a word, then spell it while they play it.

Letters are assigned and taped to various percussion instruments. The letters chosen are those that are most commonly used to spell the Word Wall words. Students use the instruments to play Word Wall words while spelling them.

Logical-Mathematical

Each student works with a partner. One is the timer and the other is the writer. Students determine how many times each can correctly and legibly write a Word Wall word that has been a challenge for that student. They take turns either timing a minute or writing. In a variation, students see how many words from the Word Wall can be written in a minute.

Students use cards containing Word Wall words to develop a sorting system for the words. They might use beginning sounds, spelling patterns, sounds found within a word, or parts of speech. After the words are sorted, students create a graph showing their results.

Naturalist

Students build words when given a set of scrambled letters that make a big word. Students look for two-, three-, four-, and five-letter words before arriving at the big word. Students can list or sort the words by word family, spelling pattern, number of letters, or part of speech.

One student writes a Word Wall word using a cotton swab dipped in water on a chalkboard. The challenge is to see how many times the word can be written before the first one dries up and disappears. Another student tries different techniques to make it evaporate more quickly—blowing, fanning, or adding heat.

Poetry

PURPOSE:
Using children's literature as a springboard for writing poetry, this lesson provides students with the framework for successful poetry writing.

LINGUISTIC

PRIMARY

LANGUAGE ARTS

MATERIALS:
Category 1 books: *Six Hogs on a Scooter* by Eileen Spinelli, *Good Night, Gorilla* by Peggy Rathmann, *Quick as a Cricket* by Audrey Wood, and *My Friend Rabbit* by Eric Rohmann, or any other simple picture book that follows a clear sequence

Category 2 books: *Chicky Chicky Chook Chook* by Cathy MacLennan or *Roadwork* by Sally Sutton, *Apt. 3* by Jack Keats, and *The Rain Came Down* by David Shannon, or any other picture book that is written with simple sound words, onomatopoeias

Chart paper

PROCEDURE:
1. Read one of the books from the first category to the students.
2. Break the book down into its story elements of character, setting, and plot.
3. Divide the students into small groups. The students take the different elements and come up with several descriptors for each of the elements. Teachers should encourage the students to think about words that describe the appearance, the movement, and the sound created by each of the elements.
4. In a large group, compile a list of the descriptors that each group came up with, creating one large list.
5. Now switch gears and read through several of the books listed in the second category. Talk about how the author used sound words and other descriptors to create a simple story or poem. Introduce the term *poetry* and share the way it is used as the format for the second book.
6. Students transform the first story they read into a poem, using the descriptors of the story elements recorded on the class chart.
7. Students share their poems with the class.

ASSESSMENT/REFLECTION:
Evaluate the final poem. Does the poem convey the story and the story elements? Does it include appropriate word choices from the list?

MI EXTENSIONS:
This lesson also uses the Interpersonal Intelligence.

Bodily-Kinesthetic: On the playground, half the class uses the equipment while the other half observes. Students list what they see, hear, and feel during ball play. The groups change places and record again. Students might record words like *exciting, bounce, round, high, low, you're out, tired, fun, whoomph.* Use these to create a Playground Poem.

Musical: Listen to a piece of instrumental music. Brainstorm words evoked by the sounds created by different instruments, tempos, and moods of the piece. While listening to fast-paced music, children might envision someone running and record words like *fast, pitter pat, glide, swoosh, dart, heavy breath, excitement, scary,* and *gasp.* Use these descriptors to create a Music Poem.

Linguistic: Students take different instruments and describe their look, feel and sound. A drum might illicit words like *boom, round, smooth, loud, fun, crash, whack,* and *bang.* Use these descriptors to write an Instrument Poem.

Naturalist: Visit a garden or other natural setting. Students record what they see, hear, feel, and smell. Create a Nature Poem.

Spanish Scavenger Hunt

PURPOSE:
Children work in groups to practice and memorize vocabulary words using a digital camera. Although this uses Spanish words, it can be adapted for use with any word study or thematic vocabulary.

MATERIALS:
One digital camera for each group, index cards, list of vocabulary words in a different order for each group, an answer key for the list

PROCEDURE:
1. Divide the class into small groups. Each group should have one digital camera.
2. Give the students a list of vocabulary words. The list should contain objects the students can find and photograph in school. This can also be done using a list of emotions, verbs, or anything that can be photographed.
3. Clarify the parameters for the hunt. Are students allowed to venture through the whole building, on a specific floor, only in the classroom, or outside?
4. Set the time limits. The total amount of time allotted is decided by the teacher. The first group that comes back gets five bonus points, the second group gets four points, and so on. Points are subtracted if children do not return by the ending time.
5. Points are subtracted if students make excessive noise, run, or travel outside the designated area.
6. When you say, "Go," students gather with their groups and set out to find the objects on their list. Start the timer. As they find each listed item, they write a label for the item, place the label on the item, and take a picture.
7. Collect the cameras and the lists. Print the pictures. Give the students an answer key. They can award themselves a point for each correctly labeled picture and another point if the label is spelled correctly.

ASSESSMENT/REFLECTION:
Can students correctly pronounce and match the Spanish word with its English counterpart?

MI EXTENSIONS:

This lesson also uses the Interpersonal Intelligence.

Bodily-Kinesthetic: Rather than have the students find various objects, students can play charades and act out a list of vocabulary.

Spatial: Use the "Pictionary" game format to practice vocabulary words.

Naturalist: How could the students sort and categorize the words on the list?

Book Reports the MI Way

PURPOSE:

Students show their understanding of a book they have read by completing a project using an intelligence of their choosing.

PROCEDURE:

Musical

- Write and perform a song that interprets story elements. Choose popular songs that the characters might enjoy and explain why.
- Choreograph a dance that expresses the theme or the mood.

Spatial

- Create a story board, mind map, claymation, cartoon, or movie.
- Create a board game.
- Build a diorama.
- Draw a map of the changing setting.
- Visualize and represent the most important event.
- Create a mobile.

Bodily-Kinesthetic

- In reader's theater, act out a scene.
- Pantomime the feelings of the characters.
- Role-play a conflict.

Linguistic

- Rewrite the ending or add another chapter.
- Write a book review and to submit to a children's magazine.
- Create a crossword puzzle using vocabulary from the book.
- Write riddles or clues about characters.

Logical-Mathematical

- Make a timeline showing the events as they take place in the story.
- Create a Venn diagram to show connections between the main character and yourself.
- Make a compare and contrast chart with another book.

Intrapersonal

- Dress up as a character and share a monologue.
- Create journal entries of feelings you had and connections made.
- Choose a way to show how you would have resolved the conflict differently.

Interpersonal

- Create a puppet show.
- While one student portrays a character, another serves as a TV news reporter conducting an interview.
- Have a debate.

Naturalist

- Create a collection that would appeal to one of the characters.
- Make a travel brochure to show where a character would have enjoyed spending time outdoors.
- Compare and contrast characters within the story.
- Rewrite the pivotal events using a different setting.

Sincerely Yours: Parts of a Letter

PURPOSE:
Students learn the structure and function of the five parts of a letter: heading, greeting, body, closing, and signature.

MATERIALS:
An English textbook or handout explaining the parts of a letter, sample letters, markers or colored pencils, props for skits

PROCEDURE:
1. Teach students "The Parts of a Letter" workout. While standing, students

   • Place their hands on their heads and say, "Heading."
   • Place hands in front of mouth and extend arms while saying "Greeting."
   • Run hands down sides of body while saying "Body."
   • Knock knees together while saying "Closing."
   • Stomp their feet three times as the teacher says "Signature."

2. Using sample letters, have students identify and color code the parts of a letter.

3. Divide the class into five groups and assign each group one of the five letter parts. Groups define the purpose of their letter part. They develop a skit that helps classmates visualize the purpose and function. For example, the heading of a friendly letter includes the street address of the sender plus the city, state, zip code, and date. Group members may place phonebooks, maps, and calendars on their heads and interview one another about where they are "heading."

4. The class acts out a letter by performing the five parts in order.

5. As a class, write a sample letter that shows the proper positions for the letter parts.

ASSESSMENT/REFLECTION:
Students write a letter to a friend. They may use the samples provided in class as references. Do students include all the letter parts? Do they use the parts appropriately? Do they structure the letter correctly?

MI EXTENSIONS:
This lesson also uses the Bodily-Kinesthetic and Interpersonal intelligences.

Interpersonal: Students take opposing positions and debate which part of the letter is the most important. Which part a letter cannot be left out?

Intrapersonal: Which part of the letter are you most like and why?

Living History

> "Be aware of the life you are living . . .
> history is created in the present."
> —*CRAIG YAGER*

PURPOSE:

Students create living histories and learn from primary sources by corresponding with a family member of another generation. Students become historians as they gather and respond to resources that exist in their lives. They demonstrate their ability to communicate their personal life experience through a letter-writing exchange.

MATERIALS:

Paper, envelopes, postage stamps, photographs, writing and drawing materials, various art supplies, binders

PROCEDURE:

This is integrated as part of a Social Studies unit on Primary Sources, asking the essential questions, "How do we know about the past?" "What resources do historians use to learn about past events?" and "How were varying perspectives communicated?"

1. During the first week of school, students are asked to invite a family member or family friend from an older generation to become their Living History partner. They ask their partners to commit to a semester- or year-long letter-writing exchange. Letters, which address monthly themes, are handwritten and mailed each month.

2. Teach the students the format of letter writing and how to address an envelope.

3. Explain the monthly theme through an outline or a web. Examples of monthly themes are:

   Letter 1: Introduction, heritage/family; who am I and where have I come from?

   Letter 2: Goals and academic experiences; what is school like for you, and what was it like for your partner?

   Letter 3: Childhood experiences and a request for primary source documents from their childhood, photographs, copies of report cards, and mementoes.

   Letter 4: Then and now, share differences in life and culture, what does a movie cost, how do you spend free time?

   Letter 5: Family; what is family, what are your family traditions?

Letter 6: Ask questions about your partner's life to do research for a profile that will be written later; what historical events do they remember?

Letter 7: Thank-you letter that shares the written profile and the portrait of the partner.

4. Each letter is written in draft form, self-edited, and teacher-edited before being mailed. Each letter shares events from the students' lives and their perspective on the theme. The children pose questions that ask their partners to share events and their perspectives on these events. The letters are photocopied and the copies are placed in the student's Living History binder. By the end of the project, the binder will be a story of the relationship between the Living History partners, containing the letters exchanged, photographs, drawings, and any other primary sources shared.

5. Using photographs received from their partners, students will paint a portrait of their Living History partner to accompany a written profile they write about their partner's life. They share these in their final letter to their Living History partners.

ASSESSMENT/REFLECTION:

Students decide on a format to share the ways their feelings and ideas have changed as a result of this project. Through their chosen medium, they share how their relationship with their partner has grown; changes in their perceptions of older people, especially confronting any stereotypes they may held regarding those from other generations, and cultural changes that affect the way they live their lives today. Students might create a performance art piece, a play, a song, a written piece, or a spatial representation.

MI EXTENSIONS:

This lesson also uses the Spatial, Intrapersonal, and Interpersonal intelligences.

Interpersonal: Students act as historians and share the primary sources they collected to create bulletin boards or a mini-museum. They share passages from their letters, photographs, and other artifacts they have collected.

Logical-Mathematical: Students create a Living History timeline of events, both personal and historical, that have occurred in their lives and their partners' lives. Students use one color on the timeline for themselves and another for their partners.

Bodily-Kinesthetic: Students write and perform a play taken from the historical events and the collective lives of the partners.

Extra, Extra, Read All About It

PURPOSE:

Students use the who, what, when, where, why, and how techniques of a journalist to summarize newspaper articles.

MATERIALS:

Copies of three different newspaper articles from a daily newspaper, paper, highlighters

PROCEDURE:

1. To introduce the five W's and H, students read a short newspaper article. As the students share single words that relate to the article, the teacher matches the words with the corresponding lead elements: who, what, when, where, why, and how. The words from the list are used to create six-word sentences that identify the main idea of the article. A phrase can count as a single word. Explain that the five W's and H questions are given within the first two paragraphs of every well-written newspaper article.

2. Divide the class into small groups. Give each group a copy of a different article from a daily newspaper. All group members must agree on the symbols or marks used to designate the 5W's and H before marking the articles. They mark up their copies of the articles.

3. Groups share with the class the six elements they have identified. The class is then asked to create a six-word sentence for the main idea.

4. Distribute a new article to each group. Students read, identify, and record the six elements.

5. Regroup the students so that each new group contains students who have read different articles. Students summarize their articles using the six elements.

ASSESSMENT/REFLECTION:

Each student is given an article to summarize by identifying the six elements. How accurately were the students able to identify the elements in their articles?

MI EXTENSIONS:

During this lesson, students also used their Interpersonal Intelligence.

Linguistic: Using other forms of news transmission, determine whether the six elements are present. Students might view internet news pages, listen to radio news broadcasts, or watch television news programs.

Musical: Students bring in copies of their favorite songs and lyrics. The students listen to a song and see whether they can identify the six elements. They consider whether popular songs follow the same format as news articles. What conclusions can the students draw?

Spatial: Students look at a narrative painting and identify the six elements. Students compare their main idea statements about the painting and consider how the students' world experiences influence their interpretations.

Literature Responses

PURPOSE:

Using different intelligences, students show their understanding of literary elements.

PROCEDURE:

Logical-Mathematical

Characters on a Venn Diagram: Students compare two or three characters from either the same story or different stories using a Venn diagram. Students can also compare themselves with a character. A student could use a Venn diagram with two or three circles. The goal is to push students from the literal (physical traits) to the more abstract (personality traits). Students should use textual references to support their ideas.

Interpersonal

Character Webbing: To understand how the characters in a story are connected and relate to each other, students in small groups generate a list of characters from a story. The names are written to form a circle on a large sheet of paper. Students connect characters by drawing a line from one to another and writing on each line words or phrases describing the connection between the two characters. Students must reach consensus on the phrases or words used on the web.

Spatial

Setting: Using evidence from the narrative, students create a visual representation of the main setting, which includes location, time of day, era, characters involved, and the mood. Students support their spatial choices by referencing specific evidence from the story.

Visualization: Students select a passage from the book to represent artistically. The passage is displayed with the art work.

Naturalist

Symbolic Character Mapping: The core values of each character are identified. Core values are those values that are the most important or represent the central qualities of a character; for example, loyalty, creativity, bravery, or independence. Students create spatial symbols to represent these qualities. For this assignment, color is considered to be symbolic along with the images that are created. An artist statement, which explains the reasons for their choices, accompanies the artistic piece.

Symbolism: Students are given a teacher-generated symbol for a character. Each student decides which character he thinks could be represented by the symbol and supports this decision with specific textual evidence. The class members discuss their opinions.

Linguistic

Perspective: Students rewrite a narrative passage using a different perspective than the one used by the author.

Bodily-Kinesthetic

Characters on Stage: After reading a narrative passage that consists of dialogue between characters, students act out the scene in order to demonstrate their understanding of the interchange. A good text to use is *The Pocketbook Game* by Alice Childress. Students may stick to the dialogue or add lines to help their skits flow, as long as the integrity of the story is not lost. The goal is to demonstrate an understanding of the relationships among the characters.

Intrapersonal

Character Interviews: Students compare the author's perspective and the way the character acts within the context of the story with their ideas about how they would react or respond to similar situations. Students take on the role of a particular character from a story and respond to a question posed by the teacher that relates to an issue in the story. Then they come out of character to share the way they would have reacted in that situation or their feelings about the issue.

Musical

Character Play List: Create a play list for the main character in the book. Support the choices on the list using references from the narrative.

ASSESSMENT/REFLECTION:

Students reflect individually about which intelligence worked best for them and which intelligences were easiest and hardest to use to portray literary elements. They then gather in small groups of four or five to share their experiences and impressions.

Activities to Support the Linguistic Intelligence

INTERPERSONAL

- Oral presentations or story telling
- Collaborative writing
- Panel discussions or debates
- Writing a persuasive article or how-to story
- Partner and choral reading

INTRAPERSONAL

- Show-and-tell activities and person-of-the-week interviews
- Selecting books for pleasure reading
- Personal narratives, journal writing, or experience charts
- Tape recording reflections
- Answering questionnaires

BODILY-KINESTHETIC

- Scavenger hunts
- Typing for the word processor and handwriting
- Finger plays and puppet shows
- Charades and pantomime
- Dramatic play

LOGICAL-MATHEMATICAL

- Story mapping
- Reasoning skills, like analogies, palindromes, and comparing and contrasting
- Crossword puzzles
- Logical humor; for example, riddles, puns, and jokes
- Flow charts

MUSICAL

- Creating poetry
- Writing lyrics to songs
- Detecting meter and pattern in poetry (limerick, haiku)
- Performing an opera
- Karaoke and lip syncing

SPATIAL

- Book making
- Alphabetizing
- Playing games like *Scrabble* and *Boggle*
- Labeling diagrams
- Cartooning

NATURALIST

- Creating field guides or how to books related to nature
- Taking an ABC hike, finding things that start with each letter of the alphabet
- Creating new names for plants or animals
- Keeping a nature journal
- Tweeting what is observed in a natural setting

Identifying the Linguistic Intelligence in Your Students

Children function at many different levels within the intelligences. Through observation of everyday activities, one can create a profile showing the level of functioning within a particular intelligence and the intelligences in relation to each other. The levels described show increased engagement and proficiency.

YES NO **APPRECIATES:**

❑ ❑ Consistently demonstrates interest, respect, and enjoyment within the intelligence and is able to differentiate qualities

❑ ❑ Enjoys expressive/receptive language

❑ ❑ Enjoys listening to stories, poems, plays

❑ ❑ Asks questions about words, sounds, or definitions

❑ ❑ Asks, "What does this say?" making the connection between meaning and the written word

YES NO **PERFORMS:**

❑ ❑ Is able to apply the intelligence to recreate an exhibit or demonstration or problem-solve with a given situation

❑ ❑ Uses language to solve problems and convey meaning in other disciplines

❑ ❑ Is adept at learning languages

❑ ❑ Uses figurative or descriptive language in speaking and writing

❑ ❑ Is able to make oral presentations

❑ ❑ Understands and responds to plays on words (such as puns, riddles, jokes)

❑ ❑ Memorizes easily

YES NO **CREATES:**

❑ ❑ Is able to apply this intelligence to generate original work, to develop unique solutions to problems or create prototypes

❑ ❑ Develops an author's voice

❑ ❑ Modifies an existing form of communication

❑ ❑ Has distinctive writing or speaking style

Reader: _____ Date: _____

Reading Survey

Do you like reading? _____

Do you read at home? _____

Do you visit the library? _____

Are you a good reader? _____

Do you think it is important to be a good reader? _____

Do you like speaking in front of people? _____

What is your favorite book? _____

What do you like reading about? _____

What would you like to learn about this year? _____

Writer: _____ Date: _____

Writing Survey

Do you write at home? _____

Are you a good writer? _____

Do you think it is important to be a good writer? _____

Do you like to write stories? _____

What do you like writing about? _____

Are you a good listener? _____ Why? _____

What is something you are good at? _____

What do you need to work on? _____

What do you like to do when you are not at school? _____

Children's Resources

Books and Recordings

Ahlberg, Janet P. and Allan. *Jolly Postman*. Little, Brown, 1986.

Aliki. *How a Book Is Made*. Crowell, 1986.

Anno, Mitsumasa. *Anno's Counting House*. Philomel Books, 1982.

Arnold, Tedd. *The Signmaker's Assistant*. Dial Books, 1992.

Banks, Kate. *Max's Words*. Farrar, Straus & Giroux, 2008.

Baylor, Byrd. *The Desert Is Theirs*. Aladdin Books, 1987.

Beisner, Monika. *Monika Beisner's Book of Riddles*. Sunburst Books, 1983.

Brisson, Pat. *Your Best Friend, Kate*. Bradbury Press, 1989.

Bruel, Nick. *Bad Kitty*. Roaring Brook Press, 2005.

Carle, Eric. *The Very Hungry Caterpillar*. Philomel Books, 1970.

Catalanotto, Peter. *Matthew A.B.C.* Atheneum Books, 2002.

Charlip, Remy. *Fortunately*. Four Winds, 1980.

Cohen, Miriam. *When Will I Read?* Dell, 1983.

dePaola, Tomie. *Andy*. Prentice-Hall, 1973.

DuQuette, Keith. *Cock-A-Doodle-Moo: A Mixed Up Menagerie*. Putnam, 2004.

Edwards, Pamela. *The Neat Line: Scribbling Through Mother Goose*. Katherine Tegen Books, 2005.

Elting, Mary, and Folson, Michael. *Q Is for Duck: An Alphabet Guessing Game*. Clarion Books, 1980.

Feelings, Muriel. *Moja Means One*. Dial, 1971.

Franco, Betsy. *Mathematicles: Words + Math + Seasons*. Souil-Si: Toso Ch'ulp'am Marubol, 2004.

Galdone, Paul. *Little Red Hen*. Clarion, 1973.

Giovanni, Nikki (editor). *Hip Hop Speaks to Children: A Celebration of Poetry with a Beat*. Sourcebooks Jabberwocky, an imprint of Sourcebooks, Inc., 2008.

Gorey, Edward. *Amphigorey: Fifteen Books*. Pedigree, Putnam, 1972.

Gravett, Emily. *Orange Pear Apple Bear*. Simon & Schuster, 2007.

Griffiths, Andy. *Cat on the Mat Is Flat*. Feiwel and Friends, 2007.

Heller, Ruth. *A Cache of Jewels*. Grosset & Dunlap, 1987.

_____. *Kites Sail High*. Grosset & Dunlap, 1988.

_____. *Merry-Go-Round: A Book About Nouns*. Putnam, 1990.

_____. *Up, Up and Away: A Book About Adverbs*. Grosset & Dunlap, 1991.

Hennessy, B. G. *Jake Baked the Cake*. Viking Penguin, 1990.

Hopkinson, Deborah. *Sweet Clara and the Freedom Quilt*. Knopf, 1993.

Hudson, Cheryl Willis. *Afro-Bets ABC Book*. Just Us Books, 1987.

Hutchins, Pat. *The Doorbell Rang*. Greenwillow, 1986.

_____. *The Tale of Thomas Mead*. Mulberry Books, 1980.

Janeczko, Paul. *A Kick in the Head*. Candlewick Press, 2005.

_____. *A Poke in the I*. Candlewick Press, 2001.

Kalman, Maria. *Max Makes a Million*. Viking Penguin, 1990.

Keats, Jack. *Apt. 3*. Viking, 1999.

Keller, Charles. *Tongue Twisters*. Simon & Schuster, 1989.

Kellogg, Steven. *Much Bigger Than Martin*. Dial, 1986.

Kipling, Rudyard. "How the Leopard Got His Spots," in *Just So Stories*. Doubleday, 1972.

Kloske, Geoffrey. *Once Upon a Time, the End (Asleep in 60 Seconds)*. Atheneum Books, 2005.

Lechner, Jack. *Mary Had a Little Lamp*. Bloomsbury Children's Books, 2008.

Lepscky, Ibi. *William Shakespeare*. Barron's Educational Series, 1988.

Lester, Alison. *Imagine*. Houghton Mifflin, 1990.

Levine, Ellen. *I Hate English*. Scholastic, 1989.

Lionni, Leo. *Inch by Inch*. Astro, 1960.

MacLachlan, Patricia. *Three Names*. HarperCollins, 1991.

MacLennan, Cathy. *Chicky Chicky Chook Chook*. Boxer Books, 2007.

Maxner, Joyce. *Nicholas Cricket*. HarperCollins, 1989.

McMillan, Bruce. *One Sun: A Book of Terse Verse*. Holiday House, 1990.

Merriam, Eve. *12 Ways to Get to 11*. Simon & Schuster, 1993.

Most, Bernard. *There's an Ant in Anthony*. Mulberry Books, 1992.

Murphy, Stuart *Pepper's Journal: A Kitten's First Year*. HarperCollins, 2000.

Osborne, Mara Pope. *American Tall Tales*. Scholastic, 1991.

Pallotta, Jerry. *The Icky Bug Alphabet Book*. Children's Press, 1991.

Patterson, Francine. *Dr. Koko's Kitten*. Scholastic, 1985.

_____. *Dr. Koko's Story*. Scholastic, 1987.

Paulson, Jim. *The Beanstalk Incident*. Carol Publishing Group, 1990.

Pulver, Robin. *Punctuation Takes a Vacation*. Holiday House, 2003.

_____. *Silent Letters Loud and Clear*. Holiday House, 2008.

Purviance, Susan, and O'Shell, Marcia. *Alphabet Annie Announces An All-American Album*. Houghton Mifflin, 1988.

Rankin, Laura. *The Handmade Alphabet*. Dial Books, 1991.

Rathmann, Peggy. *Good Night, Gorilla*. Putnam, 1994.

Ringgold, Faith. *Dinner at Aunt Connie's House*. Hyperion, 1993.

_____. *Tar Beach*. Crown, 1991.

Robb, Diane. *The Alphabet War: A Story About Dyslexia*. Whitman, 2004.

Rockwell, Anne. *The Story Snail*. MacMillan, 1974.

Roehrig, Catherine. *Fun with Hieroglyphs*. Metropolitan Museum of Art, 1990.

Rohmann, Eric. *My Friend Rabbit*. Roaring Brook Press, 2002.

Roop, Peter and Connie. *Ahyoka and the Talking Leaves*. Lothrop, Lee and Shepard Books, 1992.

Schwarz, David M. *How Much Is a Million?* Lothrop, 1985.

_____. *If You Made a Million*. Lothrop, 1989.

Scieszka, Jon. *The True Story of the Three Little Pigs*. Scholastic 1991.

Seeger, Laura. *Walter Was Worried*. Roaring Brook Press, 2005.

Shannon, David. *The Rain Came Down*. Blue Sky Press, 2000.

Sharmat, Marjorie Weinman. *My Mother Never Listens to Me*. Whitman, 1984.

Spinelli, Eileen. *Six Hogs on a Scooter*. Orchard Books, 2000.

Stanek, Mureil. *My Mom Can't Read*. Whitman, 1986.

Steptoe, John. *The Story of Jumping Mouse*. Lothrop, Lee and Shepard Books, 1984.

Sutton, Sally. *Roadwork*. Candlewick Press, 2008.

Terban, Marvin. *The Dove Dove: Funny Homograph Riddles*. Houghton Mifflin, 1988.

_____. *Mad as a Wet Hen*. Clarion Books, 1987.

Truss, Lynne. *Eats, Shoots & Leaves*. Putnam, 2006.

Van Allsburg, Chris. *The Mysteries of Harris Burdick*. Houghton Mifflin, 1984.

Van Allsburg, Chris. *The Z Was Zapped*. Houghton Mifflin, 1987.

Waber, Bernard. *Dear Hildegarde*. Houghton Mifflin, 1980.

Williams, Jay. "The Wicked Tricks of Tyl Uilenspiegel," in *Junior Great Books*, Series 4. The Great Books Foundation, 1987.

Wood, Audrey. *Quick as a Cricket*. Child's Play, 1982.

Essay

Childress, Alice. "The Pocketbook Game" in *Like One of the Family*. Beacon Press, 1986.

Poetry

Feelings, Tom. *Something on My Mind*. Dial Books for Young Readers, 1978.

Ferris, Sean. *Children of the Great Muskeg*. Black Moss Press, 1985.

Fleischman, Paul. *Joyful Noise: Poems for Two Voices*. HarperCollins, 1988.

Giovanni, Nikki. *Spin a Soft Black Song*. Farrar, Straus & Giroux, 1985.

Lee, Dennis. *The Ice Cream Store*. Scholastic, 1991.

Lesser, Carolyn. *Flamingo Knees*. Oakwood Press, 1988.

Mathis, Bell Sharon. *Red Dog/Blue Fly Football Poems*. Viking, 1991.

Prelusky, Jack. *The New Kids on the Block*. Greenwillow, 1986.

Silverstein, Shel. *A Light in the Attic*. HarperCollins, 1974.

_____. *Where the Sidewalk Ends*. HarperCollins, 1984.

Sullivan, Charles. *Children of Promise*. Abrams, 1991.

Thayer, Ernest. *Casey at the Bat*. Raintree, 1985.

Withers, Carl. *A Rocket in My Pocket*. Scholastic, 1948.

Games

Alphabet Soup: The Letter Matching Game. Parker Brothers, 1992.

Balderdash: The Hilarious Bluffing Game. Gameworks Creations, 1984.

Boggle: Three Minute Word Game. Parker Brothers, 1992.

Brainquest. University Games, 1993.

Corduroy's Birthday Games. Ravensburger, 1999.

Electronic Dream Phone Game. Milton Bradley, 1991.

Guess Who? Milton Bradley, 1987.

Hangman. Milton Bradley, 1988.

Holly Hobbie: Wishing Well Game. Parker Brothers, 1976.

Outburst Junior. Hersch, 1989.

Quiddler. SET Enterprises, 1996.

Read My Lips, Kids. Pressman, 1991.

Scattergories Junior. Milton Bradley, 1989.

Scrabble. Milton Bradley, 1989.

Scrabble: Sentence Cube Game. Selchow & Richter, 1983.

Scrabble Slam. Parker Brothers, 2008.

See and Read Dominoes. Random House, 1989.

Teachers' Resources

Boushey, Gail, and Moser, Joan. *The Daily 5, Fostering Literacy Independence in the Elementary Grades.* Stenhouse Publishers, 2006.

Bullock, Doris. *Designed to Delight.* The Library, 1977.

Burke, Kay. *Authentic Learning.* Corwin, 2009.

Caduto, Michael. *Keepers of the Earth.* Fulcrum, 1989.

Caudron, Jill M. *Alphabet Activities.* Fearon Teacher Aids, 1983.

———. *Alphabet Fun and Games.* Fearon Teacher Aids, 1984.

———. *Alphabet Stories.* Fearon Teacher Aids, 1983.

Chen, Jie-Qi, ed. *Project Spectrum: Early Learning Activities.* Teachers College Press, 1999. (This is volume 2 of Project Zero Frameworks for Early Childhood Education.)

Chisholm, Virginia. *After School Spanish Games & Activities.* Instructional Fair, 2003.

Daniels, Harvey. *Literature Circles—Voice and Choice in Book Clubs and Reading Groups.* Stenhouse Publishers, 2002.

De Wall, Frans. *The Age of Empathy.* Harmony Books, 2009.

Hamilton, Virginia. *The People Could Fly: American Black Folktales.* Knopf, 1985.

Helm, Judy Harris, and Katz, Lilian. *Young Investigators: The Project Approach in the Early Years.* Teachers College Press, 2001.

Oliver Keene, Ellin, and Zimmerman, Susan. *Mosaic of Thought, The Power of Comprehension Strategy Instruction.* Heinemann, 2007.

Rothlein, Ed.D., and Vaughn, Ph.D., *Learning Through Literature: Ecology.* Teacher Created Materials, Inc., 1996.

Sebranek, Patrick. *Writers Inc.* Educational Publishing House, 1989.

Smith, Havilan and Lyn. *Easy Plays for Preschoolers to Third Graders: A Movie.* Quail Ridge Press, 1985.

Wormeli, Rick. *Summarization in Any Subject: 50 Techniques to Improve Student Learning.* ASCD, 2005.

Zimmerman, Bill. *How to Tape Instant Oral Biographies.* Better Way Press, 1992.

"A mathematician, like a painter or a poet, is a maker of patterns."

—G. H. HARDY

5

Photograph: Patti Gabriel

The Logical-Mathematical Intelligence

Web of the Logical-Mathematical Intelligence

Student Quotes

"The Logical-Mathematical Intelligence is very, very, very, very, very awesome!"

"I'm Logical-Mathematical because I like to do logic puzzles and computation."

"The Logical-Mathematical Intelligence can be applied to just about anything: art, music, money, nature, science, and even getting a job!"

Characteristics

- Notices and uses numbers, shapes and patterns, is precise, is able to move from the concrete to the abstract easily, uses information to solve a problem, loves collections, enjoys computer games and puzzles, takes notes in an orderly fashion, thinks conceptually, can estimate, explores patterns and relationships, constantly questions, likes to experiment in a logical way, organizes thoughts, employs a systematic approach during problem-solving

Famous People

STEPHEN HAWKING explained the universe.

ALBERT EINSTEIN discovered scientific relationships related to matter.

BILL GATES, philanthropist and founder of Microsoft, has dyslexia.

MARILYN BURNS is an innovative math educator who is in the forefront of educational reform.

ALEXA CANADY was the first black woman neurosurgeon in the United States.

Adult Quotes

"A mathematician, like a painter or poet, is a maker of patterns."
—G. H. HARDY

"Pure mathematics is, in its way, the poetry of logical ideas."
—ALBERT EINSTEIN

The Logical-Mathematical Intelligence: Identification and Implementation

BY CHANAYA JACOBS AND CLAIRE REINBOLD

Imagine students choosing between getting lost in a puzzle, alphabetizing a bookshelf, creating a pattern with blocks, counting and sorting change in a piggy bank, playing chess, or guessing how many candies are in a jar. All of these options would appeal to a child who thrives on using his or her Logical-Mathematical intelligence. Think of your own students. Which students would be interested in any or all of these tasks? How can you best meet the needs of these learners?

CHARACTERISTICS OF STRONG LOGICAL-MATHEMATICAL STUDENTS

Children strong in the Logical-Mathematical Intelligence will display many common characteristics: they enjoy showing relationships and patterns; they learn information more easily when it is presented in an orderly way and they are given opportunities to question; they will often categorize or classify information; and they like computer activities, logic puzzles, and strategic games like chess. These types of learners are in every classroom and every population. At New City School, we feel the best way to teach them is by consciously including other intelligences within each Logical-Mathematical activity or lesson and, likewise, consciously including Logical-Mathematical activities in as many other lessons as possible.

Teachers need to incorporate the Logical-Mathematical Intelligence into many lessons to reinforce these kinds of thinking skills. For students who are particularly mathematical, it becomes all the more significant to tap into their thought processes in other subjects. For example, we have noticed that our Logical-Mathematical students approach a spatial problem from a different angle. These students tend to use the tools from math class (ruler, compass, protractor, geometry templates, and the like) as they work through creative processes. Additionally, these same students often brainstorm linguistic pieces using charts and webs. Such a methodical approach is a necessary beginning for these learners, and it can be seen in other subject areas.

In the first few weeks of school we offer our students many Interpersonal opportunities to work together through team building activities. This gives teachers the chance to see students' strengths and weaknesses. This group effort also enables children to capitalize on other intelligences. When we present students with challenges such as the "Human Knot" activity, by watching their approach we learn how they choose to solve problems. In this activity students are asked to form a circle and grab the left hand of someone, then grab the right hand of another student; no two students should be holding only each other's hands. Students then work together to untie the knot by physically adjusting as needed. The final goal is to have all members of the group standing in a circle, hand in hand.

It's not surprising that when they have the opportunity to do so, children choose to solve problems by using the intelligences in which they are the strongest (so do adults!). Logical-Mathematical kids frequently contribute to the problem-solving process, drawing on the skill set that is often perceived as being logical (and sometimes mathematical). These are the students who take time to consider the task and analyze what is needed so that they can come up with a plan before they begin. We listen to hear what type of comments all of our students express, and often this is where we tend to hear these students suggest plans that include numerical values, logical placement of bodies or limbs, or a step-by-step approach to "untying" the knot.

Another natural entry point for incorporating the Logical-Mathematical Intelligence is through the use of timelines in social studies. Discussing the importance of historical events and how they flow from one another can be enhanced with a visual timeline. This timeline also reinforces the idea of historical cause and effect and gives a concrete example of concurrent events. Given the tendency in social studies to often focus on dates, the timeline offers an opportunity to "see" how history has played out and allows students to look deeply at historical context and the correlation of events. The timelines can be simple line graphs or students can draw on their spatial intelligence as well as by adding pictures and drawings.

Characterization is a vital component of our curriculum, and we incorporate the Logical-Mathematical Intelligence when comparing and contrasting characters from stories during language arts class. We frequently ask our students to create a Venn diagram to show personality traits that are exhibited by characters. In their drawings and orally, students give examples of how the characters are both similar and different. The Venn diagram can be made more challenging by asking the students

Teachers need to incorporate the Logical-Mathematical Intelligence into many lessons. For students who are particularly mathematical, it becomes all the more significant to tap into their thought processes in other subjects.

It's not surprising that when they have the opportunity to do so, children choose to solve problems by using the intelligences in which they are the strongest. Logical-Mathematical kids frequently contribute to the problem-solving process, drawing on the skill set that is often perceived as being logical.

to include additional characters or themselves, or by being given a select list of descriptors to apply. This format allows a more logical and visual approach to look critically at the characters and story development. Many times students who struggle with the Linguistic Intelligence are able to understand the characters in a story and grapple with its nuances by approaching it through the strengths of their Logical-Mathematical Intelligence.

THE REAL WORLD IN MATH

Our students bring a variety of intelligences to our math classes, and it is fitting that we not only acknowledge but also incorporate these into the math curriculum. Through the use of problem-solving, we are able to see both how students approach a given problem and what intelligence(s) they call upon as they work. The Logical-Mathematical Intelligence is the foundation for the process, but each child uses his or her own set of tools to accomplish the task. When we have used a problem like the Locker Problem that requires logical thinking to reach a solution, students will capitalize on other strengths as well. The locker problem is just one example of word problems used in the sixth grade to develop Logical-Mathematical ability.

THE LOCKER PROBLEM

You are about to enter your brand-new school for the first time. The teachers, however, have gotten together and decided to perform a little ritual. All 150 students need to line up and enter the school one at a time. The first student entering will open all 150 lockers. The second student will enter and close every second locker. The third student will change every third locker, and so on. You are the last in line! But as you are waiting for your turn you realize you can figure out which lockers will be open after your turn. You amaze your teachers! Which lockers are open?

MI Approaches

Bodily-Kinesthetically Minded Children. These students will get up and physically touch the lockers or create a tangible model to represent the problem. This movement is necessary in the thinking process. Although these students may look like they are playing, in reality they are internalizing the mathematical patterns.

Linguistically Minded Children. These students will write down their thought process as they work through the problem. This written record acts as a transcript, explaining the steps they are taking. They may also prefer to orally communicate their strategy and solution.

Spatially Minded Children. These are the students who need to create a visual representation to show their thinking process. Drawing a diagram of the locker set-up and marking off the patterns they use helps to guide them to the solution.

Although the intelligence strategies in this lesson are quite obvious, children often find ways to use their strongest intelligence(s) in solving a problem, and because we believe in MI, we want to give them the opportunity to do so whenever it is possible. Word problems like these can be structured to allow a chance for students to use their Interpersonal and Intrapersonal intelligences. We regularly give the chance for students to collaborate in small groups or pairs, as well as time for independent work. Group work presents a format for Interpersonally minded children to share their ideas and learn from their peers. We also expect our students to comment on the problem-solving process; this Intrapersonal reflection only deepens their understanding of the mathematical concept and their own learning process.

Our challenge is to help students recognize their Logical-Mathematical affinity and to provide experiences to facilitate its development. It is equally important to expose children to the Logical-Mathematical Intelligence through other lenses, as well as to bring Logical-Mathematical activities into subjects in which they are traditionally not found. By offering these experiences in and out of math class, we find that all students, regardless of their interests, will be more likely to grab for the pattern blocks, count and sort coins, or put a puzzle together, and strengthen their Logical-Mathematical Intelligence by doing so. We believe that all children are capable of drawing on their own strengths when presented with a variety of ways to learn on multiple occasions.

Children often find ways to use their strongest intelligence(s) in solving a problem.

Numbers

PURPOSE:
This lesson shows ways to use various intelligences to develop and reinforce mathematical concepts including number sense, addition, time, geometry, and estimation.

MUSICAL: TIME

Materials:
Timers or a clock

Procedure:
To develop a sense of duration, children guess how many times they can sing a familiar song in one minute. One partner times one minute as the other partner sings a song, such as, "Happy Birthday," "Twinkle, Twinkle, Little Star," or "Row, Row, Row Your Boat." The partners switch roles. Try it several times using different songs to see if the guesses become more accurate.

BODILY-KINESTHETIC: ADDITION

Materials:
Twister mat with the numbers 0 through 10, some of which appear more than once

Procedure:
The "caller" chooses a number between 2 and 20. The first player finds numbers on the mat that add up to the given number. She may use feet and hands to cover two to four numbers that equal the sum. Players take turns finding different addition facts for the numbers the "caller" says.

LINGUISTIC: PROBLEM-SOLVING

Materials:
Number books, paper, art materials, binding supplies

Procedure:
Make a word problem story book related to a theme of study. Students might make books related to community helpers, the bees on the flowers in the garden, or kids in the basketball game at recess. Each child makes one page for the book.

SPATIAL: NUMBER SENSE

Materials:
Matrices of one hundred squares printed on various colors of paper

Procedure:
Use the hundred matrixes to create individual puzzles. Each student cuts his or her grid on the lines into six, seven, or eight pieces, making interesting shapes. Children put their initials on the back of each piece. Children put them together using both number order and the shapes of the pieces.

LOGICAL-MATHEMATICAL: ESTIMATION

Materials:
Clear estimating jar; worksheet strips to record dates, estimates, tallies, and actual counts

Procedure:
Each week, the Estimation Jar goes home with a student and is filled with fewer than one hundred similar objects. Students each record how many objects they think are in the jar. Talk about strategies to help with estimating, such as counting the number of objects visible on the bottom or relating the height or size to objects from a previous week. Post the guesses and talk about the mode. Although the objects are being counted by ones, twos, fives, or tens, students tally the numbers and record the actual amount. During the counting, students are given an opportunity to revise their estimates. If the objects are edible, discuss how they could be distributed fairly among classmates. Estimates and actual counts are kept during the year so students can see whether their estimating skills improve.

NATURALIST: TIME

Materials:
A window with direct sunlight during the day, masking tape

Procedure:
Record the passage of time as the sun's position changes. With masking tape, put an X on the window so the shadow of the X is visible in the classroom on the floor or wall. Every half hour, mark on the wall or floor its position and the time. Do this over the course of several days and discuss the pattern implications of the movement in relationship to telling time.

INTERPERSONAL: GEOMETRY

Materials:
Two yards of one-inch-wide elastic sewn together to form a circle, one for each group of four students

Procedure:

Each group of four students uses an elastic band to make shapes. The teacher asks for different shapes to be formed: a triangle, a trapezoid, a rotating square, rectangle around the knees, or a hexagon with one side longer than the tallest person in the group. One group could give instructions to another, checking for accuracy.

INTRAPERSONAL: REFLECTION ON MATH

Procedure:

Students think about their likes, dislikes, strengths, and weakness in various aspects of math. Use as sentence starters: "I wish my teacher would . . . ," "I am really good at . . . ," " . . . is hard for me because . . . ," "If only I knew how to . . . , then I could . . ."

Measurement Drawing

PURPOSE:

Students will learn to draw lines of specified lengths using a ruler. The mathematical concepts of inches, centimeters, intersecting lines, geometric shapes, and fractions will be reinforced. The spatial concepts of line, texture, and hue will also be reinforced.

MATERIALS:

Drawing paper, rulers, coloring materials, such as markers, pastels, or crayons

PROCEDURE:

1. Distribute a ruler, pencil, and paper to each student. Review the concepts of inches and centimeters and have students identify each unit of measure on the ruler. Practice measuring a few random things such as a pencil, paper, finger, and book.

2. Model how to draw a measured, straight line using the ruler by holding the ruler firmly and showing where to start and end the line.

3. Direct the students to draw a six-inch line anywhere on their paper. Monitor to see that they are measuring and drawing correctly. Tell them to next draw a nine-centimeter line anywhere on their paper so that it intersects the first line. Again, monitor and assist as needed.

4. Continue giving directions to add lines of varying length to their drawings. Some lengths could include half and quarter inches. Give instructions about how many lines each new line should intersect.

5. After the students have drawn approximately twelve lines, their paper should be covered with intersecting lines forming many geometric shapes. Briefly review art concepts such as texture, pattern, line, and hue. Demonstrate how to fill each geometric shape with a different texture, pattern, type of line, or color.

ASSESSMENT/REFLECTION:

Observe whether or not students can accurately draw the measured lines during the lesson.

MI EXTENSIONS:

This lesson also incorporates the Spatial Intelligence.

Linguistic: Students write step-by-step directions for drawing measured lines.

Interpersonal: Students are assigned partners. One student creates a line drawing using four measured lines. Without letting her partner see what she has drawn, she gives instructions so her partner can replicate the same drawing. The student giving the directions should use the language of mathematics.

Spatial: Students are seated in a circle. Each student is given a piece of paper. Tell them that as a group they are going to draw an elephant. Instruct the students to draw a four-inch line and then pass their paper to the person on their right. Keep giving directions about lines that are to be drawn as the children draw one line and pass the paper. All the elephants will develop differently. After the drawings have gone around the circle, they can be colored.

Scaling the Miles

LOGICAL-
MATHEMATICAL
PRIMARY
SOCIAL STUDIES

PURPOSE:

The students learn to use the scale of miles on a map to determine distances. Other map skills are reinforced, such as cardinal directions, using a key, and locating pertinent locations on maps. Other mathematical concepts are reinforced, such as using different units of measurement, making direct comparisons, and estimation. This lesson is used during a year-long theme of Westward Expansion, but could be modified to fit any geography lesson.

MATERIALS:

A large class map, individual smaller maps, string, scissors, ruler, teacher-made worksheet, teacher-made map for assessment

PROCEDURE:

1. Begin by asking the children to estimate how far it is from one place to another in their immediate environment. Since it's hard for students to visualize a mile, remind them of a landmark that is about a mile away. For homework, children find out how many miles they travel to school to reinforce their understanding of distance.

2. Show students a map connected to your area of study. While looking at the map, ask questions to get them thinking about relative distances between places on the map and the symbols on the map key.

3. Model how to use a string to measure distances, using the scale on the map. First, show them the scale of miles on a map and explain that it is a key used to measure distances. Estimate the distance between two points on the map.

4. Show the students how to measure with the string by placing it on one point and stretching it to the other point, cutting it to that length. Use a ruler to measure the string and use the scale to convert the inches to miles.

5. Practice measuring a river. Estimate the distance and demonstrate how to lay the string along the winding river, cut and measure the string, and convert the inches into miles.

6. Students practice estimating and measuring, recording their answers on the worksheet.

ASSESSMENT/REFLECTION:

Given a scale of miles, a starting landmark, and a compass rose on a piece of paper, students add other landmarks, given step-by-step instructions to complete the map. Example: *The starting location is a cabin. There is a cave four miles north of the cabin. Add a symbol to show the cave. Six miles east of the cave is a spring. Draw a symbol to show the spring. A river flows from the spring eight miles south. Add the river.* After adding the landmarks, instruct them to make a key and title.

MI EXTENSIONS:

This lesson also uses the Spatial Intelligence.

Logical-Mathematical: Give students different maps with various scales for distances, such as centimeters or kilometers.

Spatial: Draw a map to scale of real-life places, such as the classroom, playground, or school garden area. Make a key that shows how many inches equal how many feet.

Mathematical Masterpieces

PURPOSE:

Students use the problem-solving strategy of logical reasoning while practicing skills related to ratio and proportion, geometry, and addition. Given the value of one pattern block shape, students calculate the value of all the pattern blocks used to create a spatial piece.

MATERIALS:

Pattern blocks, paper pattern blocks, teacher-made Task Sheets #1 and #2, black construction paper (approximately seven by seven inches), glue

PROCEDURE:

1. Distribute sets of pattern blocks to small groups. Pose the question, "If a green triangle is worth three cents, how much is a red trapezoid worth?" Students use the blocks to figure this out. Invite students to show and tell how they figured out that the trapezoid is worth nine cents. Model on the board how their ideas could be written using pictures, words, and numbers. Encourage them to use as much mathematical language as possible.

2. Ask students to determine the value of other blocks. Show their thinking on the board until you feel confident that students understand how the values can be determined and how to write about their thinking.

3. Distribute Task Sheet #1. Explain that the green triangle is now worth twenty-five cents and they are to figure out the values of the other pattern blocks. Remind them to show their thinking on the task sheet.

4. After sufficient time has been given for students to complete the task, reconvene and discuss how students figured out the values. It is important to point out that there are numerous routes that students may have taken to reach their answers. Allowing students greater mathematical flexibility and justifying answers when there are discrepancies is an excellent reflective piece of the process.

   Note: It is likely that students will have difficulty figuring out how much the orange square and tan rhombus are worth because the triangles do not fit nicely into the same area. If so, distribute a paper triangle to each student and demonstrate how to cut into two equal pieces. Have them use these paper pieces, along with the blocks, to see if that helps them figure out the values.

5. The following day, brainstorm a list with the names of famous artists and how much their art might sell for at an auction. Distribute Task Sheet #2, black paper, paper pattern blocks, and glue. Their job is to become a great artist and, using the paper pattern blocks and

information they learned about the value of the blocks, create a masterpiece worth a high value. Suggest students try several possibilities before they glue their pieces in place on the black construction paper.

6. After creating their spatial pieces, students use the task sheets to show how they have figured out the value of their work.

7. Create a gallery with a label showing the value of their piece.

ASSESSMENT/REFLECTION:

Examine the work that students have done on the task sheets to assess their accuracy and understanding of the mathematical concepts.

MI EXTENSIONS:

The Spatial Intelligence is also used in this lesson.

Interpersonal: Students work together to create a collaborative work of art with a particular value: $4.75. Students take turns adding one pattern block and everyone keeps a running tally of the total value.

Spatial: Once the values of the blocks are determined, students build 3-D sculptures that have a given value.

Task Sheet #1

If the green triangle is worth twenty-five cents, how much are each of the other pattern block shapes worth?

Pattern blocks include an orange square, red trapezoid, yellow hexagon, blue parallelogram, and tan rhombus.

Use pictures, numbers, and words to show your work. Use as much math language as you can to explain your ideas.

Task Sheet #2

Create a design using pattern block pieces. All pieces must fit on the paper without overlapping or sticking off of the paper. Using what you've learned about the prices of the pattern blocks, figure out how much your design costs. Show your work here.

Civil War Mural and Timeline

PURPOSE:

Students demonstrate an understanding of the events leading up to the Civil War by creating a proportionally accurate timeline of these events that indicates the degree to which each event was an advantage for the North or the South.

MATERIALS:

White twelve- by eighteen-inch construction paper, colored pencils, watercolors, markers, rulers, list of events leading up to the Civil War

PROCEDURES:

1. After reading a text book or other trade books about the time period before the Civil War, discuss and chart with the students ways in which the North and South developed differently.

2. Students turn the white construction paper so the eighteen-inch dimension runs horizontally (landscape format) and fold it in half. A line is drawn along the fold line. They create a mural showing how the North developed on the top half of the paper, and one showing how the South developed on the bottom half. The paper should be completely colored in.

3. During the next class period, hand out a list of events leading up to the Civil War. The events should have dates beside them. Choose one event to use with the class to model the thought process needed to complete the project. Discuss whether the chosen event worked to the advantage of the North or the South. The event is rated on a five-star rating scale to show the degree of advantage, one star being low. Independently, students rate each of the events on the list. Opinions will differ, but as long as the position can be supported historically, it is acceptable. For example, the Fugitive Slave Act of 1850, requiring northern states to return runaway slaves, might be considered a five-star advantage for the South. Others might say it was a catalyst for the Abolitionist movement, and thus deserves only two stars.

4. Use the line on the mural as a timeline. Place the first mark one and a half inches from the left side of the paper. This will be the year 1800. Use the scale of one inch = four years. Have the students label the years beginning at 1800 and ending at 1860.

5. Students create a label for each event on the list. They arrange the labels on the murals so that each event lines up with the correct date on the timeline. They demonstrate by the placement of each event above or below the line whether it favors the North or the South. The distance away from the line shows the degree of the advantage. Events

that favor both sides, or are more neutral, are placed on the timeline, but events that favor the North are placed up toward the top of the paper. The more an event is considered to favor the North, the closer to the top of the paper it belongs, and the more it favored the South, the closer to the bottom of the paper it belongs. The Fugitive Slave Act example will line up with the year 1850 on the timeline; if given the five-star rating for the South, it will be placed far down toward the bottom of the page.

6. After the events are glued onto the mural, connect them chronologically with straight lines. The lines will look like a graph when they are finished, demonstrating not only the sequence of events but also whether each event was to the advantage of the North or the South.

7. Students then write three paragraphs explaining their mural timelines. The first paragraph summarizes how the North developed; the second tells how the South developed in the years preceding the Civil War. In the third paragraph, each student chooses one event from the timeline and explains it in more detail. Students do research and reading to add significant details about their chosen events, justifying their star ratings of the events. These paragraphs are attached to the timeline.

8. When finished, have the students share in small groups. Did other students place items differently? If so, why? Can students defend their placement of events?

9. Close with a whole group discussion. Looking at the timeline, students should be able to see that many of the events were to the advantage of the North. Why was that? Can they see why the South may have felt that the federal government no longer represented their interests?

ASSESSMENT/REFLECTION:

This activity can be assessed with a rubric and points assigned. Categories could include the following:

- Timeline is mathematically correct.
- Directions are followed.
- Murals represent the regions.
- Events are placed accurately.
- Paragraphs are accurate and complete.
- Third paragraph shows adequate justification for placement.
- Rules of grammar are followed.

MI EXTENSIONS:

This lesson also uses the Linguistic, Spatial, and Intrapersonal intelligences.

Interpersonal: In a mock debate, students defend their placement of an event.

Speed Demons

LOGICAL-
MATHEMATICAL

INTERMEDIATE

SCIENCE

PURPOSE:

Students make hypotheses about instantaneous speed as they develop the skills to measure, time, record, round, and calculate their average speeds over a distance of one hundred meters.

MATERIALS:

Stopwatches, tape measure, calculators, space to run

PROCEDURE:

1. Discuss with the students the difference between instantaneous speed (the speed that you are going at a certain moment, such as when the radar gun of a police car catches you or the speed of a pitched baseball is measured) and the average speed of an object in a certain time over a certain distance (calculated by distance divided by time).

2. Demonstrate the use of a stopwatch before the actual data collection begins.

3. Measure out one hundred (or fifty) meters on a track or field in ten-meter increments. One student is the runner while ten (or five) others are stationed at each of the ten-meter marks. With a stopwatch, each student is responsible for recording the time it takes the runner to travel the ten-meter section that ends where they are standing. The runner shouts "Go!" and begins to run, at which point the first timer begins her stopwatch. When the runner passes the first timer, that timer stops her stopwatch and shouts "Go!"—thereby signaling the second timer to start timing. When the runner passes the second timer, she stops her watch, shouting "Go!"—which signals the next timer to begin. Continue in this fashion until the race is completed.

4. The runner, when through running, collects and records the data from each of the time keepers.

5. The runner calculates the average of the instantaneous speeds recorded by each of the timers.

6. Students compare their results with their hypothesis. They make generalizations and comparisons based on the data collected about their instantaneous versus their average speed. They make predictions about how to improve their overall speed.

7. Discuss at what point the fastest instantaneous speed and the fastest average speed were reached for each runner, and give reasons why the fastest speed was reached at that point in the race. When did the slowest instantaneous speed occur? Runners compare their total speeds. Who won the race? Did this the runner have the fastest average?

ASSESSMENT/REFLECTION:

Students create a plan of action based on their predictions for improving their overall speeds through an awareness of their instantaneous speeds. This plan is tested. Assessment is based on the data collected and how it is analyzed by each student.

MI EXTENSIONS:

This lesson also uses the Interpersonal, Intrapersonal, Logical-Mathematical, and Bodily-Kinesthetic intelligences.

Linguistic: Create a play-by-play account, using the scientific terminology and the data collected.

Spatial: Create graphs or charts to represent the data and compare one student's data to that of another.

Everything and the Net

PURPOSE:
Students calculate the percentage of basketball baskets scored and determine the probability of making a basket.

MATERIALS:
Basketballs, hoops, paper

PROCEDURE:
1. On a basketball court, give the students time to practice shooting baskets. If no basketball court is available, a trash can and ball can be used.
2. Each student estimates how many baskets he or she will make, given ten attempts from a fixed spot on the court.
3. As one student shoots, another tallies the number of shots taken and baskets made. Students use this information to figure the percentage of their successful shots.
4. Repeat this process at least two more times to collect more data. Based on this information, students predict the probability of success if they take ten more shots.

ASSESSMENT/REFLECTION:
Students take ten more shots and see how closely their prediction matched the outcome. If given twenty shots, is their percentage prediction more accurate? Students determine the percentage of baskets made by classmates.

MI EXTENSIONS:
This lesson also uses the Bodily-Kinesthetic Intelligence.

Interpersonal: Divide students into small groups to make teams and determine the probability of the team's making baskets, based on the data collected. What team behaviors might be used to improve the percentage probability, given that each team member must attempt the same number of shots?

Intrapersonal: Evaluate what feelings or behaviors may have an impact on the number of shots made. Reflection questions might include: "Did I put forth my best effort?" "Was I thinking about the process?" "What other personal factors could affect the percentage of shots made from one day to another?"

Bodily-Kinesthetic: Try the same activity using soccer goals, hockey nets, or bowling pins. Discuss how the percentage of successful shots may change depending on the sport and one's exposure to that sport.

Linguistic: Students each write a sports article detailing the statistical outcome of the basketball activity. Compile the articles in a sports section of a newspaper.

Logical-Mathematical: Students have been determining the probability of success for all ten shots; for example, that they will make six out of ten shots. Have the students figure the probability of success as each shot is attempted. If a student has made six of ten shots in the past, for example, and now makes the first six shots, is the student likely to miss the last four shots or will the student's chances of making more than six be increased?

Musical: Discuss how each player may develop their own rhythm of bouncing the ball before shooting and how it may affect their shot.

Spatial: Design a basket or goal that would increase your probability of making more shots. Create a graph that compares the percentage of shots made with old and new designs.

Naturalist: Students plant ten seeds and record how many germinate. They calculate the germination rate, then predict how many will sprout on their next attempt. Conduct the experiment several times to determine the germination rate for the packet of seeds.

Restaurant Project

PURPOSE:

Students participate in a month-long simulation reviewing the math skills of data analysis, geometry, computation with fractions and decimals, and calculating percentages. Students create their own restaurants, including menus, recipes, and floor plans.

MATERIALS:

Variety of menus from area restaurants, poster board, construction paper, graph paper, markers, rulers, calculators, cookbooks, internet access, protractors, plates, napkins, eating utensils

PROCEDURE:

1. *Data Collection:* Students create surveys to develop their restaurants. They pose one numerical and one categorical question, collect responses, and analyze their data. Possible questions could address: cuisine preferences, restaurant design, prices, portion sizes, colors, or food preferences. The survey results are reflected in the choices made for the final project.

2. *Menu:* Students look at menus from local restaurants before selecting themes and names for the restaurants. They develop their own menus that include appetizers, entrees, drinks, and desserts, describing each dish using colorful restaurant language. Students can use cookbooks or the Internet to get recipes and must include at least one on their menus, utilizing fractions in the measurement of ingredients. This recipe is prepared and shared at the grand opening celebration. The students' menus should model the sample menus and include drawings and images.

3. *Restaurant Design:* On poster board, students design the floor plans of their restaurants to scale. They must include various geometric shapes and angles. The teacher determines the requirements list, based on student needs. Students calculate the area and perimeter of their floor plans and determine realistic numbers for occupancy and furniture.

4. *Problem-Solving:* Students use their menus to solve a series of math problems. Possible problems could include the following:
   - Calculate the total bill for a party of four including tax and tip.
   - Calculate the amount of ingredients needed to triple a recipe.
   - Determine the amount of ingredients needed to make your recipe serve one hundred people.
   - Determine how many different meal combinations are possible, including one item from each menu category.
   - Estimate the price of a dinner for a party of fifty.

5. *Grand Opening:* Each student prepares one recipe from their menu at home and brings it to the grand opening of the class restaurant. The

students create tags that describe the dishes and the ingredients used and state the price. Students eat at the restaurant. They calculate their final bills, which include tax and tip. The students learn how to fill out checks that are used to pay for their meals.

ASSESSMENT/REFLECTION:

Create rubrics with the class for each of the components. Final grades can be given based on points achieved on the rubrics.

MI EXTENSIONS:

During this lesson, students also used their Interpersonal, Linguistic, and Spatial intelligences.

Naturalist: Plan a meal from your menu. Sort the ingredients by food groups. Did you plan a balanced meal?

Musical: Pick the music that would be playing in the background that corresponds to your restaurant theme.

Intrapersonal: Think about personal food preferences. Write in your journal about your willingness to try something new and the kinds of foods you like and dislike.

Activities to Support the Logical-Mathematical Intelligence

INTERPERSONAL

- Plexirs (picture puzzles of words and phrases)
- Board games
- Strategy games
- Cooperative skill building
- Problem-solving

INTRAPERSONAL

- Estimate or predict
- Deductive reasoning
- Math journals
- Your own story problems, created from your life experiences
- Math problems you deal with in your own life

BODILY-KINESTHETIC

- Orienteering
- Duration activities
- Building and constructing with blocks
- Use of your body for constructing graphs, Venn diagrams, patterning, and people sorting
- Probability activities such as shooting basketballs or rolling dice

LINGUISTIC

- Thinking strategies; for example, *Warm-Up Mind Benders* by Anita Harnadek
- Timelines
- Use of statistical analysis to create your own story problems
- Computer programming
- Problems that students make up based on an answer you provide

MUSICAL

- Your own time signatures and musical notations
- Number problems set to music
- Logic stories turned into chants or raps
- Instruments played to different time signatures
- Clapping patterns and rhythms

SPATIAL

- Manipulatives like Unifix cubes, Cuisenaire rods, pattern blocks, GeoSolids, and geoboards
- Puzzles and mazes
- Story mapping
- Tessellations
- Tangrams

NATURALIST

- Recording of the life found within one square foot of land during the four seasons
- Exploration of the Fibonacci patterns in nature
- Mapping of an outdoor area
- Collecting, recording, and displaying of data about a classroom pet
- Use of recipes to create plant dyes

Identifying the Logical-Mathematical Intelligence in Your Students

Children function at many different levels within the intelligences. Through observation of everyday activities, one can create a profile showing the level of functioning within a particular intelligence and the intelligences in relation to each other. The levels described show increased engagement and proficiency.

YES NO **APPRECIATES:**

☐ ☐ Consistently demonstrates interest, respect, and enjoyment within the intelligence and is able to differentiate qualities

☐ ☐ Shows curiosity about numbers, shapes, patterns, and relationships

☐ ☐ Shows an interest in how things work

☐ ☐ Listens to math stories and notices numbers

☐ ☐ Sees patterns and relationships in the environment; for example, brick walls or spelling patterns

YES NO **PERFORMS:**

☐ ☐ Is able to apply the intelligence to re-create an exhibit or demonstration or problem-solve in a given situation

☐ ☐ Demonstrates skill in the use of numbers, shapes, patterns, and relationships in problem-solving

☐ ☐ States the problem

☐ ☐ Is able to demonstrate "How to"

☐ ☐ Takes a survey and incorporates the data into a graph

☐ ☐ Is able to use information to solve a problem

☐ ☐ Notices and counts the children who are absent

☐ ☐ Independently obtains and uses resources to solve a problem

☐ ☐ Creates rhythm patterns

☐ ☐ Recognizes math concepts outside the math context

YES NO CREATES:

- ☐ ☐ Is able to apply this intelligence to generate original work or to develop unique solutions to problems or create prototypes
- ☐ ☐ Develops a new problem or strategy
- ☐ ☐ Designs a new game format
- ☐ ☐ Forms hypotheses and develops own experiments and proofs
- ☐ ☐ Without a recipe, creates a new substance
- ☐ ☐ Creates a new type of graph to show information
- ☐ ☐ Is able to pose and solve problems

Children's Resources

Books and Recordings

Aker, Suzanne. *What Comes in 2's, 3's and 4's?* Simon & Schuster Books for Young Readers, 1990.

Allen, Pamela. *Who Sank the Boat?* Coward-McCann, 1983.

Anno, Mitsumasa. *Anno's Counting Book.* HarperCollins, 1992.

———. *Anno's Counting House.* Philomel Books, 1982.

———. *Anno's Math Games.* Philomel Books, 1987.

———. *Anno's Mysterious Multiplying Jar.* Philomel Books, 1983.

———. *Topsy-Turvies.* Weatherhill, 1970.

Axelrod, Amy. *Pigs Go to the Market.* Simon & Schuster, 2006.

Bang, Molly. *Ten, Nine, Eight.* Scholastic, 1983.

Base, Graeme. *The Eleventh Hour.* Abrams, 1989.

Blocksma, Mary. *Reading the Numbers.* Penguin Books, 1989.

Brett, Jan. *Goldilocks and the Three Bears.* Dodd, 1987.

Briggs, Raymond. *Jim and the Beanstalk.* Coward-McCann, 1970.

Carle, Eric. *Rooster's Off to See the World.* Picture Book Studio, 1972.

———. *The Secret Birthday Message.* Harper Trophy, 1986.

———. *The Very Hungry Caterpillar.* Philomel Books, 1987.

Clements, Andrew. *A Million Dots.* Simon & Schuster, 2006.

Crews, Donald. *School Bus.* Mulberry Books, 1993.

———. *10 Ten Black Dots.* Greenwillow Books, 1986.

Dee, Ruby. *Two Ways to Count to Ten.* Henry Holt, 1990.

Dunbar, Joyce. *Ten Little Mice.* Harcourt, 1990.

Ehlert, Lois. *Planting a Rainbow.* Harcourt Brace, 1988.

Feelings, Muriel. *Moja Means One.* Dial Books for Young Readers, 1976.

Fisher, Valorie. *How High Can a Dinosaur Count?* Schwartz & Wade, 2006.

Galdone, Paul. *The Three Billy Goats Gruff.* Seabury, 1973.

Giganti, Paul Jr. *How Many Snails?* Greenwillow Books, 1988.

Glass, Julie. *The Fly on the Ceiling: A Math Myth.* Random House, 1998.

Goldberg, Hirsch M. *The Book of Lies: History's Greatest Fakes, Frauds, Schemes, and Scams.* Quill/William Morrow, 1990.

Goldstone, Bruce. *Great Estimations.* Henry Holt, 2006.

Gray, Kes. *Cluck O'Clock.* Holiday House, 2004.

Gretz, Susanna. *Teddy Bears Go Shopping.* Puffin Books, 1983.

Haber, Louis. *Black Pioneers of Science and Invention.* Harcourt Brace, 1970.

Hague, Kathleen. *Numbears.* Henry Holt, 1986.

Hartman, Gail. *As the Crow Flies: A First Book of Maps.* Bradbury Press, 1991.

Haskins, Jim. *Count Your Way Through Africa.* Carolrhoda Books, 1992.

———. *Count Your Way Through China.* Carolrhoda Books, 1987.

———. *Count Your Way Through Italy.* Carolrhoda Books, 1989.

Hoban, Tana. *Shapes, Shapes, Shapes.* Greenwillow Books, 1986.

Hoffman, Mary. *Amazing Grace.* Dial, 1991.

Hubbard, Woodleigh. *Two Is for Dancing.* Chronicle Books, 1991.

Humez, Alexander, Humez, Nicholas, and Maguire, Joseph. *Zero to Lazy Eight: The Romance of Numbers.* Simon & Schuster, 1993.

Hutchins, Pat. *1 Hunter.* Greenwillow Books, 1982.

———. *Changes, Changes.* Collier MacMillan, 1987.

———. *The Doorbell Rang.* Mulberry Books, 1989.

Kitamuro, Satoshi. *When Sheep Cannot Sleep: The Counting Book.* Farrar, Straus & Giroux, 1986.

Langstaff, John. *Over in the Meadow.* Harcourt Brace, 1957.

Leedy, Loreen. *The Great Graph Contest.* Holiday House, 2005.

Lepscky, Ibi. *Albert Einstein.* Barron's, 1992.

Lionni, Leo. *Inch by Inch.* Astor-Honor, 1960.

Lord, John. *Giant Jam Sandwich.* Houghton Mifflin, 1972.

MacDonald, Suse. *Numblers.* Dial Books for Young Readers, 1988.

Mack, Stan. *Ten Bears in My Bed.* Pantheon Books, 1974.

Macy, Sue. "*Bison Americanus:* America's Great Shaggy Beast." *Cobblestone* 2, no. 8 (August 1981).

Manushkin, Fran. *101 Dalmatians: A Counting Book.* Disney Press, 1991.

Marzolla, Jean. *I Spy.* Scholastic, 1992.

McElligott, Matthew. *The Lion's Share: A Tale of Halving and Eating It Too.* Walker, 2009.

McKissack, Patricia. *A Million Fish . . . More or Less.* Knopf, 1992.

McMillan, Bruce. *Eating Fractions.* Scholastic, 1991.

McPhail, David. *Lost.* Little, Brown, 1990.

Mohy, Margaret. *17 Kings and 42 Elephants.* Dial Books for Young Readers, 1990.

Moore, Lilian. *My First Counting Book.* Golden Book, 1956.

Morozumi, Atsuko. *One Gorilla.* Farrar, Straus & Giroux, 1990.

Munsch, Robert. *Moira's Birthday.* Annick Press, 1987.

Murphy, Stuart. *Elevator Magic.* HarperCollins, 1997.

Neuschwander, Cindy. *Amanda Bean's Amazing Dream: A Mathematical Story.* Scholastic Press, 1998.

———. *Sir Cumference and the First Round Table: A Math Adventure.* Charlesbridge, 1997.

Numeroff, Lauren. *If You Give a Mouse a Cookie.* Harper Festival, 1992.

Oppenheim, Joanne. *Left and Right.* Harcourt Brace, 1989.

Pallotta, Jerry. *The Icky Bug Counting Book.* Charlesbridge, 1992.

Perry, Sarah. *If.* Children's Library Press, 1995.

Pinczes, Elinor J. *One Hundred Angry Ants.* Houghton Mifflin, 1993.

Raskin, Ellen. *The Westing Game.* Puffin Books, 1992.

Reisberg, Joanne. *Zachary Zormer: Shape Transformer.* Charlesbridge, 2006.

Sachar, Louis. *Sideways Arithmetic from Wayside School.* Scholastic, 1989.

Saunders, Hal. *When Are We Ever Gonna Have to Use This?* (updated 3rd ed.). Dale Seymour, 1988.

Sayre, April. *One Is a Snail; Ten Is a Crab.* Candlewick Press, 2003.

Schwartz, David M. *How Much Is a Million?* Lothrop, Lee and Shepard Books, 1985.

———. *If You Made a Million.* Lothrop, Lee and Shepard Books, 1989.

Shannon, George. *Stories to Solve: Folktales from Around the World.* Beech Tree, 1991.

Smith, David. *If the World Were a Village.* Kids Can Press, 2002.

Tang, Greg. *The Best of Times: Math Strategies That Multiply.* Scholastic, 2002.

———. *The Grapes of Math.* Scholastic, 2001.

Tompert, Ann. *Grandfather Tang's Story.* Crown Publishers, 1990.

Tudor, Tasha. *Bedtime Book*. Platt and Munk, 1977.

Viorst, Judith. *Alexander, Who Used to Be Rich Last Saturday*. Aladdin Books, 1988.

Games

4-Way CountDown. Cadaco, 2004.

Abalone Galoob. Abalone Games, 1989.

Body Bingo. Lakeshore, 1993.

Boggle Junior Math. Parker Brothers, 1993.

Candyland Bingo. Milton Bradley, 1984.

Chess. Pavillion, Geoffry, 1989.

Chinese Checkers: Classic Game. Golden: Western, 1989.

Color and Shape Bingo. Trend Enterprises, 1984.

Color and Shape Lotto. Trend Enterprises, 1985.

Heximoes. Educational Insights, Inc., 2004.

Little, Big, Medium: Discovering Opposites. Creative Toys.

Mastermind. Invicta, 1976.

Penguin Math. CB Publishing, 2006.

Perfection. Lakeshore, 1975.

Set: The Family Game of Visual Perception. SET Enterprises, 2004.

Somebody: The Human Anatomy Game. Artistoplay, 1990.

The Original Memory: Card Matching Game. Milton Bradley, 1989.

Tip Top Tally. Purple Pebble Games LLC, 2004.

What's for Dinner? Rapid Mounting and Fishing, 1989.

Where in the USA Is Carmen Sandiego? University Games, 1993.

Teachers' Resources

Anderson and Bereites. *Thinking Games*. Fearon, 1980.

Baker, Ann, and Baker, Johnny. *Raps and Rhymes in Math*. Heinemann, 1991.

Baratta-Lorton, Mary. *Mathematics Their Way*. Addison-Wesley, 1976.

Braddon, Kathryn, Hall, Nancy, and Taylor, Dale. *Math Through Children's Literature: Making the NCTM Standards Come Alive*. Teacher Ideas Press, 1993.

Burke, Kay. *Authentic Learning*. Corwin, 2009.

Burnam, Tom. *The Dictionary of Misinformation*. HarperCollins, 1975.

Burns, Marilyn. *A Collection of Math Lessons*. Math Solutions, 1988.

————. *About Teaching Mathematics: A K–8 Resource*. Math Solutions Publications, 2000.

————. *Math for Smarty Pants*. Little, Brown, 1982.

————. *The Book of Think*. Little, Brown, 1976.

————. *The I Hate Mathematics Book*. Little, Brown, 1975.

————. *This Book Is About Time*. Little, Brown, 1978.

Butzow, Carol. *Science Through Children's Literature*. Teacher's Ideas Press, 1989.

Chen, Jie-Qi, ed. *Project Spectrum: Early Learning Activities*. Teachers College Press, 1999. (This is volume 2 of Project Zero Frameworks for Early Childhood Education.)

Draznin, Sharon Z. *Writing Math, Project-Based Activities to Integrate Math and Language Arts*. Good Year Books, 1995.

Egan, Lorraine Hopping. *25 Super Cool Math Board Games*. Scholastic Professional Books, 1999.

Franco, Betsy. *Write-and-Read Math Story Books*. Scholastic Inc., 1998.

Grimm, Gary, and Mitchell, Dan. *The Good Apple Math Book*. Good Apple, 1975.

Harnadek, Anita. *Warm-Up Mind Benders*. Midwest Publications, 1979.

Helm, Judy Harris, and Katz, Lilian. *Young Investigators: The Project Approach in the Early Years.* Teachers College Press, 2001.

Macy, Sue. "*Bison Americanus:* America's Great Shaggy Beast." *Cobblestone* 2, no. 8 (August 1981).

Moscovich, Ivan. *Fiendishly Difficult Math Puzzles.* Sterling, 1991.

Palmer, Hap. *Learning Basic Skills Through Music,* I. Educational Activities, AR 514.

Read, Ronald C. *Tangrams: 330 Puzzles.* Dover, 1965.

Reimer, Luetta, and Reimer, Wilbert. *Mathematicians Are People, Too: Stories from the Lives of Great Mathematicians.* Dale Seymour, 1990.

Russell, Stone. *Used Numbers.* Dale Seymour, 1990.

Skinner, Penny. *It All Adds Up!* Math Solutions Publications, 1999.

Sloane, Paul, and MacHale, Des. *Challenging Lateral Thinking Puzzles.* Sterling, 1993.

Stenmark, Jean, Thompson, Virginia, and Cossey, Ruth. *Family Math.* Lawrence Hall of Science, 1986.

Thiessen, Diane. *The Wonderful World of Mathematics: A Critically Annotated List of Children's Books in Mathematics.* National Council of Teachers of Mathematics, 1992.

Welchman-Tischler, Rosamond. *How to Use Children's Literature to Teach Mathematics.* National Council of Teachers of Mathematics, 1992.

Whitin, David, and Wilde, Sarah. *Read Any Good Math Lately?* Heinemann, 1992.

Wormeli, Rick. *Summarization in Any Subject: 50 Techniques to Improve Student Learning.* ASCD, 2005.

"Where there's music there can be no evil."

—MIGUEL DE CERVANTES

6

Photograph: Patti Gabriel

The Musical Intelligence

Web of the Musical Intelligence

Student Quotes

" I think my greatest intelligence is Musical because I like to act, sing and put on shows. "

" I'm Musical because I play a few instruments and every day I sing a song in my head. "

" I hum and dance all the time everywhere. "

Characteristics

- Enjoys singing and playing musical instruments, remembers songs and melodies, enjoys listening to music, keeps beats, makes up her own songs, mimics beat and rhythm, notices background and environmental sounds, differentiates patterns in sounds, is sensitive to melody and tone, body moves when music is playing, has a rich understanding of musical structure, rhythm, and notes

Famous People

JOHN WILLIAMS, laureate conductor of the Boston Pops Orchestra, is one of the most prolific and popular composers of our time.

MARIAN ANDERSON is considered the greatest contralto of her generation and one of the golden voices of the twentieth century.

MIDORI is an international violinist and recording artist.

By the age of five, WOLFGANG AMADEUS MOZART was competent on the keyboard and violin and began composing his own work.

Although blind from birth, STEVIE WONDER is one of the most well-known R&B/Blues musicians.

Adult Quotes

"Music expresses that which cannot be said and on which it is impossible to be silent. "
    —VICTOR HUGO

" To stop the flow of music would be like the stopping of time itself, incredible and inconceivable. "
    —AARON COPELAND

" Music is a moral law. It gives soul to the universe, wings to the mind, flight to the imagination, and charm and gaiety to life and to everything. "
    —PLATO

" Music is the universal language of mankind. "
—HENRY WADSWORTH LONGFELLOW

Minding the Music

BY BEN GRIFFITHS

About twelve weeks post-conception, a fetus normally begins to develop a sense of hearing. From then until birth, hearing serves as the fetus's primary source of information about the surrounding world. By the time of birth, it has already spent months following the rhythm of its mother's heartbeat, hearing the steady pulse of fluids in transit, and learning to identify the voices of family members. With such early exposure to rhythmic patterns, it's no surprise the Musical Intelligence is the first to emerge, or that it is present in each of us.

Musical Intelligence involves an understanding of pitch, rhythm, and the timbre or texture of a sound. There are some children and adults who believe they are not "musical," yet those same individuals can quickly tell you their favorite radio station, composer, or band, and detail their distaste for numerous others. The truth is, we are all (even those with hearing impairments) musical beings with definite musical abilities and intellect. Of course, that does not mean that we are all capable of playing in an orchestra or singing the lead in a musical. There are ways a person might exhibit Musical Intelligence beyond performing, including composing music for others to play, identifying patterns in sounds, recognizing subtle inflection in language, reviewing music others have produced, or simply selecting music for enjoyment.

> It's no surprise the Musical Intelligence is the first to emerge, or that it is present in each of us.

Although compositional styles and instrumentation vary greatly across different societies, music is present in every culture around the world. It is a universal language spoken by people across all boundaries. We all connect with music in one way or another, and, given the opportunity, we can learn about our culture, our history, our thoughts, our emotions, and each other through music.

> Musical Intelligence involves an understanding of pitch, rhythm, and the timbre or texture of a sound. We are all (even those with hearing impairments) musical beings with definite musical abilities and intellect.

There are many ways to help students access and use Musical Intelligence in the classroom, even if the classroom is not the *music* classroom, per se. Many ways involve little or no preparation and can be implemented regardless of a teacher's personal level of experience with music.

BRINGING MUSIC INTO THE CLASSROOM

Musical Cues. Music can be a wonderful way to grab your students' attention or signal a transition between activities. Try clapping a rhythm for them to repeat when you need them to stop and listen. Play a certain piece of music to signal the end of an activity or as a timer for a cleanup session requiring completion by the end of the song. Choose a song to sing or a rhythmic poem to start an activity and get everyone focused.

Music can be a wonderful way to grab your students' attention or signal a transition between activities.

Once you've established some common cues, your class will know what to do without being told.

Supporting Intrapersonal and Interpersonal Growth. Music can help you to develop a creative, welcoming atmosphere while providing exposure to a variety of musical composers and genres. Have music playing when your students arrive and begin their morning routines. Establish theme days and traditions, like "Mozart Mondays" or "Fifties Week." Have your students create a soundtrack filled with some of their own favorite songs that could greet them in the morning. Establish a listening center where students can access the music at other times of the day as well. Time allowed in such centers can be a powerful motivator for students. Try to incorporate background music in other parts of the day as well and you may find it becomes a part of your classroom community. You'll have a musical subculture of your own.

Music as Context for Content. There are endless ways to support your students' understanding across content areas. As you study math, offer opportunities to hear selections from composers who have written music using mathematical calculations, such as Brian Transeau (better known as BT) or James Tenney. During a science investigation into sound waves and pitch, play a portion of *The Brain Opera* by Tod Machover. As you learn about the Civil War, play the soundtrack to *Gettysburg* in the background. Or as you explore poetry, provide examples of poetry set to music, such as the Whiffenpoofs' version of Yeats' poem, "Down by the Sally Garden." Music from a variety of composers around the globe is increasingly available and accessible through the Internet. Playing music or making it available in centers will deepen any learning experience.

Targeting Specific Content. Music is also a powerful tool to help with memorization and retention. Most of us probably learned our ABCs by singing the alphabet song. Similarly, a song about the names of the fifty states, the rules for division, or the table of elements is a powerful mnemonic device for your students. Play the *Animaniacs*' rendition of "The Nations of the World," and you'll have your kids begging for a chance to hear it again. They'll be studying geography without even knowing it. Songs like "The Galaxy Song" by Monty Python and "Why Does the Sun Shine?" by They Might Be Giants are infused with information about the solar system, but cleverly arranged in a humorous, entertaining manner. There are similar songs for all the content areas. The *Schoolhouse Rock* series has a DVD with every song they've produced, and other companies, such as Songs for Teaching, have realized the power of music in the classroom and provide broad collections of music available for purchase.

The key is realizing that students are indeed musical beings who will benefit from any and every opportunity to learn through the Musical Intelligence.

Content-Based Compositions. Students often enjoy the opportunity to write their own songs about the content they are learning. As students study Civil Rights protests, they will benefit from the opportunity to write their own protest songs. Students learning about spiders or the life cycle of a butterfly can arrange a series of facts to a well-known melody. Rewriting a song or a portion of it is also a way to offer your students the opportunity to express themselves through song without having to start from scratch.

Although the Musical Intelligence is present in all of us, experiences with music in the classroom will vary greatly based on many factors. Depending on your situation, it may indeed be a daunting task to fully integrate music into your classroom. Start with what you know you can handle and build from there. The key is realizing that students are indeed musical beings who will benefit from any and every opportunity to learn through the Musical Intelligence. If you are open to it, you will soon discover that music will find its way into your teaching, and into the hearts and minds of your students as well.

Digestion in the Human Body

PURPOSE:

Children name the parts and function of the digestive system. This lesson could also be adapted for units on body characteristics, the brain, the skeletal system, the circulatory system, and general well-being.

MATERIALS:

Chart paper or dry erase board; words to "The Digestion Song" by Monette Gooch-Smith written on chart paper and a copy of the song lyrics for each child; musical instruments; video camera; crayons and paper; copies of *What Happens to a Hamburger* by Paul Showers, *Mysterious You: Burp!* by Diane Swanson, *What Happens to Your Food?* by Alistair Smith, and *101 Science Poems and Songs for Young Learners* by Meish Goldish.

PROCEDURE:

1. Write the word *digestion* on the chart paper and have the children pronounce it. Start a *KWL chart* listing the things they *know* about digestion, what they *want* to know, and finally what they have *learned*.
2. Teach "The Digestion Song" to the class. Discuss the lyrics. Compare these responses to those that were recorded on the chart.
3. Dramatize the digestive process, using musical instruments and movement. Have each child select a musical instrument to represent various parts of the digestive system. The children then play the instruments in order as a "piece of food" passes through the system.
4. Children think about the song and movement activities and tell something they learned about digestion, which is added to the chart.

ASSESSMENT/REFLECTION:

Have students draw and label a map of the digestive system. Review the drawings for content and accuracy.

MI EXTENSIONS:

This lesson also uses the Bodily-Kinesthetic, Interpersonal, Spatial, and Linguistic intelligences.

Interpersonal: Working in pairs, students use a stethoscope to listen to the partner's digestive tract as he or she eats a carrot. Listen at the cheek, throat, and stomach. Use sound words to label a diagram of the digestive system.

Linguistic: Each child chooses a part of the digestive tract. If that body part could talk, what would it say and to whom would it speak? Write a dialogue that shares what this body part likes and dislikes about its job, and why.

Spatial: Create a model of the digestive system using paper towel tubes (esophagus), clear plastic storage bags (stomach) and pink crepe paper streamers (intestines).

Digestion Song
BY MONETTE GOOCH-SMITH
(SUNG TO THE TUNE OF "THE WHEELS ON THE BUS")

The teeth in my mouth chew, grind, tear,
chew, grind, tear, chew, grind, tear.
The teeth in my mouth chew, grind, tear,
whenever food is there.
The glands in my mouth squirt saliva,
squirt saliva, squirt saliva.
The glands in my mouth squirt saliva,
all day long.
The tongue in my mouth moves food down,
moves food down, moves food down.
The tongue in my mouth moves food down,
down the esophagus.
Esophagus takes it to my stomach,
to my stomach, to my stomach
Esophagus takes it to my stomach
and breaks down food much more.
The stomach takes food to my intestine,
to my intestine, to my intestine.
The stomach takes food to my intestine
the small, then the large.
That's how my body digests food,
digests food, digests food.
That's how my body digests food,
Every time I eat. YUM! YUM!

Caterpillars to Butterflies

PURPOSE:

Students learn the lifecycle of a butterfly and demonstrate metamorphosis through dance.

MATERIALS:

Monarch Butterfly by Gail Gibbons, several sets of pictures of the stages of a butterfly's metamorphosis, scarves or material to be used as wings and chrysalises, music, chart paper, teacher-created checklist that tells the stages of metamorphosis

PROCEDURE:

1. Read *Monarch Butterfly* by Gail Gibbons. After reading, create a mind map of the process of metamorphosis on a chart.

2. Children sort and put in order the pictures illustrating metamorphosis.

3. Children lie down with their eyes closed and listen to music you have selected to represent metamorphosis. They visualize the four stages and the transitions between these stages. In their minds, they become eggs that hatch into caterpillars. As caterpillars, they crawl, eat, grow, and change into a chrysalis. In their imaginations they transform into a butterfly.

4. Children are asked how they might move their bodies to the music to illustrate each stage of metamorphosis. Have them volunteer to demonstrate how they could move their bodies to show the different stages. Allow them time to practice different movements experimenting with the scarves and materials.

5. Children order their movements to choreograph a dance that represents metamorphosis.

ASSESSMENT/REFLECTION:

During the performances, note on a checklist whether the stages of metamorphosis are depicted in the correct order.

MI EXTENSIONS:

This lesson also uses the Naturalist and Bodily-Kinesthetic intelligences.

Naturalist: Research other animals that go through metamorphosis. Create panels that share this information with other students.

Spatial: Decorate a knee-length sock to look like a caterpillar. The toe of the sock is the head of the caterpillar. Make a butterfly out of felt. Holding the wadded-up butterfly in your hand, put your hand inside the sock and pull the sock up to your elbow. Turn the sock inside out as the chrysalis is formed, hiding the caterpillar. Pull the sock off your hand as the chrysalis opens, exposing your hand with the butterfly inside.

Human Rhythm

PURPOSE:

Students explore how sounds can be made by the human body and then organized into rhythmic patterns to create music. Students use symbols to represent sounds and rhythms.

MATERIALS:

Paper, chalkboard or whiteboard and chalk or markers, internet access to YouTube for video by a group called "Body Rhythm Factory" related to body percussion

PROCEDURE:

1. Challenge the students to think of ways to make sound with their bodies in appropriate ways. Agree on a symbol to represent each sound. Include symbols to represent pauses and stops.
2. Demonstrate a rhythm: *Clap, clap, snap, pause. Clap, clap, snap, pause. Clap, clap, snap, stop.* On the board, translate this into the sound symbol notation.
3. Students compose body rhythms and write the symbols. These are posted or displayed in a gallery walk.
4. Students move from composition to composition, playing the body rhythms.

ASSESSMENT/REFLECTION:

During the gallery walk, note the following: Were students able to read and write music using the common set of symbols? Were they able to perform the music accurately?

MI EXTENSIONS:

This lesson also uses the Bodily-Kinesthetic Intelligence.

Interpersonal: Put students in small groups and ask them to integrate their patterns into a musical composition to be performed for other groups.

Spatial: Students use their symbols to create art using watercolors, pastels, or the medium of their choice. Use the art of Wassily Kandinsky as inspiration. Display the art and perform the music that results from the spatial representation.

Naturalist: Use objects found in nature to create sounds. Select symbols to represent the sounds created by the objects. Record and play the compositions.

Making Music

PURPOSE:

Students learn basic facts about vibration and sound as they work together to create musical instruments using recycled materials.

MATERIALS:

A letter to parents asking them to send in materials, which could include boxes of various shapes and sizes, tubes, cans, string, rubber bands, paper plates, beans, or rice

For teacher demonstrations: salt, tuning forks, cups with balloons taped tightly across the top, wooden rulers or yardsticks, string of various lengths

PROCEDURE:

1. Send home the parent letter so you can begin to collect materials for the musical instruments the students will make after they have explored sound and vibration.

2. In pairs, one student holds one end of a string up to her ear while stretching the other end away from her face. Her partner gently plucks the taut string. They listen for the sound that is created. Next, the students try a piece of string of a different length. Discuss the differences in the sounds heard and formulate a hypothesis for those differences.

3. Why does the string make a sound, and why are the sounds different? Use the rulers to show what is happening to the string. Place a ruler on the table, letting it extend well beyond the edge. Push down on the ruler and then release. The students will hear a sound and see the ruler vibrating. Shorten the length of ruler extending beyond the edge and push down once again. The vibration they see and the sound they hear will be different. Let each child try the experiment that you have demonstrated. Afterward, talk about what they noticed and have them share their reasons for what they observed.

4. Repeat steps #2 and #3, this time focusing on the force with which the string is plucked and the ruler is struck. Plucking and pushing gently creates a quieter sound, whereas plucking and pushing harder creates a louder sound. Have children experiment with string and rulers to create quiet and loud sounds.

5. Use a cup with a balloon stretched tightly across the top like a drum head to demonstrate vibration. Put some salt on the top of the balloon. After striking the tuning fork to make it vibrate, lightly touch it to the top of the balloon. The salt will jump. What do the students notice?

6. Students use the collected materials to make musical instruments. They might create shakers, guitar-like instruments, or drums.

ASSESSMENT/REFLECTION:

Use a ruler or a piece of string to create a tone. Ask students to make a tone that is higher or lower with the same material. Observe the students to see whether they are able to lengthen or shorten their material appropriately to obtain the desired result.

MI EXTENSIONS:

This lesson also uses the Spatial Intelligence.

Interpersonal: With like instruments grouped together, children create an orchestra. As a group, decide what hand signals the conductor will use to direct the orchestra to play louder, softer, higher, or lower. Children take turns conducting the orchestra.

Naturalist: Children collect natural materials and experiment with creating sounds. Try blowing on a blade of grass, swishing a willow branch, tapping rocks of various sizes, or dropping pebbles into different depths of water.

Linguistic: Children write cause and effect statements; for example, "If I pluck a string hard, then the sound is louder."

Poetry in Sounds

PURPOSE:
Students create poetry using the sounds they hear while they are outside.

MATERIALS:
Chart paper, blindfolds

PROCEDURE:
1. Students sit outside in a circle somewhere on the playground or in the schoolyard. The students affix blindfolds and listen for one minute. With blindfolds in place, after you give a signal, they call out phrases sharing what they have heard. Record the phrases on chart paper so that they can later be cut apart.

2. Again, the students listen. After two minutes, record the phrases the students share to describe what they have heard. This continues until you feel there have been enough poetic phrases shared to create poems.

3. In the classroom, the phrases are cut apart and sorted by categories. These might include transportation sounds, the sounds of children playing, animal sounds, or neighborhood sounds.

4. Groups of students are given phrases within the chosen categories to arrange into a poem. The poem is copied and published.

5. Students display and read their poems for classmates.

ASSESSMENT/REFLECTION:
Note the interest, respect, and enjoyment students demonstrate during this project.

MI EXTENSIONS:
This lesson also uses the Linguistic and Interpersonal intelligences.

Bodily-Kinesthetic: Watch the movement of children on the playground at recess and record phrases describing those movements. Sort the phrases by categories and create poems.

Spatial: Record phrases that illustrate the colors, shapes, and textures the students see on the playground or an interesting place in the school building. Use these to create poetry.

Spatial: Children draw the source of the sound they heard: Was it an insect, bird, or animal, or was the wind rustling the leaves?

Naturalist: Listen to sounds in nature from birds, frogs, waves, wind in the trees, and the like; create a corresponding poem.

Naturalist: Children work to improve the environment by picking up at least two pieces of litter.

Literary Soundtrack

PURPOSE:

After reading a novel or short story, students work in small groups to create a piece of music that represents the story. Students identify and incorporate various aspects of plot development, such as introduction, rising action, climax, falling action, and resolution.

MATERIALS:

Plot development sheet, copy of the novel or short story for each student, a variety of instruments, audio or video recording equipment

PROCEDURE:

1. Plot development is introduced and discussed during literature circle as the class reads the story in which the elements of plot can easily be identified. Introduce the idea of using a roller coaster ride as a metaphor for plot development within the text.

2. Introduction: How does a roller coaster ride begin and how is that like the introduction of the plot in a story? The students might share anticipation and questions about what will happen next.

   Rising action: When does the tension begin to mount during the ride? How does suspense build within the story?

   Climax: What is the most exciting and tense moment during the ride or in the story?

   Falling Action: How does it feel as the end is approaching and the car is slowing down? Where does the reader get a similar feeling in the story?

   Resolution: How do the ride and story end? At the end, do you feel as though you want to try it again?

3. When the story is finished, ask the students to imagine that a new movie is going to be made of the story, and they have been asked to be the musical directors. In small groups, their job is to develop a soundtrack for the story they just analyzed. Each group will be responsible for creating music that represents each of the five elements of plot.

4. Each soundtrack is recorded and reviewed by the class. Members of the performing group explain each musical section and its connection to the corresponding element of plot.

ASSESSMENT/REFLECTION:

Students can explain the correlation between the music, the elements, and the story.

MI EXTENSIONS:

During this lesson, students also used their Linguistic and Interpersonal intelligences.

Intrapersonal: Students identify the emotions they feels as they listen to each piece of music and compare those feelings to the feelings of the main character. Attention is given to the plot elements portrayed by the music and the events within the story they represent. Is there a connection?

Bodily-Kinesthetic: Students create an interpretive dance to accompany the musical pieces.

Spatial: Students create a storyboard to illustrate each element of plot using the roller coaster as a metaphor.

Naturalist: Use the life cycle of a plant or animal as the metaphor for plot development.

A Record of Time

MUSICAL

INTERMEDIATE

SOCIAL STUDIES

PURPOSE:

Students identify current issues and events that are evident in the lyrics of popular songs. Students compare lyrics of today with lyrics of other generations or cultures to learn that music is a primary source that documents social issues and actions.

MATERIALS:

Recorded songs with lyrics from various time periods and cultures, popular songs brought in by students, graph paper

PROCEDURE:

1. Students bring in a teacher-approved piece of current music.

2. As a class, listen to one sample of music and start a chart of social issues mentioned in the lyrics. This may include issues such as materialism, ecology, love, commitment, loneliness, alienation, war, and peace.

3. In small groups, students listen to songs they have brought to class and list any social issues or events evident in the songs.

4. Come back together as a whole group and add to the chart started in step #2.

5. Discuss how the popular music of today reflects current societal issues. Help students make the connection that music can be used as a primary source when studying a culture or generation.

ASSESSMENT/REFLECTION:

Give students a recorded song from a different era or culture. They will use this primary source to determine what issues were important at that time or in that place. Students take on the persona of the songwriter and present to the class the reasons behind their lyrics. For example, a student could dress as Bono and explain the historical significance of *Pride, in the Name of Love* as it relates to the assassination of Dr. Martin Luther King Jr.

MI EXTENSIONS:

This lesson also uses the Interpersonal Intelligence.

Spatial: Use works of art as primary sources to discuss cultural and historic context.

Intrapersonal: What social issues are important to you that were not addressed in the music we explored? Why might that be? Students write possible answers in a journal.

Logical-Mathematical: Chart the top ten songs in the pop category over a period of time. Conduct research to determine what social issues were most prevalent during that time. Create a frequency graph to show how often popular music addressed the concerns of the day.

Get the Beat

PURPOSE:

Students learn how to keep a tempo and use rhythm patterns to create a musical piece. Students develop strategies that allow them to perform within an ensemble.

MUSICAL

INTERMEDIATE

PERFORMING ARTS

MATERIALS:

Various percussion instruments, construction paper for teacher-created beat cards

PROCEDURE:

1. Students sit in a circle to learn how to properly play the percussion instruments they are working with for this lesson. Each instrument is demonstrated and then passed around the circle for each child to explore. As a new instrument is introduced, it is passed to the right or left. In this way, each instrument makes its way around the circle.

2. Students are given an instrument to use as they learn about musical notation. They are first introduced to the quarter note and how it is played in a 4/4 measure. The students play a measure with four quarter notes. Whole notes, half notes, eighth notes, and rests are also introduced.

3. Use teacher-made beat cards to show students different ways to play rhythms that could be found in a 4/4 measure. For example, one card might contain two quarter notes and a half note. Another card might have two eighth notes, a quarter note, and a half note. Make several cards with various combinations.

4. Over several days, students practice playing the different beat card rhythms using different instruments.

5. Students record their own beat patterns in 4/4 time on construction paper. Working in groups, they form percussion ensembles, playing the patterns they created. Students problem-solve ways to ensure that they start at the same time and keep the same tempo. They might choose to count off or have one person serve as the leader or conductor.

ASSESSMENT/REFLECTION:

Collect the student-created beat cards to determine whether the notation works for a 4/4 measure. During the ensemble performances, notice each group's ability to keep the beat and the ways the members choose to solve problems that arise.

MI EXTENSIONS:

This lesson also uses the Interpersonal and Logical-Mathematical intelligences.

Logical-Mathematical: Create and perform rhythms using a different time signature.

Linguistic: Find poetry that has a rhythm; for example, a limerick. Determine the pattern and assign a time signature.

Naturalist: Listen to the sounds made by local birds. Is there a pattern? Can it be transferred to a time signature?

Bodily-Kinesthetic: Students use their bodies to create the beat pattern from their beat cards and then play their bodies in an ensemble.

Activities to Support the Musical Intelligence

INTERPERSONAL

- Play musical board games such as instrument bingo or composer concentration.
- Turn a song into a finger game, story, puppet show, or play.
- Play circle games like "Miss Mary Mac," "Down, Down Baby," or "Sally Walker."
- Learn musical games from other countries.
- Practice and invent jump rope rhymes.

INTRAPERSONAL

- Have music playing in the background during other activities.
- Create a music montage.
- Become a DJ for ten minutes and record selections to fit your mood.
- Listen to music and think about how it affects you. What makes you move, lie still, smile, turn off the music?
- Compare yourself to a musical instrument or piece of music.

BODILY-KINESTHETIC

- Make up a dance with instrumental accompaniment.
- Experiment with unconventional instruments and sound.
- Interpret a rhythm through role playing.
- Lip-sync a song.
- Use your body to make music.

LINGUISTIC

- Compose a song, rap, jingle, or melody.
- Say things to a rhythm.
- Spell to music by singing each letter to a beat.
- Retell a story by rewriting the words to a familiar tune.
- Find music to accompany parts of a story which demonstrate the mood.

LOGICAL-MATHEMATICAL

- Assign sounds to pattern elements and play the pattern.
- Connect fractions with music, such as whole notes, half notes, sixteenth notes.
- Compare and contrast musical styles from a historical perspective.
- Sort instruments into the four basic groups.
- Sort and classify music by style, genre, or instrumentation.

SPATIAL

- Paint a picture of musical instruments.
- Make apple doll or puppet composers.
- Listen to a musical work and draw the visual image you get or what you think the composer looks like.
- Design a new musical instrument.
- Create a symbol system to record music.

NATURALIST

- Use various seeds to create shakers, noticing the different sounds created.
- Organize a class band that plays instruments made from natural objects.
- Record outdoor sounds and put them together to create a song.
- Learn to blow grass whistles.
- Learn to identify bird, frog, or other animal songs or sounds.

Identifying the Musical Intelligence in Your Students

Children function at many different levels within the intelligences. Through observation of everyday activities, one can create a profile showing the level of functioning within a particular intelligence and the intelligences in relation to each other. The levels described show increased engagement and proficiency.

YES NO **APPRECIATES:**

☐ ☐ Consistently demonstrates interest and enjoyment; is able to differentiate qualities

☐ ☐ Enjoys music as a performing art

☐ ☐ Recognizes many tunes

☐ ☐ Can distinguish among musical styles or instruments

☐ ☐ Asks to listen to music

☐ ☐ Hears beat and rhythm in environmental sounds, such as a copy machine, a ticking clock

☐ ☐ Hums or mimics

☐ ☐ Body moves when music is playing

☐ ☐ Talks about musical performances, attends events, writes about it

YES NO **PERFORMS:**

☐ ☐ Is able to apply the intelligence to create an exhibit or demonstration, or problem-solve in a given situation

☐ ☐ Demonstrates skill (voice or instrument) in using pitch and rhythm

☐ ☐ Sings, plays an instrument

☐ ☐ Easily memorizes information presented musically

☐ ☐ Is able to differentiate patterns and sounds

☐ ☐ Integrates musical activities into projects, centers, theme; for example, writes raps, makes instruments

☐ ☐ Uses body to make musical sounds, such as taps on chest, cheek pops, knee slaps

☐ ☐ Uses sound to enhance language experience, such as poetry, math facts, spelling words

☐ ☐ Mimics intricate beats or rhythms

☐ ☐ Reads music

CREATES:

☐ ☐ Is able to apply this intelligence to generate original work, to develop unique solutions to problems or create prototypes

☐ ☐ Designs and/or produces an original composition incorporating musical elements

☐ ☐ Designs or constructs a unique musical instrument

☐ ☐ Composes original music; for example, writes songs, sound accompaniment to poetry

☐ ☐ Develops original notation related to the musical elements, such as rhythm, melody, harmony, form

Children's Resources

Books and Recordings

Ackerman, Karen. *Song and Dance Man.* Knopf, 1988.

Adams, Ron. *There Was an Old Lady Who Swallowed a Fly.* Child's Play, 1973.

Aliki. *A Play's the Thing.* HarperCollins, 2005.

Aliki. *Ah, Music.* HarperCollins, 2003.

Archambault, John. *Boom Chicka Rock.* Philomel Books, 2004.

Bang-Campbell, Monika. *Little Rat Makes Music.* Harcourt, 2007.

Base, Graeme. *Animalia.* Scholastic, 1986.

Bryan, Ashley. *All Night, All Day.* Atheneum, 1991.

Bryan, Ashley. *Let It Shine.* Atheneum Books for Young Readers, 2007.

Buffett, Jimmy and Susannah. *Jolly Mon.* Harcourt Brace Jovanovich, 1988.

Burnford, Sheila. *The Incredible Journey.* Little, Brown, 1960.

Busse, Sarah. *Banjo Granny.* Houghton Mifflin, 2006.

Byrd, Baylor. *When Clay Sings.* Aladdin Books/MacMillan, 1972.

Campbell, Bebe Moore. *Stompin' at the Savoy.* Philomel Books, 2006.

Christenson, Bonnie. *Woody Guthrie: Poet of the People.* Dragonfly Books, 2001.

Cohlene, Terri. *Dancing Dream.* Rourke, 1990.

Downing, Julie. *Mozart Tonight.* Bradbury Press, 1991.

Emberly, Rebecca. *City Sounds.* Little, Brown, 1989.

Falwell, Cathryn. *Scoot.* Greenwillow Books, 2008.

Fillegard, Dee. *Brass.* Children's Press, 1988.

_____. *Percussion.* Children's Press, 1987.

_____. *Strings.* Children's Press, 1988.

_____. *Woodwinds.* Children's Press, 1987.

Fleischman, Paul. *Rondo in C.* HarperCollins, 1988.

Fleming, Candace. *Gabrielle's Song.* Atheneum Books for Young Readers, 2005.

Gerstein, Mordicai. *What Charlie Heard.* Farrar, Straus & Giroux, 2002.

Gibbons, Gail. *Monarch Butterfly*. Holiday House, 1989.

Griffith, Helen. *Georgia Music*. Greenwillow Books, 1986.

Gustafson, Scott. *Scott Gustafson's Animal Orchestra*. Contemporary Books, 1988.

Guthrie, Woody. *Pastures of Plenty: A Self-Portrait*. Harper Perennial, 1990.

Hard, Thacher. *Mama Don't Allow*. HarperCollins, 1985.

Haseley, Dennis. *The Old Banjo*. Aladdin Books/MacMillan, 1990.

Hayes, Ann. *Meet the Orchestra*. Harcourt Brace Jovanovich, 1991.

Holl, Adelaide. *Sylvester, The Mouse with the Musical Ear*. Golden Press, 1963.

Hopkinson, Deborah. *Home on the Range: John A. Lomax and His Cowboy Songs*. Putnam, 2009.

Husherr, Rosmarie. *What Instrument Is This?* Scholastic, 1992.

Isadora, Rachel. *Ben's Trumpet*. Greenwillow, 1979.

_____. *Bring on the Beat*. Putnam, 2002.

Keats, Jack. *Apt. 3*. Aladdin Books, 1986.

Komaiko, Leah. *I Like the Music*. HarperCollins, 1987.

Kraus, Robert. *Musical Max*. Simon & Schuster, 1990.

Kroll, Virginia. *Wood-Hoopoe Willie*. Cambridge, 1992.

Kuslein, Karla. *The Philharmonic Gets Dressed*. HarperCollins, 1982.

Lionni, Leo. *Geraldine, the Music Mouse*. Pantheon, 1979.

Madison Alan. *Pecorino's First Concert*. Atheneum Books for Young Readers, 2005.

Martin, Bill Jr., and Archambault, John. *Barn Dance*. Henry Holt, 1986.

_____. *Brown Bear, Brown Bear, What Do You See?* Henry Holt, 1992.

Martin, Bill Jr., and Archambault, John. *Chicka Chicka Boom Boom*. Simon & Schuster Books for Young Readers, 1989.

Maxner, Joyce. *Nicholas Cricket*. HarperCollins, 1989.

Mitchell, Barbara. *Raggin': A Story About Scott Joplin*. Carolrhoda Books, 1987.

Parker, Robert. *Piano Starts Here: The Young Art Tatum*. Schwartz & Wade, 2008.

Peek, Merle. *Mary Wore a Red Dress and Henry Wore His Green Sneakers*. Clarion Books/Tichnor & Fields, 1985.

Pinkney, Brian. *Max Found Two Sticks*. Simon & Schuster, 1994.

Pinkwater, Daniel. *Doodleflute*. MacMillan, 1991.

Polhemus, Coleman. *Crocodile Blues.* Candlewick Press, 2007.

Raschka, Christopher. *Charlie Parker Played Be Bop.* Orchard Books, 1992.

Rosen, Michael. *Little Rabbit Foo Foo.* Simon & Schuster Books for Young Readers, 1990.

Ryan, Pam. *When Marian Sang: The True Recital of Marian Anderson—the Voice of the Century.* Live Oak Media, 2004.

Sage, James. *The Little Band.* McElderry Books, 1991.

Seeger, Pete. *Abiyoyo.* Macmillan, 1986.

Seeger, Pete. *The Deaf Musicians.* Putnam, 2006.

Showers, Paul. *The Listening Walk.* HarperCollins, 1991.

_____. *What Happens to Hamburger.* Harper Trophy Book, 1985.

Steinbeck, John. *The Pearl.* Barron's Educational Series, 1985.

Troupe, Quincy. *Little Stevie Wonder.* Houghton Mifflin, 2005.

Van Kampen, Vlasta, and Eugen, Irene C. *Orchestranimal.* Scholastic, 1989.

Volkmer, Jane Anne. *Sing a Song of Chimimia: A Guatemalan Folktale.* Carolrhoda Books, 1990.

Walter, Mildred. *Ty's One Man Band.* Four Winds Press, 1980.

Williams, Vera B. *Music for Everyone.* Mulberry Books, 1988.

Winter, Jeanette. *Follow the Drinking Gourd.* Dragonfly Books/ Knopf, 1992.

Yolen, Jane. *An Invitation to the Butterfly Ball: A Counting Rhyme.* Caroline House, 1976.

Zemach, Margot. *Hush Little Baby.* Dutton, 1976.

Games

Creating Word Pictures, The Five Sense Store. Aesthetic Education Program, CEMREL, Viking Press/Lincoln Center for the Performing Arts, 1981.

Instrument Bingo. Jenson, 1989.

Music Maestro. Aristoplay, 1988.

Music Mind Games. CPP, Belwin, 1993.

Musical Instrument Lotto. Nath, Jeux Nathan, S.A., 1987.

Note Ability for Juniors. Tiger Electronics, 1991.

Rhythm Bingo. Jenson, 1989.

Simon. Milton Bradley, 1994.

Songburst: The Complete the Lyric Game. Hersh, 1992.

Teachers' Resources

Agnes and Aubrey, *Art Songs, Ten songs About Artists*. Tate Publishing, 2005.

Beall, Pamela, and Nipp, Hagen Susan. *Wee Sing and Play*. Price Stern Sloan, 1984.

Burgie, Irving. *Caribbean Carnival*. Tambourine Books, 1992.

Burke, Kay. *Authentic Learning*. Corwin, 2009.

Burton, Leon, and Kurola, Kathy. *Arts Play*. Addison-Wesley, 1981.

Cassidy, John and Nancy. *The Book of Kids Songs: One and Two*. Klutz Press, 1988.

Chapin, Harry and Sandy. "The Cat's in the Cradle," *Verities and Balderdash*. Story Songs, 1974.

Chen, Jie-Qi, ed. *Project Spectrum: Early Learning Activities*. Teachers College Press, 1999. (This is volume 2 of Project Zero Frameworks for Early Childhood Education.)

Cline, Dellas. *Homemade Instruments*. Oak Publications, 1976.

Colin, Amy. *From Sea to Shining Sea*. Scholastic, 1993.

De Regniers, Beatrice Schenk. *Sing a Song of Popcorn: Every Child's Book of Poems*. Scholastic, 1988.

Ellington, Duke. "Bojangles." Recorded on Vi26644.

Goldish, Meish. *101 Science Poems & Songs for Young Learners*. Scholastic Professional Books, 1996.

Guthrie, Woody. "My Dolly," *Woody's 20 Grow Big Songs*. Harper-Collins, 1948.

Hart, Avery and Mantell. *Kids Make Music*. Williamson Publishing, 1993.

Haskins, James. *Black Music in America*. Harper Trophy, 1990.

Helm, Judy Harris, and Katz, Lilian. *Young Investigators: The Project Approach in the Early Years*. Teachers College Press, 2001.

Keynton, Tom. *Homemade Musical Instruments*. Drake Publishers, 1975.

Krull, Kathleen. *Gonna Sing My Head: American Folk Songs for Children*. Knopf, 1992.

Lomax, John and Alan. "Git Along Little Dogies," folk song. New American Library, 1947.

Luvenia, George. *Teaching the Music of Six Different Cultures*. World Music Press, 1987.

Mattox, Cheryl. "Let's Get the Rhythm of the Band," *Let's Get the Rhythm of the Band: A Child's Introduction to Music from African-American Culture.* JTG of Nashville, 1993.

Mattox, Cheryl. *Shake It to the One That You Love the Best.* Warren-Mattox Productions, 1991.

Palmer, Hap. *Homemade Band.* Crown, 1990.

Palmer, Hap. *Turn on the Music.* HiTops Video, 1988.

Price, Christine. *Dancing Masks of Africa.* Scribner, 1975.

Rubin, Roslyn, and Wathen, Judy. "Are You Sleeping?" *The All-Year-Long Songbook.* Scholastic, 1980.

———. "Wheels on the Bus." *The All-Year-Long Songbook.* Scholastic, 1980.

———. "Today Is Monday," *The All-Year-Long Songbook.* Scholastic, 1980.

Showers, Paul. *What Happens to a Hamburger.* HarperCollins, 2001.

Smith, Alistair. *What Happens to Your Food?* Usborne Books, 2003.

Swanson, Diane. *Mysterious You: Burp!* Scholastic, 2001.

The Metropolitan Museum of Art. *The Treasury of Children's Song.* The Metropolitan Museum of Art and Henry Holt and Company, LLC, 2003.

United Nations Association. *Musical Instruments of the World.* Facts on File Publications, 1975.

Walther, Tom. *Make Mine Music.* Little, Brown, 1981.

Warren, Jean. *Piggyback Songs.* Tatline Press, 1983.

Weisman, Julie. *Kids in Motion.* Alfred, 1993.

Wiseman, Ann. *Making Musical Things.* Scribner, 1979.

Wormeli, Rick. *Summarization in Any Subject: 50 Techniques to Improve Student Learning.* ASCD, 2005.

"Art is the only way to run away without leaving home."

—*TWYLA THARP*

7

Photograph: Shannah Burton

The Spatial Intelligence

Web of the Spatial Intelligence

Student Quotes

❝ The Spatial Intelligence is not just about being an artist; it's about being creative. I use it as a tool to help with all the other intelligences. ❞

❝ I'm good at finding details and examining everything I see. I love putting puzzles together. ❞

❝ I'm spatial because I like to create original things. I like to bead necklaces, earrings, and bracelets. ❞

❝ My favorite spatial activities are playing with fabric, drawing portraits with different mediums, visualizing things while listening to music, and looking at other artists' pieces. ❞

❝ I use the Spatial Intelligence to express myself and to show that I am who I am without having to use words. ❞

Characteristics

- Enjoys maps and charts, likes to draw, build, design, and create things, thinks in three-dimensional terms, enjoys putting puzzles together, loves videos and photos, enjoys color and design, enjoys pattern and geometry in math, likes to draw and doodle

Famous People

FRIEDA KAHLO was a famous Mexican artist who painted using vibrant colors.

MARIA MARTINEZ, a Pueblo Indian, is synonymous with black pottery.

WALT DISNEY was an Academy-award-winning film producer and innovator in the field of animation.

FRANK LLOYD WRIGHT was a leader of the Prairie School movement of architecture.

Adult Quotes

❝ We cannot create observers by saying "observe," but by giving them the power and the means for this observation, and these means are procured through education of the senses. ❞
—MARIA MONTESSORI

❝ If there were only one truth, you couldn't paint a hundred canvases on the same theme. ❞
—PABLO PICASSO

Spatial Intelligence: Through the Mind's Eye

BY MONETTE GOOCH-SMITH

The Spatial Intelligence is more than seeing, and it is more than art! Kate is an astute observer of her world, of people in her world, and of changes—she notices subtleties and details that most of us miss. Jacob can navigate through town and provide several ways to arrive at each destination. While blindfolded, Zoe can identify all of her classmates by touch. Harbor can assemble puzzles upside down or sideways with as much speed and accuracy as his peers who are doing them the traditional way. Abby demonstrates chess moves to her kindergarten class. Daniel has a remarkable ability to observe, to focus his attention and produce images through art; his work is extraordinary. Betsy can offer constructive criticism about any visual/spatial display with regard to composition, color, balance, or form. James uses his fascination with numbers, counting, and patterns whenever he builds or constructs with blocks, LEGOs, or any other manipulative material.

These youngsters are often found closing their eyes to think, to concentrate, and to problem-solve. Visualizing images and seeing through their mind's eye is a way of life for them. These children think in pictures and images. They can orienteer through space or navigate a chess board. They can become connoisseurs of art. When they couple their Spatial Intelligence with Bodily-Kinesthetic abilities, they can assemble, build, draw, construct, paint, arrange, and sculpt. They all possess an intuitive sense of space.

The aforementioned youngsters are quite remarkable in their spatial aptitude, but it is important to note that everyone possesses spatial ability in varying degrees. Our job is to identify and educate these spatial learners.

> Development of spatial intellect involves much more than just seeing. One must perceive the world accurately by recognizing, interpreting, and understanding what is seen.

WHAT IS SPATIAL INTELLIGENCE?

Spatial Intelligence is defined by Howard Gardner in *Frames of Mind* as "the ability to perceive the visual world accurately, to perform transformations and modifications upon one's initial perceptions, and to re-create experiences, even in the absence of physical stimuli." Involvement in the spatial arena is primarily, but not exclusively, out of the visual experience. Development of spatial intellect involves much more than just seeing. One must perceive the world accurately by recognizing, interpreting, and understanding what is seen. One need not have sight to possess Spatial Intelligence. Blind youngsters can recognize shapes through tactile means. They can interpret tactile maps and navigate to

> The ability to take an object and then manipulate that object in space can take anyone completely into the spatial realm.

locations. They can make transformations internally and externally. And they can produce wonderful works of art through various artistic genres. The ability to take an object and then manipulate that object in space can take anyone completely into the spatial realm.

WHO IS THE SPATIAL LEARNER?

Visual-spatial learners, according to Linda Kreger Silverman (*The Visual-Spatial Leaner: An Introduction*, 2002) are nonsequential, whole-to-part learners who need to see the big picture before they learn the details. They are system thinkers who can orchestrate vast amounts of information from different domains. Silverman goes on to say that these individuals are often gifted creatively, mathematically, mechanically, technologically, or emotionally.

People with a spatial orientation are likely to have characteristics that manifest as abilities to:

- Organize information visually and discern minute details
- Think in pictures or in three-dimensional terms
- Navigate through space with a strong sense of direction
- Enjoy creating, inventing, and building
- Use visual information as a segue to other disciplines
- Enjoy doodling, painting, sculpting, drawing, and other art and craft activities
- Decode maps, graphs, charts, and diagrams
- Become fascinated with machines, contraptions, and things to take apart
- Enjoy visuals like movies, slides, computers, videos, television shows, and photographs
- Get excited about color, shapes, patterns, and designs
- Understand perspective and manipulate images
- Make figure-ground distinctions and remember scenes
- Appreciate gestalt shifts and optical illusions
- Visually sequence events and form mental images
- Actively imagine; vividly recall dreams

> Children relish opportunities to engage their talents and minds by experimenting with a variety of materials and strategies in both traditional and nontraditional ways.

DEVELOPING THE SPATIAL INTELLIGENCE IN THE CLASSROOM

Integrating spatial activities throughout the curriculum is a way to support and cultivate this intelligence. Spatial potential can be developed, nurtured, and improved. Howard Gardner contends that intelligences can be considerably modified by changes in resources, and we know that children relish opportunities to engage their talents and minds by experimenting with a variety of materials and strategies in both traditional and nontraditional ways. These spatial experiences should also include occasions to develop visual perception and enhance visual processing. Spatial acuity can be developed by letting children solve problems in their own way in their own time. Using portfolios allows children to view their work over time and to document their growth. We can teach to students'

> Spatial acuity can be developed by letting children solve problems in their own way in their own time.

spatial strengths by giving them an overview of the subject being taught and presenting information visually, offering opportunities for them to observe others, and modeling how to visualize spelling words and math facts and to create visual representations of concepts.

Teachers can help students develop Spatial Intelligence in the classroom by implementing some of the following strategies:

- Set up spatial centers in the classroom. The wet art center provides a place for messy projects like paints, while the dry art center offers materials like paper, markers, crayons, cloth, nature items, and "found" items. Try a "take apart" center or a center for puzzles. Provide a fine motor center with mazes, sewing, hidden pictures, and incomplete pictures. Have a game center that offers teacher-made and traditional visual games like chess, *Jenga*, *Memory*, *Guess Who?* or *I Spy*. Use graphic software on your computer. A building center might contain blocks, tiny figures of people, signs, or other small manipulative materials. Set up a sight center with telescopes, microscopes, binoculars, and magnifying glasses. Try a workbench or construction area so children have access to real tools to make real projects.

- Invite local artists and spatially talented guests to share their expertise and experiences. This is a wonderful way to help young children understand that there are many forms of art besides paint, and that there are many different kinds of artists. Help children collect reproductions and illustrations of fine art. Reproductions of paintings, prints, and drawings are available in museum gift shops, bookstores, libraries, and on-line.

- When writing, encourage students to examine alternate endings to poems, stories, and plays. Suggest they experiment using the "language" of architects, artists, sculptures, designers, and other visual-spatial thinkers. Select an artist like Edward Hopper and invite students to write about or tell about his pictures; choose an architect like I. M. Pei and invite children to compare his work with buildings in the neighborhood.

- Provide opportunities for students to use digital cameras, camcorders, and technologies like PowerPoint and Kid Pix. Children learn about perception when they design games.

- Take walks through the neighborhood or visit parks and gardens. Use the language of naturalists as you explore, examine, experiment, and analyze plants, trees, and other natural features. Children learn about their world as they observe and navigate through their environments.

During math lessons:

- Use Cuisenaire rods to teach fractions.
- Design and build with pattern blocks to reinforce shapes.
- Bake a batch of cookies to explain division.
- Use children as "live models" to demonstrate patterns or solve math problems.
- Count, add, and subtract actual students while taking attendance.
- Have a weekly guess jar to make predictions and estimations using real objects—a jar of M&Ms, a jug of water, a bag of checkers.

- Provide opportunities to think, visualize, and picture images and concepts.
- Compare and contrast art postcards featuring different artists and genres.

During language classes:

- Label art prints to reinforce vocabulary or write poems and stories about them.
- Use story boards or puppets to retell a story.
- Draw, paint, or sculpt the main character or the setting while listening to stories.
- Make a cartoon strip, flip a book, or play a board game to demonstrate understanding of concepts.
- Teach visual educational strategies like visual note-taking and mind-mapping skills.
- Create a dialogue from the artwork's perspective by asking questions such as "What could the people in this painting be discussing?" or "If you were this sculpture, who would you want to talk to and about what?"
- Perform a radio show, create a PowerPoint presentation, or produce a real estate ad about buildings in the neighborhood. Learn historical information and use it in your visual aids.
- Make a video to debate the pros and cons for preserving the school building. If they were to design a new school, how might it look different?
- Provide opportunities for demonstration.
- Translate key concepts into poems, stories, or songs.
- Make picture dictionaries or keyword pictures.
- Explore social studies through the art or the architecture of different cultures. Youngsters can compare and contrast buildings, Greek temples, medieval cathedrals, or sculptures from around the world. Children can appreciate art as it speaks to them—like music, like nature, like color. Art affects mood and feelings.

There is no finite box for Spatial Intelligence. It is tied to the concrete world of objects and their place in space. Our challenge is to provide opportunities for youngsters to recognize their spatial talent and to provide experiences to facilitate its development.

WHAT DO SPATIAL LEARNERS DO?

People with strong spatial intellect can be found in all walks of life. Albert Einstein gathered his basic insights and inspirations from spatial models and imagery. Kevin Trudeau developed the Mega Memory system using images and picture association techniques. All students possess some degree of spatial talent. Spatial visualizers are often attracted to the arts when pursuing vocations and avocations. Some become artists, sculptors, designers, photographers, painters, and architects. Others find outlets in advertising, graphic design, computers, and drafting. Navigators, chess masters, mechanics, coaches, and inventors are talented in the visual-spatial realm, as are florists, carpenters, engineers, and surgeons.

There is no finite box for Spatial Intelligence. It is tied to the concrete world of objects and their place in space. Intelligences are expressed in the context of specific tasks, domains, and disciplines. Spatial is so much more than art! Our challenge is to provide opportunities for youngsters to recognize their spatial talent and to provide experiences to facilitate its development.

Painting the O'Keeffe Way

PURPOSE:

Students observe giant flower still life paintings by Georgia O'Keeffe. While identifying and imitating the style of the artist, children develop the ability to categorize works of art using color, shape, line, and media. This lesson could be used throughout the year with a variety of artists. The students learn facts about the artist.

MATERIALS:

Several pictures or postcards of Georgia O'Keeffe flower paintings, *Georgia O'Keeffe* by Robyn Montana Turner, *Georgia O'Keeffe* by Mike Venezia, *Through Georgia's Eyes* by Rachel Rodriguez, or *My Name Is Georgia* by Jeanette Winter, white poster board, watercolors or tempera paint and brushes, permanent medium point black markers that will not bleed, index cards

PROCEDURE:

1. Hang pictures and postcards of Georgia O'Keeffe's paintings around the room and give students a chance to observe them. Choose a few to discuss with the class and ask such questions as: When you look at the colors in this work of art, which color did you see first? Was color the first thing that you noticed? What else caught your eye?

2. Make a chart with these headings: Color, Shape, Pattern, Line, and Media. Have the students take turns describing what they see in the paintings. They might say, "I see a thin, curving line"; "I see a heavy, white square." List the children's responses under the correct categories.

3. Read some of the suggested books to the class. Point out key points so students gain information about O'Keeffe's life, such as why and where she painted, to create a context for her work.

4. Students add information to the classroom chart based on what they learned while reading the books. These elaborations strengthen their understanding of the artist's style. For example, the flowers are so big because Georgia O'Keeffe wanted everyone to notice all the parts of a flower. There are different hues of the same color in each flower to show depth and to make them look real.

5. Students work independently or with a partner, using the O'Keeffe paintings as their inspiration, to create a painting of a flower in her style. After closely observing the painting they have chosen, the students use black marker to outline, and watercolors to create their picture on white construction paper. Direct the students to pay close attention to the line, pattern, size, shape, and colors used by Georgia O'Keeffe in her painting.

6. The students' works are displayed with written artists' statements that include information about Georgia O'Keeffe's art and the connection between their art work and the work of the master artist. Students refer to the chart when comparing the works.

ASSESSMENT/REFLECTION:

Students are given a set of postcards with works by various artists and asked to sort the cards, labeling the criteria used. To assess what they learned about the artist, use a quiz show format to ask children true or false questions relating to facts about O'Keeffe's life and art work.

MI EXTENSIONS:

During this lesson, children also used the Linguistic Intelligence.

Naturalist: Students sort pictures of Georgia O'Keeffe paintings according to various characteristics of the flowers. What generalizations can the students make based on their prior knowledge of flowers?

Interpersonal: Give a pair or group of students postcards of pictures of flowers by different artists and ask them to sort the postcards by artist. They could sort by the artist's names or instead by just noticing what is similar about the style of the works.

Bodily-Kinesthetic: Use clay to make miniature sculptures of Georgia O'Keeffe flowers.

Aurora Borealis

PURPOSE:

After an introduction to the aurora borealis phenomena, students learn what causes this scientific occurrence and create a spatial representation of the northern lights.

SPATIAL

PRIMARY

SCIENCE

MATERIALS:

Watercolor paper of various sizes, watercolor paints, brushes, black construction paper, scissors, glue, pictures of the aurora borealis or northern lights, web sites:

http://ds9.ssl.berkeley.edu/auroras/

www.exploratorium.edu/learning_studio/auroras

http://lewis-clark.org/content/searchresults.asp?cx=01548899424077833
2427%3A0fcj_oscabi&cof=FORID%3A11&q=aurora1borealis1#508

PROCEDURE:

1. Students make discoveries about the scientific phenomenon known as the Northern Lights by looking at the pages on http://ds9.ssl.berkeley.edu/auroras/. After the exploration, discuss pertinent information and encourage questions.

2. Display various pictures of the aurora borealis, making sure you have a variety of colors and formations. Ask the children: "What colors do you see?" "What shapes do you see?" "Does it look like the colors are moving or still?" "How can you tell?" "Are the colors in a column?" "Are they spread out over the horizon?" Notice the black silhouette foreground in the photographs.

3. Model how to create a picture of the northern lights using watercolors. First, thoroughly wet the watercolor paper with a brush. Next, wet the watercolor cake that you choose to use. Keep the colors simple so that the children don't use too many colors and end up with a brown sky. Then saturate the brush with watery paint.

4. With watercolor, emphasize that the color should be transparent and the paint should not be overworked. Show them how to control the deepness of the hue by using more or less water on the paper and on the brush. Experiment with different techniques. One is to let the paint drip onto the wet paper rather than applying with brushstrokes and to move the color around the paper by moving the paper, allowing the paint to follow the water's path. Another is to simply brush the paint on.

5. Most often, the northern lights are seen far away from urban areas, so you see evergreens, mountains, hills, or outlines of tents on the horizon. Demonstrate how to cut a continuous silhouette of a landscape, from black construction paper, that fits across the paper and becomes the horizon line. After the paper is dry, glue this onto the lower half of the painting to serve as a foreground.

ASSESSMENT/REFLECTION:

Display the paintings. Students match photographs of the northern lights to the paintings and reflect on similarities between the artwork and the photographs, noticing the colors, shapes, and semblance of movement.

MI EXTENSIONS:

This lesson also uses the Linguistic Intelligence.

Bodily-Kinesthetic: Using long pieces of fabric or scarves as props, perform an interpretive dance of the northern lights.

Linguistic: Read about how different cultures across the world interpret the northern or southern lights. Read the poem *The Ballad of the Northern Lights* by the Canadian poet Robert Service. Children write poems showing an interpretation of the phenomenon.

Spatial: Introduce the artist Anne Madden through her website, www.anne-madden.com/MaddenPages/paintings6.html. Read her artist's statement, explaining her interpretations of the aurora borealis, and view her artwork. Children experiment with pastels to imitate her style.

Dream On! Designing Your Ideal Room

PURPOSE:

The students reflect on who they are and what they need and interpret this awareness by creating a representation of a physical space to accommodate these insights.

MATERIALS:

Large construction paper, notebook paper, markers

PROCEDURE:

1. Children find a place in the room or outside to lie down and relax for a teacher-led visualization activity.

2. Offer this reading: "While you were away at summer camp, an amazing thing happened. When you returned home, your bedroom had been redecorated. It was wonderful! You had been dreaming about your room while you were away, and now there it was—just as you had imagined! You are at the open door, looking inside your fantastic bedroom. Walk inside. Look at the ceiling. Someone who knows you very well painted something there. What do you see? Why did that person choose to paint that particular picture? What does the picture tell others about you? How has the furniture in your room changed? What do you see now? Next to your bed are all the things you always wanted but you thought were impossible to have. What do these things tell about your interests? Picture in your mind what is on the walls and on the floor. What sounds do you hear? What colors do you see? What music is playing?"

3. Continue with leading questions so the children's visualizations define who they are rather than allowing them to be purely materialistic. Children share their dream rooms with a partner who serves as a note taker and records what main features will be included in their partner's room.

4. Give the students a large piece of construction paper to draw their dream room as it appeared in their minds' eyes. Students draw several views of the room.

ASSESSMENT/REFLECTION:

Students meet with their note-taking partners, who refer to the notes that were taken before drawing. The partners verify that all the details were included in the drawing. Display the dream rooms. The children guess (partners excluded) to which student each room belongs.

MI EXTENSIONS:

Students also used their Interpersonal and Intrapersonal intelligences in this lesson.

Linguistic: Write a narrative that describes the dream room with sensory detail that allows the reader to visualize the room and shares why the room looks as it does.

Logical-Mathematical: Have the students draw their dream rooms to scale.

Naturalist: Students compare their actual rooms with their dream rooms by creating a Venn diagram. One circle is "actual" and the other is "dream."

Shrink Me

PURPOSE:
Students use nonstandard units of measurement to explore ratios and create a half-size representation of their bodies.

MATERIALS:
White butcher paper, string, scissors, chart paper, art supplies

SPATIAL

PRIMARY AND INTERMEDIATE

MATHEMATICS

PROCEDURE:
1. Cut a piece of string that measures your height. Ask students to estimate how many times this piece of string will go around your head and record the estimates on chart paper.

2. Wrap the string around your head to show the ratio of body length to head circumference. The string will usually wrap about three times around the head. Record the ratio: 3:1.

3. Brainstorm a list of other body ratios for the students to explore.

4. With a partner, students cut a piece of string the length of their heights and explore body ratios independently. Students are free to explore other relationships that are not on the list.

5. Students record the ratios they have discovered. As a class, compare ratios to show differences and similarities. Make a chart of the similar ratios as a reference.

6. Students cut their strings in half. Cut butcher paper exactly the same length as each student's new string.

7. Students use the ratios they discovered earlier to accurately draw the size of other body parts on the butcher paper.

8. When the entire body is drawn, it can be colored.

ASSESSMENT/REFLECTION:
Visually check the relative measurements of the shrunken body parts.

MI EXTENSIONS:
This lesson also uses the Logical-Mathematical and the Interpersonal intelligences.

Linguistic and Logical-Mathematical: Students create puppets that are one-quarter of their body size and use them for a puppet show.

Naturalist: Given a set of ratios, the students create a new animal.

Intrapersonal: Students use their favorite stuffed animal and create a double-sized image using ratios.

Self-Portrait: I See Me, You See Me

PURPOSE:

Each year at New City, students create self-portraits using various mediums. These are collected during the student's tenure at the school and show learning and growth over time.

MATERIALS:

Examples of self-portraits, mirrors, various art supplies, paper, poster board, digital editing software, digital camera, computer

PROCEDURE:

Kindergarten: Students draw a self-portrait at the beginning and at the end of the year and reflect on their physical changes and personal growth by comparing the two portraits.

First Grade: On the computer, the teacher uses photographs taken of individual students to create four black-and-white, high-contrast images of each student. Students design four unique self-portraits: a "Natural Me" (a true-to-life colored self-portrait), a "Camouflage Me" (an Andy Warhol–inspired abstract self-portrait), a "Design Me" (a Chuck Close–inspirited self-portrait), and a "Rainbow Me" (a Joan Miró–inspired geometric self-portrait).

Second Grade: Students are introduced to artist Paul Klee and explore and analyze his geometric self-portraits. Students then use mirrors to create self-portraits in the style of Paul Klee, using geometric shapes to communicate a visual interpretation of themselves.

Third Grade: Students create self-portraits using symbols to show their physical attributes, hobbies, interests, and life ambitions.

Fourth Grade: Students draw a self-portrait in the middle of a large piece of construction paper, with eight branches extending from the image in a mind-map fashion. At the end of each branch, students draw pictures to show their strengths or interests in each of the intelligences. A photograph is added to show the student engaged in his or her favorite intelligence.

Fifth Grade: Students research portraits as primary sources of information. Portraits convey information about the status, location, personal interests, and heritage of the person depicted. Students paint self-portraits to share more information than just what they look like.

Sixth Grade: Students explore the theme of identity in the photographic self-portrait works of Cindy Sherman (*Bus Riders* series) and Kimiko Yoshida (*Bride* series). After brainstorming ways to use a single white piece of paper to portray their identity, students decide what identity to create for their portrait. Using a blank piece of white or black paper as a conceptual starting point, students cut, fold, and manipulate the piece of paper to communicate an element of their personality. Photograph the students from the shoulders up holding their paper. For example, one student who has a strong naturalist personality might create a flower out of a white piece of paper and be photographed looking through the center of the flower.

Native American Storyteller Dolls

PURPOSE:

While learning about the history and importance of Native American storytellers and storyteller dolls, students explore the clay medium and create their own dolls.

MATERIALS:

Pictures of storyteller dolls, drawing paper, pencils, markers, crayons, colored pencils, low-fire or air-dry clay, slip (clay that has been wetted down), clay tools, acrylic paint and small and medium-sized paintbrushes, *Keepers of the Earth* by Joseph Bruchac and Michael J. Caduto, *Pueblo Stories and Storytellers* by Mark Bahti, *Storytellers and Other Figurative Pottery* by Douglas Corigdon, the magazine *Faces*, volume IX number VIII, April 1993

PROCEDURE:

1. Tell a Native American folktale, such as "Gluscabi and the Game Animals," found in the book *Keepers of the Earth* by Joseph Bruchac and Michael J. Caduto. Explain the importance of the storyteller in the culture. Through the storyteller, the children learned how to behave and how to live properly. Traditions were passed on from generation to generation through stories. Children learned social skills and how the members of a group were supposed to interact. They did not read or have books, so the storyteller became very important to Native American society.

2. Discuss Helen Cordera, from the Cochiti Pueblo, the artist who began making storyteller dolls many years ago. Information can be found in the magazine *Faces*, volume IX number VIII, April 1993.

3. Show pictures of storyteller dolls. Examples can be found in the book *Storytellers and Other Figurative Pottery* by Douglas Corigdon and *Pueblo Stories and Storytellers* by Mark Bahti. Discuss the costumes, facial features, and body structure of the dolls. It is important to point out that the dolls are seated, the mouth is open because the doll is telling a story, and the eyes are closed because it is thinking. There are usually children attached to the doll.

4. Lead the students in a visualization exercise. They become the storyteller. Your family sits around you. What are you wearing? How are you holding your head and hands? Are your eyes open or closed? How does your appearance reflect the story being told?

5. Students draw what they visualize, using lots of detail and color.

6. Demonstrate techniques for working with the clay, including how to attach clay by scratching the areas to be joined and adding a little water (a technique called "score and slip"). Be sure not to use too much water. Start by making a pinch pot and then turn it upside down. This becomes the body to which the head, arms, legs, and other details are added.

7. Students shape their storyteller dolls, using their drawings as their guides.

8. Let the clay figures dry, firing slowly if necessary. Students paint the details, using their drawings as a guide.

ASSESSMENT/REFLECTION:

Students write artist statements for their work, including a title and a brief narrative explaining the doll. The storyteller dolls are displayed with the artists' statements in preparation for a gallery viewing.

MI EXTENSIONS:

The Linguistic and Bodily-Kinesthetic intelligences are also used in this lesson.

Linguistic: Create an original story that your doll would tell that teaches social skills and how the members of the class are supposed to interact.

Interpersonal: Become a storyteller like the doll you have made. Imagine your classmates are your family. What stories would they like to hear? What stories do they need to hear? Find stories that teach those skills to share with the class.

Intrapersonal: In your journal, write about the stories from your family that a storyteller should tell to the next generation. What stories have your parents or grandparents told you?

Shadow Puppets

SPATIAL

INTERMEDIATE

ART

PURPOSE:

Students research the ancient art of shadow puppetry and explore its cultural connections. Students follow directions to create their own shadow puppets.

MATERIALS:

Sketch paper, black cardstock or poster board, pencils, scissors, X-Acto knife, thin wooden dowels, 22-gauge floral wire, small brads, packing tape, small hole punch, projector or other light source, teacher-created shadow puppet, internet access, web sites:

> www.artsedge.kennedy-center.org/shadowpuppets/
>
> www.owlyshadowpuppets.com/

PROCEDURE:

1. On the Internet, students research the art of shadow puppetry. The Artsedge Kennedy Center website offers exploratory online learning that covers the history and culture of shadow puppetry in addition to the basic components of shadow puppets.

2. Based on their knowledge of traditional stock characters, students sketch ideas for their own shadow puppet. The sketches are developed into a final concept that includes interior details that need to be cut out.

3. Students plan which parts move and draw those parts separately. These moving parts are drawn to overlap the main part of the shadow puppet so they can be connected with brads. Draw a small x where the moving pieces connect with the brads.

4. Students cut out the main pieces and trace them on the black paper. They need to outline the interior details and x marks for the brads.

5. Students cut out the main parts of the shadow puppet using scissors. Interior cutting can be done with an X-Acto knife. Pieces can be laminated to make them sturdier. Students can use markers on the clear laminated pieces to add color to the shadow.

6. Punch holes on the x marks. Students connect the moving pieces to the main shadow puppet using brads. They tape dowels on the back of the puppet. Wire can be added to help make some parts move more easily. Students are given the opportunity to experiment and use ingenuity to find a moving mechanism that works for their design.

7. Use a projector or other light source to cast light on a wall or screen. Place the puppets between the light source and the wall to create a shadow.

8. Photograph the shadows cast by the puppets for a display. Include students' artist statements that show what they have learned from their research and the methods used to create the puppet.

ASSESSMENT/REFLECTION:

Artist statements are used to determine what was learned about the ancient art of shadow puppetry. By looking at the final product, assess the student's ability to follow directions to create a shadow puppet with working moveable parts.

MI EXTENSIONS:

This lesson also uses the Linguistic and Bodily-Kinesthetic intelligences.

Intrapersonal: Introduce *The Cave Allegory* from the Greek philosopher Plato, in which shadows play an important role. Students become philosophers and begin a discourse on the meaning of this allegory. *Little Big Minds* by Marietta McCarty is an excellent resource for more information.

Interpersonal and Linguistic: Divide students into teams to write and perform a play using their shadow puppet characters.

Naturalist: Light is an essential art material in shadow puppetry. Use different opaque, transparent, or translucent materials to cast shadows. Experiment with the placement of the light to produce shadows.

Colonial Portraits

PURPOSE:

Students use portraits made during the colonial period as primary sources for a historical study of that time period. They learn about portraiture as an artistic genre, then create a portrait of a real or fictitious person who might have lived during that time.

MATERIALS:

History books, American history text books, books of colonial portraits, art supplies, teacher-created worksheet, computer with internet access

PROCEDURE:

1. This lesson requires teacher background knowledge. Begin by visiting the following website: http://www.famsf.org/fam/education/publications/guide-american/part2.html. Using this website, you will learn about the importance of symbols, setting, clothing, posture, position of those in the portrait, and how to interpret paintings from the colonial time period.

2. Using this background knowledge, lead the students in a discussion of this artistic genre while looking at portraits from this historical period. This can be done during a field trip to a local art museum or on an online virtual field trip. Conduct an internet search of colonial portrait galleries.

3. As students view the portraits, ask them to think about details they notice in the pictures. What objects are in the painting, and why do they think the person being painted wanted these things in the painting? What do the setting and the clothing tell the viewer about the person in the painting? What historical references are evident? Why do the students think the portrait was painted? What message was the sitter hoping to convey about his or her life? What can the students determine about this time period through this image? What perspective or point of view was the artist hoping to convey?

4. Create a worksheet using these questions. Students use web sites, books from the library, or prints of portraits to independently answer questions about colonial portraits.

5. In small groups, students discuss their written observations of what they have noticed in the portraits. Other group members have the opportunity to add what they notice in the artistic work being discussed and draw conclusions.

6. Students create a portrait of someone who lived or could have lived during the colonial period. In the painting, consider aspects of the time and the region in which the subject lived. Choose some elements to include in your portrait: landscape, homes, wealth, status, religion, conditions of life, family life, work, products, artifacts, and important

historical events. Plan how to reflect them in your painting and make them evident in the pencil draft.

7. After receiving feedback from peers to the question, "What do you notice in my painting?" students create a final portrait.

ASSESSMENT/REFLECTION:

Create a rubric with the students, based on the guided discussion and worksheet questions, to assess the portrait. In an artist statement, students answer the following questions about their paintings: What can you determine about colonial times through this image? What details of the subject's life can be seen in this portrait? In what region did your subject live? What are you trying to say in this painting?

MI EXTENSIONS:

This lesson also uses the Linguistic and Interpersonal intelligences.

Linguistic: Students create journal entries that could have been written by the subject of their painting. The entries must be accurate to the time and setting. Prior to creating the journal, students look at journals from that time as primary source documents.

Naturalist: Before beginning the paintings, students do research to learn about different natural features found in the northern, middle, or southern colonies of the United States to use as landscape background in their paintings.

Musical: Students listen to music from the colonial period to get another perspective about differences in the lives of the colonists. There are songs about being an indentured servant, a slave, a land owner, and an immigrant. Songs were brought to America from many countries and reflect the cultures that were integrated into colonial culture. A good reference is *Colonial and Revolution Songbook* by Keith and Rusty McNeil. Choose a song that would be played or sung by the person in your portrait.

Activities to Support the Spatial Intelligence

INTERPERSONAL

- Murals
- Collages
- Choreographing a dance
- Blindfold activities
- Finger puppets

INTRAPERSONAL

- Creating an environment
- Dioramas
- Design costumes
- Creating architectural designs and construct floor plans
- Body awareness

BODILY-KINESTHETIC

- Building with geometric solids, blocks, or manipulatives
- Painting with different tools
- Arts and crafts like quilting, clay, and papier-mâché
- Orienteering
- Constructing models, from plastic kits to origami animals

LINGUISTIC

- Story mapping
- Flannel boards
- Comic strips
- Mind mapping
- Posters and display boards

LOGICAL-MATHEMATICAL

- Puzzles and mazes
- Pattern blocks and Cuisenaire rods
- Scale models
- Constructing maps and timelines
- Chess, checkers, and other strategy games

MUSICAL

- Setting up an orchestra using paper models of instruments
- Creating a floor plan of the symphony
- Learning a dance
- Developing a musical notation system
- Making musical instruments

NATURALIST

- Creating a nature video
- Making a book similar to *Zoom* by Istvan Banyai
- Constructing a nature weaving
- Producing a PowerPoint presentation with a theme from nature or science
- Making leaf or nature prints to notice patterns

Identifying the Spatial Intelligence in Your Students

Children function at many different levels within the intelligences. Through observation of everyday activities, one can create a profile showing the level of functioning within a particular intelligence and the intelligences in relation to each other. The levels described show increased engagement and proficiency.

YES NO **APPRECIATES:**

☐ ☐ Consistently demonstrates interest, respect, and enjoyment within the intelligence and is able to differentiate qualities

☐ ☐ Enjoys building and taking things apart

☐ ☐ Shows interest in line, shape, color, pattern, texture

☐ ☐ Shows interest in concrete artistic expression of other cultures (such as clothing, jewelry, body ornamentation, crafts)

☐ ☐ Shows interest in manipulatives (such as LEGOs, tangrams)

☐ ☐ Enjoys working with art material (such as paint, markers)

☐ ☐ Enjoys looking at pictures and talking about others' art work

☐ ☐ Identifies different artistic styles

YES NO **PERFORMS:**

☐ ☐ Is able to apply the intelligence to recreate an exhibit or demonstration or problem-solve in a given situation

☐ ☐ Demonstrates skill in use of line, shape, color, texture, pattern in projects

☐ ☐ Draws and reads maps

☐ ☐ Takes items apart and puts them back together, such as toys, appliances

☐ ☐ Draws a different perspective without seeing it

☐ ☐ Easily puts things together after hearing directions

☐ ☐ Copies other artist's work with accuracy

☐ ☐ Draw mazes and intricate patterns

☐ ☐ Draws with varied lines and uses color with intention

☐ ☐ Uses texture to create depth in art work

☐ ☐ Has inner sense of where one is in space

YES NO **CREATES:**

❑ ❑ Is able to apply this intelligence to generate original work, to develop unique solutions to problems or create prototypes

❑ ❑ Produces an original work that conveys meaning visually

❑ ❑ Uses materials in a unique way

❑ ❑ Creates artwork with a recognizable style

❑ ❑ Designs and constructs an original 3-D structure

Children's Resources

Books

Ahlberg, Allan. *The Pencil.* Candlewick Press, 2008.

Banyai, Istvan. *Zoom.* Viking Juvenile, 1995.

Baum, Arline and Joseph. *Opt: An Illusionary Tale.* Puffin Books, 1989.

Bjork, Cristina. *Linnea in Monet's Garden.* Farrar, Straus & Giroux, 1987.

Bolton, Linda. *Hidden Pictures.* Dial Books, 1993.

Catalanotto, *Pete. Emily's Art.* Atheneum Books, 2001.

Clouse, Nancy L. *Puzzle Maps U.S.A.* Henry Holt, 1990.

Cottin, Menena. *The Black Book of Color.* Groundwood Books/ House of Anansi Press, 2008.

Cummings, Pat. *Talking with Artists.* Bradbury Press, 1992.

dePaola, Tomie. *Art Lesson.* Putnam, 1989.

Everett, Gwen. *Li'l Sis and Uncle Willie.* National Museum of American Art, Smithsonian Institute, 1991.

Gardner, Beau. *The Turn About, Think About, Look About Book.* Lothrop, Lee and Shepard Books, 1980.

Garner, Alan. *Jack in the Beanstalk.* Doubleday, 1992.

Hoban, Tana. *Look, Look, Look.* Greenwillow Books, 1988.

———. *Over, Under, and Through and Other Spatial Concepts.* MacMillan, 1973.

Horatcek, Petr. *Butterfly, Butterfly: A Book of Colors.* Candlewick Press, 2007.

Hutchins, Hazel. *Mattland.* Annick Press, 2008.

Jonas, Ann. *13th Clue.* Greenwillow, 1992.

———. *Color Dance.* Greenwillow Books, 1989.

———. *Round Trip.* Greenwillow Books, 1983.

———. *Round Trip.* Mulberry Books, 1990.

Kesselman, Wendy. *Emma.* HarperCollins, 1980.

Kostecki-Shaw, Jenny Sue. *My Traveling Eye.* Henry Holt, 2008.

Lawrence, Jacob. *Harriet and the Promised Land.* Simon & Schuster Books for Young Readers, 1993.

———. *The Great Migration.* HarperCollins, 1993.

Lepscky, Ibi. *Pablo Picasso.* Barron's, 1984.

Lewis, Samella. *African American Art for Young People.* Hand Craft, 1991.

MacDonald, Suse. *Alphabatics.* MacMillan, 1986.

McCarthy, Mary. *A Closer Look.* Greenwillow Books, 2007.

McCarty, Marietta. *Little Big Minds.* Penguin Group, 2006.

McKissack, Patricia. *Stitchin' and Pullin': A Gee's Bend Quilt.* Random House, 2008.

McPhail, David. *Something Special.* Little, Brown, 1988.

Micklethwait, Judy. *A Child's Book of Art, Great Pictures, First Words.* Dorling Kindersley, 1993.

Newell, Peter. *Topsy and Turvys.* Dover Publications, 1964.

Onishi, Satoru. *Who's Hiding?* Kane/Miller, 2007.

Peet, Bill. *Bill Peet: An Autobiography.* Houghton Mifflin, 1989.

Pinkwater, Daniel. *The Big Orange Splot.* Hasting House, 1977.

Portis, Antoinette. *Not a Box.* HarperCollins, 2006.

_____. *Not a Stick.* HarperCollins, 2008.

Raboff, Ernest. *Van Gogh.* HarperCollins, 1988.

Reynolds, Peter. *The Dot.* Candlewick Press, 2003.

_____. *Ish.* Candlewick Press, 2004.

Roberto, Nina Laden. *The Insect Architect.* Chronicle Books, 2000.

Rumford, James. *Silent Music: A Story of Baghdad.* Roaring Brook Press, 2008.

Rylant, Cynthia. *All I See.* Orchard Books, 1988.

Seeger, Laura. *Lemons Are Not Red.* Roaring Brook Press, 2004.

Segal, Loren. *Morris the Artist.* Farrar, Straus & Giroux, 2003.

Shannan, George. *White Is for Blueberry.* Greenwillow Books, 2005.

Sherry, Kevin. *I'm the Best Artist in the Ocean.* Dial Books for Young Readers, 2008.

Siebert, Diane. *Sierra.* HarperCollins, 1991.

Sills, Leslie. *Inspirations: Stories About Women Artists.* Whitman, 1989.

Strom, Maria. *Rainbow Joe and Me.* Lee and Low Books, 1999.

Thomson, David. *Visual Magic.* Dial Books, 1991.

Turner, Robyn Montana. *Rosa Bonheur.* Little, Brown, 1991.

_____. *Georgia O'Keeffe.* Little, Brown, 1991.

Venezia, Mike. *Getting to Know the World's Greatest Artists: Georgia O'Keeffe.* Children's Press, 1993.

Warhola, James. *Uncle Andy's*. Putnam, 2003.

Wolf, Aline D. *Mommy, It's a Renoir*. Parent Child Press, 1984.

Woodson, Jacqueline. *Show Way*. Putnam, 2005.

Yenawine, Philip. *Colors*. Delacorte Press, 1991.

———. *Lines*. Delacorte Press, 1991.

———. *Shapes*. Delacorte Press, 1991.

———. *Stories*. Delacorte Press, 1991.

Games

Art Deck: The Game of Modern Masters. Aristoplay, 1985.

Art Lotto: National Gallery of Art. Safari, 1990.

Art Memo Game. Piatnik Vienna, 1989.

Arts in Play. Intempo Toys, 1988.

Brick by Brick. Binary Arts, 1992.

Castle Logix. Educational Insights Inc., 2002–2007

Chop Stix. TDC Games, 2000.

Community Helper Lotto. Trend Enterprises, 1990.

FIGURIX. Ravensburger Spieleverlag, 1998/2002.

Good Old House: A Puzzle Game. Aristoplay, 1981.

In the Picture: The Kids' Art Game. Intempo Toys, 1990.

Jenga. Milton Bradley, 1986.

Pictionary. Pictionary, 1985.

Qwirkle. MindWare, 2006.

SEQUENCE for Kids. Jax Limited Inc., 2001.

Set: The Family Game of Visual Perception. Marsha J. Falco, 1988.

The Very Hungry Caterpillar. University Games Corp., 2006.

Teacher's Resources

Block, Richard, and Yuker, Harold. *Can You Believe Your Eyes?* Gardner Press, 1989.

Brookes, Mona. *Drawing with Children.* Tarcher, 1986.

Brundin, Judith A. "Clay Storyteller Dolls." *Faces,* volume IX, number VIII, April 1993.

Burke, Kay. *Authentic Learning.* Corwin, 2009.

Caduto, Michael, and Bruchac, Joseph. *Keepers of the Earth.* Fulcrum, 1988.

Chen, Jie-Qi, ed. *Project Spectrum: Early Learning Activities.* Teachers College Press, 1999. (This is volume 2 of Project Zero Frameworks for Early Childhood Education.)

Corigdon, Douglas. *Storytellers and Other Figurative Pottery.* Schiffer Publishing, 1999.

Evans, Livingston. "Buttons and Bows," *Gene Autry's Greatest Hits.* COL 1035.

Helm, Judy Harris, and Katz, Lilian. *Young Investigators: The Project Approach in the Early Years.* Teachers College Press, 2001.

Hieronymus, Brenda, and Moomaw, Sally. *More Than Painting.* Redleaf Press, 1999.

Margulies, Nancy. *Mapping Inner Space.* Zephyr Press, 1991.

Pentagram. *Pentamagic.* Simon & Schuster, 1992.

Rubin, Roslyn, and Wathen, Judy. "I'm a Little Teapot," *The All-Year-Long Songbook.* Scholastic, 1980.

Striker, Susan. *The Anti Coloring Book.* An Owl Book, Henry Holt, 1984.

Sullivan, Charles. *Children of Promise.* Abrams, 1991.

Vitale, Barbara Meister. *Unicorns Are Real.* Jalmar Press, 1982.

Wormeli, Rick. *Summarization in Any Subject: 50 Techniques to Improve Student Learning.* ASCD, 2005.

Wycoff, Joyce. *Mindmapping.* Berkeley, 1991.

"When we try to pick out anything by itself, we find it hitched to everything else in the universe."

—*JOHN MUIR*

8

Photograph: Patti Gabriel

The Naturalist Intelligence

Web of the Naturalist Intelligence

Student Quotes

" I'm a naturalist because I just don't want to be inside. I would rather look at nature than just talk with people. "

" I like animals and want to learn more about their habitats. "

" The outdoors gives me a 'free' feeling that I just can't get inside. "

" I love to go hiking, camping, walking through the park and spelunking. "

Characteristics

- Learns through observation and discovery of natural phenomenon; is good at comparing, categorizing, and sorting; enjoys being outdoors; excels in finding fine distinctions between similar items; feels alive when in contact with nature; appreciates scenic places; enjoys having pets; likes to camp, hike or climb; is conscious of changes in the environment

Famous People

JOHN BURROUGHS was a naturalist important in the evolution of the conservation movement.

AL GORE, former U.S. vice president, is an environmental activist who shared the 2007 Nobel Peace Prize with the Intergovernmental Panel on Climate Change.

THEODORE ROOSEVELT was instrumental in establishing the national park system.

JANE GOODALL is well-known for her study of chimpanzees in Gombe Stream National Park, Tanzania; DIAN FOSSEY was known for her observations of gorillas in the mountain forests of Rwanda.

MERIWETHER LEWIS AND WILLIAM CLARK led an overland expedition of exploration to the Pacific Coast and back.

Adult Quote

" It is not the strongest of the species that survives, nor the most intelligent that survives. It is the one that is the most adaptable to change. "
—CHARLES DARWIN

MI, Science, and the Naturalist Intelligence

BY ERIC ESKELSEN

"When do we get science?" is a question the science teacher often hears from the kindergarteners at our school. Because the science classroom is near the kindergarten rooms, the younger students have a lot of curiosity about what goes on in that classroom. They see the older students coming to and from science, and the "big kids' work" displayed in the hall.

This room is a magnet for students whether or not they are taking science class! Budding naturalists wander in with their parents after school to explore the shells, bones, teeth, and preserved animals on display for students to explore. Logical-Mathematical youngsters are drawn to the machines on display, while musical children grab various sound tubes and instruments to explore. Students' curiosity about the world around them is amazing. You can feel it with their energy as they explore at naturalist centers, and you can hear it in the many questions they ask as they learn about the human body. You can see it in the amazing spatial work they create in our garden. They are constantly using their Naturalist Intelligence, yet they still ask, "When do we get science?"

WHAT IS THE NATURALIST INTELLIGENCE?

The Naturalist Intelligence was the eighth intelligence identified by Howard Gardner. He thought of it as a way to describe those who sort, categorize, and draw on the natural environment. In the distant past the Naturalist Intelligence helped people to survive; they knew what plants they could eat, when to sow seeds, and how to use natural cures. They may have known of a plant that helped with snakebites or used the alignment of stars to know when to plant crops or prepare for winter. Today, most people in the United States don't rely on the Naturalist Intelligence for survival, but it still is a very important way for students to learn.

The Naturalist Intelligence has three main components: observing, investigating, and experimenting. Teachers have a responsibility to promote growth in each area. Most kids have a natural curiosity about the world around them; they make many great observations and ask insightful questions. They wonder why clouds are white or black, why we put cracks in the sidewalk, why ants make hills, or why leaves change colors. A teacher's job is not only to keep that curiosity growing but also to encourage them to go on to the next step of investigating.

> Today, most people in the United States don't rely on the Naturalist Intelligence for survival, but it still is a very important way for students to learn.

> A teacher's job is not only to keep that curiosity growing but also to encourage them to go on to the next step of investigating.

Investigating may mean asking more questions or making more observations as those ants create new hills. It can also lead to research in a book, asking an expert, or maybe even simple experimentation as the students work their way to the next step. The child that is really investigating may even knock over that ant hill to see whether the ants will rebuild it. Each day inquisitive minds come into the science classroom for answers to their questions. They usually receive an answer, but also another question to keep their minds going.

Keep in mind that each experiment can lead to a new one! During a unit of study on plant growth, for example, some students isolated different variables and tested to see whether gravity affected the direction of root growth. While recording their data, students noticed mold growing on some of the seeds, which led to another experiment to determine the factors that influence mold growth. Older elementary students do many experiments so they can have proof to back up their scientific claims, but they still need chances to simply observe and explore around the schoolyard or on field trips. Forcing the scientific method into their brains every day can turn kids off to science. Instead, we must take questions they formulate and then design experiments to find their answer; this is the basis of inquiry-based science. If students are curious, they are more likely to do a great experiment!

THROUGHOUT THE BUILDING

The science classroom is not the only place where science and the Naturalist Intelligence abound. How is it used in the classroom? Here at New City School the Naturalist Intelligence is used in a variety of ways during center times. Younger students have centers that involve sorting bones, shells, rocks, or seeds. The life cycles of plants are explored as students grow seeds under the grow lights. Classroom pets are used to help students learn about animal behavior. As students learn about bees and other insects, Naturalist students start to realize how nature is interconnected. They begin to understand how soil or rain can affect bees, which in turn affects our yield from fruit trees and other pollinated crops. Scientific classification is studied in science, and children learn about famous scientists such as Charles Darwin and Jane Goodall, as well as a modern-day Naturalist like *Survivorman* Les Stroud.

When students observe caterpillars making cocoons, take part in MI centers in the library, read picture books, plant seeds, and learn about the seasons, they start to see that science is not something that just happens in the science room—it happens everywhere. Toward the end of the year students begin to ask the science teacher, "When do we get science *with you*?" At an MI school there are many opportunities to bring science into center time, morning meetings, theme, or the classroom curriculum. Teachers can always find ways to incorporate the Naturalist Intelligence into their teaching. When writing paragraphs, they can have students create a paragraph explaining the parts of a flower, maybe some poetry about clouds, or perhaps a graphing activity related to plant growth. Any investigation that enables children to use their Naturalist Intelligence helps them discover that science is everywhere.

HOW IS THE NATURALIST INTELLIGENCE USED OUTSIDE THE SCHOOL BUILDING?

We are fortunate to have a great outdoor naturalist exploration area: our Centennial Garden. We have places for kids to dig for fossils and worms, and an area where they can build animal houses out of logs, leave, and vines. They can observe birds at the feeder, watch bees busily collecting nectar, see rabbits eating strawberries and ants building homes. You can pick out Naturalist kids: they become so enthralled observing an animal or creating a habitat for an animal that they block out the world around them. Much like Linguistic kids who get lost in a book or Spatial students who are wrapped up in an art project, Naturalist kids become a part of the natural world around them.

We also try to tap into our community to enhance the Naturalist Intelligence. Each grade level at our school takes several off-site trips. For example, some grades go to nature preserves or plant trees along the river to help make a difference for the environment. Other grades study water ecosystems by canoeing and observing plant and animal life in the water. Our upper grade students go on overnight camping trips during which they study nature at night by looking for owls or glowworms. Plus, we just installed a Green Roof on our dining hall. Overall, we hope the students gain an appreciation for nature and understand how the natural world connects to their lives, even if they spend very little time outside. The true Naturalist child will continue to discover more connections as he or she grows older and finds out ways to be involved in nature and help the world.

> Teachers can always find ways to incorporate the Naturalist Intelligence into their teaching.

> The true Naturalist child will continue to discover more connections as he or she grows older and finds out ways to be involved in nature and help the world.

INCORPORATING OTHER INTELLIGENCES INTO THE NATURALIST UNIT

Students learn in different ways through different intelligences, and various learners are accommodated by using all of the intelligences during each unit of study. During the fifth-grade unit on motion, for example, students do several different kinds of lab activities related to speed and acceleration. The following is a brief overview of how each of the intelligences is used throughout the unit. These ideas can easily be adapted to any Naturalist unit you may choose.

Linguistic: Students write descriptions to explain motion of objects from lab work, and they complete and create word problems related to speed. We also use our science books to compare our data to the book's information.

Spatial: Students generate different-sized arrows to represent the speed of different objects. They create graphs to convey information from labs. Data can be tracked and recorded to show whether objects are speeding up, slowing down or moving at a constant rate.

Logical-Mathematical and Bodily-Kinesthetic: Students go outside and measure a given distance. They complete a movement such as running, crab walking, or cartwheels to cover that distance while another student records the time of their movement. They then use math to calculate their average speed for each action. Students will also act out motions related to lab activities: after our acceleration activity, in which they calculate the acceleration of a marble, they must try to mimic the movement using their bodies.

Musical: We compare different musical rhythms to different speeds.

Interpersonal: Students continually discuss data, results and questions with others. They also peer teach with mini-whiteboards.

Intrapersonal: Students complete self-reflections on their effort, group work skills, and homework performance (accuracy and timeliness).

Naturalist: Students are given the top speeds of different animals and asked to compare the animal's speed to their speeds. We have also calculated the speed of falling maple seeds.

It is a challenge to incorporate all of the intelligences, but we are continually reminded of the power of teaching in different ways when a kid says, "Oh, now I get it!" As students learned about acceleration they may have done an experiment, recorded data, made an arrow map, and read about it, but not until B-K kids get a chance to act out the acceleration of a marble do they fully get it!

ASSESSMENT

It's important to use a lot of varied assessments. You may walk into the science classroom and see kids using folders as blinders as they complete a "traditional" test, but on further inspection you will see that these tests also incorporate MI. When learning about the seasons, kids are asked to show the difference between rotation and revolution using their B-K Intelligence: they become the Earth as they move in large and small circles. During a unit on electricity, some parts of the test allow them to use their Spatial Intelligence and draw circuits, while on other parts they must tap into their Interpersonal Intelligence and explain something using wires, bulbs, and batteries. There is also a section in which they create a poem to convey their knowledge of conductors and insulators. Using different intelligences on tests expands the ways that students can show what they know, and it gives them more confidence, which leads to more comfort in experimentation and in making new mistakes.

PROJECTS AND CHOICES

When students are assigned projects, they are always given a rubric of the main guidelines that they must follow. Every student must follow those guidelines, but each student decides how he or she will do it and how much more information he or she will convey. Students often come up with surprising ideas! For example, when sixth grade students were completing reports (posters, PowerPoint presentations, traditional reports) on planets, one student brought in a piece of classical music—"Mars, Bringer of War," from Gustav Holst's *The Planets* that was written and composed with their planet in mind.

Likewise, fifth-grade students all must take part in the Great Egg Drop project, in which, following strict guidelines, they create a package that protects a raw egg as it is heaved out a third-story classroom window. (The rest of the school observes the Great Egg Drop. Parents, children, and students chant "Break the egg, break the egg!") The students also create a display board to explain the process they went through to make the package and explain how they think it will protect the egg. Kids are encouraged to be creative in their presentations, and every year there are impressive new ideas. Spatial students make their packages look more like an art project than a science project. Projects have resembled space ships, chickens, cartoon characters, Humpty Dumpty, soccer balls, basketballs, and so much more. In the accompanying explanation that the students prepare on a poster board, some kids will go above and beyond by using their Logical-Mathematical Intelligence to calculate kinetic and potential energy of their package. The posters and packages are creative, but children attack the challenge using their strongest intelligence. In the end, each child creates a great product that complies with the guidelines, because all have been allowed to delve into an intelligence that gives them confidence.

Our older students are also given choices during a portion of the year to sign up for a week-long Pursuing Opportunities to Develop Skills (PODS) class that suits their favorite or strongest intelligence. Each specialist teacher (Art, B-K, Performing Arts, and so on) will meet with a group of students every day for an extended period to focus on such things as a frog dissection, bridge building, fabric making, scrapbooking, hockey, play writing, creating a rock band, or playing board games, to name a few. It is a great chance for students to work on an intelligence area of their choice. New City also offers after-school classes that give students a chance to focus on different intelligences. This year we offered classes on building and on robotics. Second grade students stayed focused for hours to complete robots made from LEGOs, six-foot-tall Ferris wheels made from K'NEX, and bridges of all shapes and sizes.

Most everyone agrees that hands-on, inquiry-based science is more meaningful to students, but when MI is incorporated, it not only allows more opportunities to be successful but also makes genuine learning more likely, more meaningful, and even more fun, while giving students more confidence.

Shadows

PURPOSE:
During a study of shadows, students observe how their bodies create shadows and how shadows change over time. Students refine their cooperative skills while improving their sense of balance, coordination, and visual perception.

NATURALIST

PRIMARY

SCIENCE

MATERIALS:
Chalk, sun

PROCEDURE:
1. For this activity, the class will go outside on a hardtop area in the morning or late afternoon. It must be a sunny day. After the students experiment with the shadows their bodies make, instruct them to create a shadow with a hole in it, a round shadow, a square shadow, and a shadow with an angle.

2. Divide the class into an even number of small groups. Each group designates one member as the tracer. Outside, the other group members create a sculpture with their bodies. The tracer uses a piece of chalk to trace around the shadow cast by the bodies.

3. When the groups have completed their shadow sculptures, they move to another group's work and try to replicate the outline of the shadow with their bodies. The tracer joins the group and another group member becomes the engineer, directing the movement and position of the students to recreate the shadow.

4. Discuss how the students made their shadow shapes. Explore the difficulties in creating the exact same sculpture shadow; for instance, the sun has moved, the children in the groups are of a different sizes and shapes, and the level of cooperation may vary among the groups. Were the students able to problem-solve ways to block the light to make a particular shadow?

ASSESSMENT/REFLECTION:
Make observations during the activity, noting who leads, who follows, who offers suggestions, and who compromises, negotiates with, or volunteers to help others. In addition, facilitate conversation about the process, getting children to reflect on how they experimented while creating the shadows and how they moved their bodies to maintain balance, coordination, and the visual accuracy of the shadow.

MI EXTENSIONS:
This lesson also uses the Spatial, Bodily-Kinesthetic, and Interpersonal intelligences.

Intrapersonal: Ask the students to think about their role within the group using the Shadow Puzzles Reflection worksheet.

Linguistic: Read *Bear Shadow* by Frank Asch. Take the students outside again on a sunny day to see whether they can make their shadows disappear.

Logical-Mathematical: Use sheets of notebook-sized paper to determine the area of each group's shadow sculpture.

Musical: Play several different kinds of music; for example, a march, soft environmental music, classical, and jazz. Hang a sheet in the classroom. Behind the sheet, place an overhead projector with its light shining on the sheet. Students take turns moving and dancing between the sheet and the light source. Other students have to guess who the performer is.

Spatial: Design a sundial.

Naturalist: Create a data table to record how the length of the shadow increases or decreases during the day. Use a tetherball pole, ruler, or tree and track the length of the shadow during the day. You could also record the length of a given shadow at different times throughout the year. Discuss how the sun's angle affects shadow length.

Name: _____   Date: _____

Shadow Puzzles Reflection

Names of the people in my group: _____

The person it was easiest to work with: _____

Because: _____

The person it was hardest to work with: _____

Because: _____

I was a leader in my group. _____ yes _____ no

I was a follower in my group. _____ yes _____ no

I was happy being the leader or the follower. _____ yes _____ no

I gave some ideas to the group. _____ yes _____ no

The group used my ideas. _____ yes _____ no

I tried to help someone who was quiet. _____ yes _____ no

One way we cooperated was: _____

One thing that didn't work was: _____

Next time I work in a group I will try to: _____

A Closer Look at Trees

PURPOSE:

Students develop classification techniques while using a field guide to identify a tree they have chosen using leaf, bark, and bud patterns.

MATERIALS:

Tree identification books, paper, crayons

PROCEDURE:

1. The students choose a tree and use a field guide to identify it using leaf characteristics; such as, simple/compound, smooth/little teeth, variegated, handlike, veining patterns, and needles/scales.

2. Use bark characteristics—for example, flaking, thick or thin, scented, or resinous—and the field guide to confirm the tree's identification.

3. Using paper and crayons, the students make bark and leaf rubbings. Each rubbing should be labeled with the kind of tree from which it came.

4. The students observe the tree they identified and write a descriptive paragraph incorporating their observations. They should note physical characteristics, fruit, animal nests, cavities in the tree, and features of the surrounding area.

5. Compile the students' observations and paragraphs to create a class field guide.

ASSESSMENT/REFLECTION:

Using the class-made field guide, the students identify other students' trees. Was the student able to categorize leaves observed by noticing similarities in the patterns?

MI EXTENSIONS:

This lesson also uses the Spatial and Linguistic intelligences.

Spatial: Create models of trees with toothpicks and clay, paying particular attention to the branching and form of the tree. Label each tree with its name.

Bodily-Kinesthetic: Students use their bodies to build a human tree, showing the branching of the tree. They notice and compare the different structures of their trees.

Logical-Mathematical: Graph the leaves by their characteristics. What generalizations can the students make?

Pollination

PURPOSE:
Children learn how bees are connected within communities by participating in a pollination simulation.

MATERIALS:
Large paper cutouts of various flower shapes; a large paper hive, divided into cells large enough for a child to curl up in; straws; small plastic baggies, each with a small hole cut in one lower corner; tape; at least three different kinds of cereal; a small cup to hold the nectar at each flower; water that has been slightly sweetened

Setup prior to simulation:

Put flower cutouts on the floor around the room. Each flower should have one kind of cereal on it to represent pollen and a cup of sweetened water to represent nectar. The paper cutout of the hive should be placed on the floor some distance from the flowers.

PROCEDURE:
1. Divide the students into three groups. One group is the larva in the hive waiting to be fed. One group is nurse bees who will feed the larva. The other group is food-foraging bees collecting pollen and nectar from the flowers.
2. Each food-foraging bee needs a straw to serve as a proboscis and a baggie taped to his or her leg to serve as a pollen basket.
3. Food-foraging bees move from flower to flower drinking nectar and collecting pollen which they put in their pollen baskets. As the bees land on a new flower, they might need to wiggle a bit so some of the pollen from their baskets falls onto that flower.
4. Food-foraging bees periodically go back to the hive. Nurse bees take the pollen from the pollen baskets and use it to feed the larva.
5. Each larva lies curled inside a cell and waits silently to be fed by the nurse bees.
6. After a period of time, change roles, and repeat the activity giving each child an opportunity to be each kind of bee.

ASSESSMENT/REFLECTION:
Discuss the simulation including questions; such as, "Why did the bees collect the pollen?" "What happened to the pollen on the flowers?" "What might happen if one of these groups in the bee community was missing?" "What would happen if there were fewer flowers?" During the discussion, record children's responses to determine their level of understanding.

MI EXTENSIONS:

During this lesson, children also used their Bodily-Kinesthetic and Interpersonal intelligences.

Intrapersonal: Children write a journal entry from the viewpoint of each role. On whom or what did you rely the most? What did you need when you were a . . . ?

Spatial: Create a class mural that depicts the entire process.

Linguistic: Are there other animals or insects that live in a community? Conduct research to find the commonalities between animals that live in communities.

Bodily-Kineshetic: Create a bee dance that will guide other members of the hive to the flowers in the classroom.

Taping the Bison

PURPOSE:
While working in small groups, the students create a life-sized outline of a bison to practice measuring and estimating accurately. This lesson is part of a unit on the Plains Indians and their relationship with the bison, but it could be adapted to any number of topics, such as the solar system, other animals, transportation, monuments, buildings, or trees.

NATURALIST

PRIMARY

SOCIAL STUDIES

MATERIALS:
"*Bison Americanus:* America's Great Shaggy Beast" by Sue Macy, *Cobblestone*, vol. 2, no. 8 (August 1981), teacher-created graphic organizer, tape measures, yardsticks, masking tape

PROCEDURE:
1. Using the article "*Bison Americanus:* America's Great Shaggy Beast" by Sue Macy, students read to learn the height and length of a male (bull) and female (cow) bison and record this information on a graphic organizer.
2. Divide the class into groups and determine which groups will create an outline of the bull and which will create an outline of the cow.
3. Using the measurements from their graphic organizers, each group uses masking tape to create a life-sized outline of a bison on the floor.
4. After the figures of the bison are complete, the students estimate how many students can fit sitting, standing, and lying down inside the outline of the bison.
5. Students place themselves in the figure in the positions mentioned to check the accuracy of their estimates.

ASSESSMENT/REFLECTION:
Observe the students' abilities to apply principles related to measuring, to create an exhibit, and to solve problems.

MI EXTENSIONS:
This lesson also uses the Spatial and Interpersonal intelligences.

Linguistic and Intrapersonal: In their journal, students reflect on their role in the creation of the bison outline. What are the steps involved when creating an exhibit? What do I need to remember when measuring?

Logical-Mathematical: Cut pieces of string the length of the bison and use these as a nonstandard unit of measurement to determine the length of various things at school.

Naturalist: Compare the size of the male and female of other species of animals. Is the relationship between the sizes the same?

Un-Natural Hike

PURPOSE:

Students develop a keener sense of visual observation by noticing incongruent colors, shapes, and textures appearing in an outdoor setting.

MATERIALS:

A variety of objects not ordinarily found in nature such as coat hangers, golf balls, clothes pins, toys, rubber bugs, twisty ties, books, Styrofoam balls, pipe cleaners, plastic cups

PROCEDURE:

1. Prior to the lesson, choose a natural area and identify a path or trail that the kids will follow. Designate a starting and finishing point. Hide the unnatural objects on the trail, making some easier to notice than others. Place the objects at different levels—some high, some eye level, and some on the ground.

2. Discuss the differences between natural and unnatural objects found in the particular environment. The students walk quietly and slowly down the trail, looking for and remembering as many of the unnatural objects as they can.

3. At the end of the trail, students share how many objects they observed. As the students repeat the exercise, challenge them to observe the objects they found on the first trip, as well as others they may have missed.

4. Meet together as a group and reveal the different items each student found.

5. Together, walk along the trail again, picking up the items. Discuss how challenging it is to find each object. Students tell why it is easier to find some items than others.

ASSESSMENT/REFLECTION:

Students create or select a new environment or habitat and hide out-of-place objects and explain in a written format why they do not belong. Later, others try to find those hidden objects and check their answers.

MI EXTENSIONS:

This lesson also uses the Spatial Intelligence.

Interpersonal: As an alternative, have kids walk together through the area and work in small groups to find the hidden objects. Is it easier to do in groups or alone?

Spatial: Create a paper collage with a unifying theme such as straight lines, cats, or city streets, and insert objects that do not fit the theme.

Naturalist: Teach the importance of camouflage in nature by showing pictures of walking sticks, praying mantises, and female birds. Discuss why some animals are brightly colored.

Get It Done!

PURPOSE:

Students identify environmental problems that exist within the school community. They create and carry out plans to increase awareness of the problems and address them.

PROCEDURE:

1. Students explore the school building and grounds looking for natural resources that need to be conserved, such as energy, water, paper, or food.

2. After the tour, students make a class list of problems they see and decide on ways they might be categorized.

3. After choosing an area that interests them, students decide what research needs to be done to establish that the problem does exist and what data would be helpful to collect to confirm that it is a problem. They might check utility bills, document the use and waste of materials, or research costs.

4. Students conduct interviews to see how others feel about the problem, possibly charting responses on a Likert scale. Questions should include how people think the problem could be solved and by whom: individual students, groups, teachers, or administrators. These results are charted to make a graph.

5. Students devise a way to bring awareness within the school community that the problem exists. Time could be spent researching how people have brought awareness of problems to the public in the past, using different intelligences. These methods might include articles, protest songs, photography, posters, marches, and speeches. Students decide on an effective way to highlight their chosen problem, using their preferred intelligence.

6. Students meet in groups, composed of people with with a similar focus, and brainstorm possible solutions to the identified problems. With a way to facilitate change in mind, they develop their own plan of action. Depending on the problem, some solutions might be using the back sides of paper when printing from their computers, adjusting the heating and cooling in the building, providing more trash cans for litter, turning off computers and printers at night, turning off lights when a room is vacant, developing a recycling program, or finding a use for food that is now being discarded.

7. Once a solution has been selected, students devise and carry out a plan to initiate action within the school community.

ASSESSMENT/REFLECTION:

Are the students able to implement their plan of action? After monitoring the problem for a period of time, students evaluate the effectiveness of their plan. Have there been positive changes?

MI EXTENSIONS:

Other intelligences used in this lesson are the Interpersonal and Logical-Mathematical.

Intrapersonal: Keep a written record of the planning and implementation of the project. Make notes about successes, frustrations, and what might have been done differently.

Linguistic: Write a newspaper article, complete with a title, picture, and caption, to bring attention to the problem and possible solutions.

Spatial: Using magazine or other pictures, create a collage that depicts the chosen problem.

Mystery Photos

PURPOSE:
Students learn how to format text, insert and edit graphics, research, and use word processing skills.

MATERIALS:
Intel-Play Computer Microscope (or any other computer microscope program) and its software, Mystery Photo examples found in *Current Science* magazine, computer, graphics software, projector, numerous objects to put under the microscope (if you do not have access to this technology, this lesson can be completed using construction paper with a window cut out over any magnified picture or photograph.)

PROCEDURE:
1. Show the students a few examples of mystery photos—pictures taken through high-powered microscopes that are not readily identifiable.

2. As you show the examples, students try to identify the unknown object. Point out that the pictures often feature a defining characteristic of the object, but not the entire object.

3. Explain to the students that they will be creating a mystery photo of an object along with a three- to four-sentence description.

4. Show the students the objects related to a unit of study—for example, mollusks, shells, and seahorses might be used during an ocean study unit—and have them choose one.

5. Demonstrate how to use the microscope and the software. The object is placed under the microscope and a picture is taken and saved.

6. Students conduct research, finding three or four facts about the chosen object.

7. They create a piece entitled "What am I?" which includes the picture and facts they have turned into clues. Students explore how to center the image on the page, change the image size, and format the font style and size. After this is printed, the name of the object is revealed on the back or under a flap on the front.

ASSESSMENT/REFLECTION:
The final project communicates facts in such a way that other students can determine the object pictured.

MI EXTENSIONS:

This lesson also uses the Linguistic and Spatial intelligences.

Interpersonal: Enough objects are provided for half of the students to complete the project. Students figure out how to share these objects while creating views and clues for the shared objects.

Logical-Mathematical: Using the magnified portion, students do a calculation to determine the magnified size of the entire object.

Sun Shines over Me

PURPOSE:
Students notice how the relationship between the position of the sun and the length of shadow it casts changes over time. They make and confirm hypotheses related to their observations.

MATERIALS:
Dowel rods cut to two-foot lengths, adding machine rolled paper, rulers

PROCEDURE:
1. In pairs, the students mark a place on the playground that will be their observation point to observe the changing length of a shadow. Five trips are made—two trips in the morning, one at noon, and two in the afternoon—to record the length of the shadows created by their dowel rods. Students place one end of the rod on the ground and hold it in a vertical position while the partner unrolls the paper on the ground to measure the length of the shadow. The lengths of the shadows are labeled with the time the shadow was cast, the date, and the length of the shadow.

2. Students display their paper shadows in chronological order. Did all the pairs of students obtain similar results? What explanations can they offer for what they observe?

3. Students, with your guidance, select a time of day as the constant for the next experiment. At the designated time, students go to their observation point and measure the shadows cast by their dowel rods. They again use the rolled paper, recording the date, length, and time of the shadow.

4. Students periodically go outside at the same time over the course of several weeks to collect data, which is displayed. Students notice any similarities among the results the class is obtaining. Hypotheses are offered. The results and the reasons presented are particularly interesting if the data is recorded before and after the solstice.

5. Students use books to confirm the reasons they have presented, determining whether other scientists agree with their suggestions.

ASSESSMENT/REFLECTION:
Note the students' abilities to formulate hypotheses, the curiosity and enjoyment they display about the natural world, and their ability to notice patterns.

MI EXTENSIONS:

This lesson also uses the Logical-Mathematical Intelligence.

Logical-Mathematical: Create a line graph of the data collected.

Linguistic: Record the findings in a scientific learning log.

Spatial: On large sheets of construction paper, make a spatial representation of the findings.

Interpersonal: Students share what they have learned with students from a younger grade, using an intelligence of their choice to reach the audience, depending on that class's prior knowledge and understanding.

Activities to Support the Naturalist Intelligence

INTERPERSONAL

- Gardening and planting
- Taking care of class pets
- Nature scavenger hunt

INTRAPERSONAL

- Naturalist survey (likes and dislikes)
- Reflecting on naturalist activities
- Comparing yourself to things in nature

BODILY-KINESTHETIC

- Field trips (nature hikes on trails, zoos, gardens, wildlife and nature centers, and so on)
- Act out life cycles and plant growth
- Gardening

LINGUISTIC

- Nature poems or stories (write)
- Nature literature
- Season or nature word webs

LOGICAL-MATHEMATICAL

- Comparing, sorting, and graphing nature items (leaves, flowers, seeds, and so on)
- Tree and leaf identification and classification
- Planting, predicting, observing, charting growth of seeds

SPATIAL

- Leaf rubbings
- Nature collages or seed mosaics
- Naturalist artists' studies (Monet, O'Keeffe, Audubon)
- Creating animal homes and habitats
- depicting living things (flowers, insects, trees, animals) using a variety of materials (paint, wood pieces, tissue paper, pipe cleaners, Model Magic, and the like)

MUSICAL

- Exploring musical instruments such as gourds, rainsticks, dried seed pods
- Making instruments from nature (such as seed shakers)
- Environmental music
- Writing songs about nature
- Drawing to music evocative of nature, such as Vivaldi's *The Four Seasons*

Identifying the Natural Intelligence in Your Students

Children function at many different levels within the intelligences. Through observation of everyday activities, one can create a profile showing the level of functioning within a particular intelligence and the intelligences in relation to each other. The levels described show increased engagement and proficiency.

YES NO **APPRECIATES:**

☐ ☐ Consistently demonstrates interest, respect, and enjoyment within the intelligence and is able to differentiate qualities

☐ ☐ Shows curiosity about and finds enjoyment in the natural and scientific worlds

☐ ☐ Notices patterns

☐ ☐ Reads books or watches videos about nature and science

☐ ☐ Asks why and how questions, making connections when learning the answers

☐ ☐ Enjoys being outside

YES NO **PERFORMS:**

☐ ☐ Is able to apply the intelligence to recreate an exhibit or demonstration or problem-solve within a given situation

☐ ☐ Formulates hypothesis

☐ ☐ Is open to new ideas and discoveries

☐ ☐ Is able to demonstrate "How to . . ."

☐ ☐ Is adept at noticing patterns and has an eye for the natural world

☐ ☐ Is able to use, organize, and categorize objects

☐ ☐ Demonstrate informed skepticism and seeks clarity and accuracy

☐ ☐ Collect things

YES NO **CREATES:**

☐ ☐ Is able to apply this intelligence to generate original work or to develop unique solutions to problems or create prototypes

☐ ☐ Develops and organizes stewardship projects

☐ ☐ Forms hypotheses and develops own experiments and proofs

☐ ☐ Shows original thinking using the scientific method

☐ ☐ Is able to pose and solve problems

Children's Resources

Books

Arnosky, Jim. *Wild Tracks! A Guide to Nature's Footprints.* Sterling, 2008.

Ayres, Katherine. *Up, Down, and Around.* Candlewick Press, 2007.

Bauer, Marion. *A Mama for Owen.* Simon & Schuster, 2007.

Berger, Carin. *The Little Yellow Leaf.* Greenwillow Books, 2008.

Berger, Melvin. *All About Seeds.* Scholastic, 1992.

Bjork, Cristina, and Anderson, Lena. *Linnea in Monet's Garden.* R&S Books, 1985.

Bogacki, Tomek. *My First Garden.* Frances Foster Books, 2000.

Brenner, Barbara, and Chardiet, Bernice. *Where's That Insect?* Scholastic, 1993.

Bunting, Eve. *Butterfly House.* Scholastic, 1999.

Cabrera, Jane. *Mommy, Carry Me Please.* Holiday House, 2006.

Campbell, Nicola. *Shi-Shi-etko.* Publishers Group West, 2005.

Caras, Roger. *Coyote for a Day.* Windmill Books and Dutton, 1977.

Carson, Rachel. *The Sense of Wonder.* HarperCollins, 1956.

Cherry, Lynne. *How Groundhog's Garden Grew.* Blue Sky Press, 2003.

———. *The Great Kapok Tree.* Harcourt Brace Jovanovich, 1990.

Cole, Henry. *On Meadowview Street.* Greenwillow Books, 2007.

Cox, Rosamund Kidman. *Usborne First Nature Flowers.* EDC Publishing, 1980.

Davies, Jacqueline. *The Boy Who Drew Birds: A Story of John James Audubon.* Houghton Mifflin, 2004.

Davis, Nicola. *Surprising Sharks.* Candlewick Press, 2003.

Denison, Edgar. *Missouri Wildflowers.* Missouri Department of Conservation, 1998.

Ehlert, Lois. *Red Leaf, Yellow Leaf.* Harcourt Brace Jovanovich, 1991.

Ering, Timothy. *The Story of Frog Belly Rat Bone.* Candlewick Press, 2003.

Fowler, Allan. *Frogs and Toads and Tadpoles, Too.* Children's Press, 1992.

Gibbons, Gail. *The Season's of Arnold's Apple Tree.* Scholastic, 1995.

Glaser, Linda. *It's Winter!* (also *Spring, Fall,* and *Summer*). Scholastic, 2003.

Gunderson, Jessica. *The Sunflower Farmer*. Picture Windows Book, 2008.

Hatkoff, Isabelle. *Owen and Mzee: A True Story of a Remarkable Friendship*. Scholastic, 2006.

Heiligman, Deborah. *From Caterpillar to Butterfly*. Scholastic, 1998.

Heller, Ruth. *Chickens Aren't the Only Ones*. Grossett & Dunlap, 1985.

———. *The Reason for a Flower*. Grossett & Dunlap, 1985.

Hulme, Joy. *Wild Fibonacci: Nature's Secret Code Revealed*. Tricycle Press, 2005.

Jenkins, Steve, and Page, Robin. *Move*. Houghton Mifflin, 2006.

———. *What Do You Do with a Tail Like This?* Houghton Mifflin, 2003.

Johnson, D. B. *Henry Builds a Cabin*. Houghton Mifflin, 2002.

Kavanagh, James. *A Pocket Naturalist Guide: Animal Tracks*. Waterford Press, 2001.

Kelly, Irene. *It's a Butterfly's Life*. Scholastic, 2008.

Koch, Maryjo. *Seed Leaf Flower Fruit*. Collins Publishers, 1999.

Kuhn, Dwight. *My First Book of Nature: How Living Things Grow*. Scholastic, 1993.

Levenson, George. *Pumpkin Circle*. Tricycle Press, 2002.

Maass, Robert. *When Spring Comes*. Scholastic, 1997.

Maestro, Betsy. *Why Do Leaves Change Color?* Scholastic, 1994.

McGinty, Alice. *Darwin: With Glimpses into His Private Journal and Letters*. Houghton Mifflin, 2009.

McKissack, Patricia and Frederick. *Messy Bessy's Garden*. Scholastic, 1991.

Merrill, Claire. *A Seed Is a Promise*. Scholastic, 1990.

Milway, Katie. *One Hen*. Kids Can Press, 2008.

Nayer, Judy. *A Tree Can Be*. Scholastic, 1994.

Nivola, Claire. *Planting the Trees of Kenya: The Story of Wangari Maathi*. Farrar, Straus & Giroux, 2008.

Oppenheim, Joanne. *Have You Seen Bugs?* Scholastic, 1999.

———. *Have You Seen Trees?* Scholastic, 1999.

Packard, Steven. *Claude Monet: Sunshine and Waterlilies*. Grosset & Dunlap, 2001.

Pallotta, Jerry. *The Icky Bug Counting Book*. Charlesbridge, 1992.

Parker, Nancy Winslow, and Wright, Joan Richards. *Bugs*. Scholastic, 1987.

Pattou, Edith. *Mrs. Spitzer's Garden*. Harcourt, 2001.

Peterson, Roger Tory. *Peterson First Guides (Wildflowers, Trees, Fish, Forest . . .)*. Houghton Mifflin Company.

Quigley, Mary. *Granddad's Fishing Buddy*. Dial Books for Young Readers, 2007.

Quinn, Greg Henry. *The Garden in Our Yard*. Scholastic, 1995.

Rao, Sirish. *Leaf Life*. Tara, 2006.

Roop, Connie and Peter. *Over in the Rain Forest*. Scholastic, 2003.

Ruddell, Deborah. *Today at the Blue Bird Café: A Branchful of Birds*. Margaret K. McElderry Books, 2007.

Sayre, April. *Stars Beneath Your Bed: The Surprising Story of Dust*. HarperCollins, 2005.

Schwartz, David M., and Schy, Yael. *Where in the Wild: Camouflaged Creatures Concealed . . . and Revealed*. Tricycle Press, 2007.

Scieszka, Jon. *Science Verse*. Juvenile Viking, 2006.

Seeger, Laura Vaccaro. *First the Egg*. Roaring Book Press, 2007.

Sellers, Ronnie. *When Spring Comes*. Caedmon, 1984.

Selsam, Millicent E. *Big Tracks, Little Tracks, Following Animal Prints*. HarperCollins, 1998.

Sherrow, Victoria. *Chipmunk at Hollow Tree Lane*. Scholastic, 1996.

Sidman, Joyce. *Red Sings from the Treetops: A Year in Colors*. Houghton Mifflin, 2009.

Steele, Mary Q. *Anna's Garden Songs*. Scholastic, 1990.

Stevens, Janet. *Tops and Bottoms*. Harcourt, 1995.

Venezia, Mike. *Georgia O'Keeffe*. Children's Press, 1993.

———. *Monet*. Children's Press, 1990.

Wallace, Nancy Elizabeth. *Paperwhite*. Houghton Mifflin, 2000.

Walters, Catherine. *When Will It Be Spring?* Scholastic, 1999.

Ward, Jennifer. *Over in the Garden*. Scholastic, 2003.

Wells, Robert. *Is a Blue Whale the Biggest Thing There Is?* Whitman, 1993.

———. *What's Smaller Than a Pygmy Shrew?* Whitman, 1995.

Worth, Bonnie. *Oh Say Can You Seed?* Random House, 2001.

Games

Hammet, Lucy. *Wildflower Bingo*

Learn to Recycle. Lakeshore, 2009.

Teachers' Resources

Books

Ashbrook, Peggy. *Science Is Simple*. Gryphon House, 2003.

Burke, Kay. *Authentic Learning*. Corwin, 2009.

Burnie, David. *Reader's Digest: How Nature Works*. The Reader's Digest Association, 1991.

Chalufour, Ingrid, and Worth, Karen. *The Young Scientist Series*. Redleaf Press, 2005.

Chen, Jie-Qi, ed. *Project Spectrum: Early Learning Activities*. Teachers College Press, 1999. (This is volume 2 of Project Zero Frameworks for Early Childhood Education.)

Cornell, Joseph. *Sharing Nature with Children*. Dawn Publications, 1979.

Curti, Anna. *My Very First Nature Craftbook*. Little Simon, 1997.

Danks, Fiona, and Jo Schofield. *Nature's Playground*. Chicago Review Press, 2007.

Glock, Jenna, Wertz, Susan, and Meyer, Maggie. *Discovering the Naturalist Intelligence: Science in the Schoolyard*. Zephyr Press, 1999.

Goldish, Meish. *101 Science Poems and Songs for Young Learners*. Scholastic, 1996.

Hamilton, Kersten. *The Butterfly Book: A Kid's Guide to Attracting, Raising, and Keeping Butterflies*. John Muir Publications, 1997.

Helm, Judy Harris, and Katz, Lilian. *Young Investigators: The Project Approach in the Early Years*. Teachers College Press, 2001.

Hickman, Pamela, and the Federation of Ontario Naturalists. *The Jumbo Book of Nature Science*. Kids Can Press, 1996.

Hume, Barbara, and Galton, Christine. *The Art of Science*. World Print Limited, 1997.

Ingram, Mrill. *Butterfly Biology*. Kendall/Hunt Publishing.

Jaffe, Roberta, and Appel, Gary. *The Growing Classroom: Garden Based Science*. Dale Seymour, 1990.

Kite, L. Patricia. *Gardening Wizardry for Kids*. Barron's Educational Series, Inc., 1995.

Krautwurst, Terry, and Gwen Diehn. *Nature Crafts for Kids*. Sterling, 1992.

Louv, Richard. *Last Child in the Woods*. Algonquin Books of Chapel Hill, 2005.

Martin, Laura C. *Nature's Art Box*. Storey, 2003.

Milord, Susan. *The Kids' Nature Book*. Williamson Publishing, 1996.

Missouri Conservation Department. *A Guide to the Planning and Development of Outdoor Classrooms*. Conservation Commission of the State of Missouri, 1993.

Mitchell, John, and the Audubon Society. *The Curious Naturalist*. Massachusetts Audubon Society, 1996.

Moore, Jo Ellen. *Learning About Plants*. Evan Moor, 2000.

Moore, Jo Ellen, and Norris, Jill. *Learning About My Body*. Evan-Moore, 2000.

Mrill, Ingram. *Bottle Biology*. Kendall/Hunt, 1993.

National Wildlife Federation. *Wading into Wetlands*. Chelsea House Publishers, 1998.

Nickelsburg, Janet. *Nature Activities for Early Childhood*. Addison-Wesley, 1976.

Project Learning Tree. *Environmental Education Activity Guide PreK–8*. American Forest Foundation, 2002.

Sheehan, Kathryn, and Waidner, Mary. *Earth Child: Games, Stories, Activities, Experiments, and Ideas About Living Lightly on Planet Earth*. Council Oaks Books, 1995.

Simon, Seymour. *Pets in a Jar*. Puffin Books, 1979.

Sobel, David. *Beyond Ecophobia*. The Orion Society, 1966.

Starbuck, Sara, Olthof, Marla, and Midden, Karen. *Hollyhocks and Honeybees*. Redleaf Press, 2002.

Swanson, Diane. *Bug Bites*. Whitecap Books, 1997.

Tagholm, Sally. *The Complete Book of Seasons*. Kingfisher, 2002.

Taylor, Beverly. *Exploring Energy with Toys*. Terrific Science Press, 1998.

Weiner, Esther. *Science Mini Books*. Scholastic, 1994.

White, Jennifer M. *Math in the Garden*. National Gardening Association, 2006.

Wormeli, Rick. *Summarization in Any Subject: 50 Techniques to Improve Student Learning*. ASCD, 2005.

Web Sites

http://www.oplin.org/tree/ (tree identification)

http://www.insectidentification.org/ (bug identification)

http://www.acornnaturalists.com (to purchase items)

Part 2

Putting It All Together with the Multiple Intelligences

9

Different Intelligences Are an Aspect of Diversity

BY SHERYL REARDON

Photograph: Patti Gabriel

New City School's philosophy statement notes that we believe that "the opportunity to learn together should be shared by children of diverse racial and socio-economic backgrounds, as well as diverse academic abilities," and that we create an atmosphere that "respects and values individual differences." This may sound similar to the mission and philosophy statements of many other schools, so what makes us different?

> One thing that truly sets New City School apart is the fact that valuing diversity was one of the founding tenets of our school.

One thing that truly sets New City School apart is the fact that valuing diversity was one of the founding tenets of our school. Since our doors opened in 1969, we have considered this unique appreciation for diversity to be a key component of who we are. It is integrated into our academics and the warm, nurturing ambience of our classrooms and halls. We know that we have not and never can arrive at some magical place where diversity work will be easy. We know that if we intend to truly reflect the needs and demographics of our school and of local and world communities, then our definition of diversity will also continue to include ongoing reflection, education, and action. Our goal is for students to leave our school with a strong academic foundation, an appreciation and understanding of diversity, and a confident sense of self.

> We view the diversity umbrella as one that covers race and ethnicity but also extends even further to include (but not limit us to) socioeconomics, religion and faith, politics, gender, learning styles, language, sexual orientation, age, physical abilities, and family structure.

At New City School, the definition of diversity is so broad that we say it "goes beyond the numbers," because we view the diversity umbrella as one that covers race and ethnicity but also extends even further to include (but not limit us to) socioeconomics, religion and faith, politics, gender, learning styles, language, sexual orientation, age, physical abilities, and family structure. Our definition of diversity acknowledges and embraces the differentness that each family, student, and faculty member brings through our doors. Appreciating MI is an important part of this commitment.

DIVERSITY AND ACADEMICS

An appreciation of diversity—understanding, accepting, and valuing others—is an important part of the academic preparation that our students receive. Teachers and administrators work together to develop curricula that teach, encourage, and reinforce awareness, respect, appreciation, acceptance, and a willingness to take action. Not only do we make decisions about what we *will* teach, but we also make choices about the things we *won't* teach. Whereas textbooks have traditionally focused on a very heterosexual, male, Eurocentric view of literature and history, we use and create resources that reflect the gifts that a broader range of people have contributed to those fields.

> An appreciation of diversity—understanding, accepting, and valuing others—is an important part of the academic preparation that our students receive.

Rather than celebrating African-American or women's history within the confines of a designated period, we include the contributions of all peoples throughout the year and throughout the intelligences. We are a secular based school, but we do not shy away from conversations about religion, holidays, and observances. Our school calendar reflects a variety of observances that are important to our families. A faculty diversity committee offers professional development opportunities for teachers and includes parents (who are an excellent resource) as part of that education process. For example, we have enjoyed presentations from families about the tenets of their faith. While each presentation was different, faculty members were able to make connections between the religions and, perhaps more important, make connections to the families. It also gave the families an opportunity to see that they are vital to our growth and development as a school community.

OTHER WAYS TO EMBRACE DIVERSITY

Our Family Support Program and need-based financial aid are also critical to creating a culture of diversity at New City School. Families can take advantage of free early care before school from 7:00 A.M. and can pay for extended day services after school until 6:00 P.M. A camp (recreational, not academic) is offered every summer, and coverage is also available for part of our spring and winter breaks. "No School at School" offers coverage for families on those days when school is closed for parent-teacher conferences or in-service programs. (As with the camps, there is a fee to participate in this program.)

Each program offers families coverage for a wide range of working hours and professional and personal time needs. Parent education and support groups are also offered for adoptive families, LGBT (lesbian, gay, bisexual, and transgendered) families, and families of color. In each case, families define themselves and decide whether they will attend the groups. In many cases, parents help set the agendas and lead activities and discussions. An evening diversity committee is composed of parents, faculty members and board members who debate current events, read and discuss group-selected books, and organize and facilitate diversity-related parent education opportunities at school and in the local community. Our need-based financial aid (over a third of our students receive some assistance to attend New City) allows us to help fulfill our goal of enrolling a socioeconomically diverse student body. Once, at a diversity conference, one of our faculty members overheard teachers from an independent school on the east coast talking about how surprised they were to learn which students were receiving financial aid at their school. Their school published a list of financial aid recipients that was shared with the teachers! Our faculty members proudly told them that we afford parents the privacy they deserve with their finances and that our teachers do not have that information.

DIVERSITY AND MI

This *is* a book about Multiple Intelligences, so you may be wondering just how this tradition of diversity and our use of MI interconnect. Quite well, thank you! Most important to us are the Personal Intelligences, reflected on the first page of our progress report. Interpersonal and Intrapersonal skills such as motivation, problem solving, and appreciation for diversity are evaluated. We strive to educate the *whole* child. To be successful in that effort means that we must first get to know the needs, strengths, and weaknesses of each child. Intake conferences in early fall allow teachers an opportunity to meet with families to discuss areas that will give a detailed picture of the child socially, emotionally, and academically. How

We strive to educate the *whole* child.

does the child deal with frustrations? What kind of problem solver is the child? What conversations has the family had about discrimination? What religious or cultural holidays or observances are important to the family? What does the family want most for the child this school year?

Teachers help students develop the tools necessary to be active participants in their own Intrapersonal and Interpersonal growth. We begin in preschool to teach our children to give and to receive constructive feedback from teachers as well as peers and to evaluate their own work with a critical eye. As students get older, they are asked to set personal goals and work as a team with classmates to reach class goals. Structured as well as spontaneous opportunities for presentations and performances abound. Initially, diversity might not come to mind when thinking of these activities, but at New City School all of these opportunities both support the understanding and appreciation for diversity within the classroom and enhance our students' personal experiences with diversity.

What about MI and diversity beyond the Personal Intelligences? Students attend specialist classes that enrich their Spatial, B-K, Musical, and Naturalist Intelligences, and classroom teachers also incorporate those intelligences into the Linguistic or Logical-Mathematical classrooms. There are many opportunities and choices that allow students to show genuine understanding of academic skills through their strongest intelligences as well as work to develop strength and comfort within intelligences that they may not feel as comfortable using. Students learn to read, write, and compute, but they do so in a way that truly speaks to them as individuals and helps them gain both mastery of facts and genuine understanding of concepts. The spatially talented fifth grader performs scenes from the Civil War using puppets to illustrate the lives of soldiers and slaves. Third graders create detailed spatial dioramas to accompany written reports about Native American tribes and their daily lives. The fourth grader who loves movement and motion can use her B-K Intelligence to help her remember the difference between acute and obtuse angles as she performs a geometry cheer. The musical kindergarten student can recall the functions of the organs by singing to himself the body song. Second graders produce naturalist journals with detailed sketches created in the field and descriptions, written "like scientists," similar to those of Lewis and Clark on their journey west.

Using MI is natural for us at New City School in many ways, because it validates that we are all different, and that these differences are more than acceptable—they're wonderful. Multiple Intelligence helps us tap into a range of student potentials and diversities.

10

Photograph: Patti Gabriel

Learning
Through
Simulations

BY SUSIE BURGE

"No more taxes! No more taxes!" The chants filled the classroom air as students popped up from behind tables and chairs, waving paper signs that they had taped onto meter sticks.

Why in the world were fifth graders protesting the payment of unfair taxes? They were experiencing learning through a simulation. Simulations are excellent educational tools that promote genuine understanding in students by immersing them in realistic experiences. In our school, for example, the fifth graders also begin a study of economics through a classroom economy simulation in which children apply for jobs and receive weekly wages. They are paid in "classroom currency" for completing daily jobs, working at centers, and turning in homework on time. They can spend their currency at the class store, which sells items like mechanical pencils. However, since we are simulating real-world conditions, they are also required to pay a weekly rent on their desks.

The simulation goes deeper than jobs and wages. As the unit of study on the American Revolution approaches, the class begins to investigate the question of taxes. The students interview their parents and ask why they pay taxes, what taxes they pay, and what is done with the tax revenue. After a discussion of what they have learned, the students learn that in order to keep our economic simulation realistic, they will be taxed. The taxes begin slowly, but tax after tax is added until the students become quite upset.

Meanwhile the fifth graders are exploring related topics in their writing journals, such as these:

- Have you ever been in a situation where you were treated unfairly?
- How did it feel?
- What did you do?
- Describe the qualities of a leader.
- What things do you think need to be changed in our country? In our state? At our school?

As they protest the taxes imposed by the British government, they read in various texts about the experiences of the American colonists. Additional taxes continue to be levied until the muttering and complaining escalate to a crisis. Emotions finally build to a boiling point; student leaders emerge to rally the others, and plans are formed during recess. The teacher walks into a full-blown protest in the classroom! The students experience first-hand the feelings of the American colonists, and they are able to connect with their desires and make efforts to bring about change.

Simulations help turn abstract concepts into concrete realities for students. Some simulations, such as the economics unit, let students try out real-world scenarios for themselves on a miniature scale. Others, like the focus on taxation, place students in conditions that require decision making with related consequences. Students share in the feelings and dilemmas that real people faced in similar situations. All simulations need to have an element of realism; paying students a wage does not mean anything if there is no place for them to spend their money. The fifth grade's classroom economy uses paper bills and plastic coins, and the prices in the store require students to make change to practice Logical-Mathematical skills in a realistic setting.

What happens to the classroom revolutionaries? They meet the same logical consequences that followed their counterparts two hundred years ago. The students are asked to write their own classroom constitution, modeled after the United States Constitution. They spend several days reading and studying the Constitution with a purpose: to learn how to set up a government. The students then form committees to write the different sections: a preamble; sections dealing with an executive branch, a legislative branch, a judicial branch; and a student bill of rights. Once the rough drafts are completed, classroom debates begin, as they read descriptions of those hot summer nights in Philadelphia in 1787. Students learn about the heated disagreements and the need to compromise through their reading, and also through their first-hand experiences of being in this very similar situation. Finally, the document is ratified and put into effect, and the classroom operates from this constitution for the remainder of the year. Elections are held, the executives set a course, the representatives pass rules, and the judicial branch settles disputes and vigorously protects the student bill of rights. (One of the first things the students quickly learn is how to create amendments, as they have inevitably forgotten to address some issues in the original document.) These students have formed a deep understanding of how our government works and the processes by which it was formed through participating in this reenactment of those events.

Of course, students use their MI in many ways in these simulations, from creating spatial banners and signs, to speaking linguistically to arouse the passions of their peers, to singing songs from the Colonial period. Persuading and protesting highlights the Interpersonal Intelligence, as does the negotiating that runs throughout the entire legislative process. There are also structured times for students to develop their Intrapersonal Intelligence by reflecting on the roles they played in particular situations as well as what they could do differently in the future.

Some simulations run the whole year and continue to build. In the economics simulation, students are offered the opportunity later in the year to open their own businesses. They must submit an application to the class's Better Business Bureau and purchase a business license if it is approved. Later in the year they move from a cash basis to checking accounts, and students practice more logical-mathematical skills as they learn that one cannot just go "get money from the bank" if money has not been deposited there in the first place. During the final third of the year they may apply for a credit card—and learn to their dismay that items charged on the cards must be paid for at a later date.

Other kinds of simulations can be briefer and more directly focused. In a rainforest simulation game carried out in science class, the objective is to help students recognize how and why different groups of people have different perspectives on vital issues such as rainforest preservation. Students are assigned to different interest groups, such as bankers, villagers, industrialists, environmentalists, and government officials who all live in a rainforest country. Although they have the same ultimate goal of developing their imaginary country in the best possible way, they soon realize that each interest group has a different approach and different interests.

Another fifth grade simulation is the poverty game. This takes place towards the end of our unit of study on the Civil Rights movement. Students have learned about the failure of reconstruction following the Civil War, the "black codes," discrimination, and segregation. They have studied people who made a difference: Rosa Parks, Dr. Martin Luther King Jr., Ruby Bridges, and the Little Rock Nine. They have read books and watched videos that capture this era. These studies are followed by a culminating event in which the entire grade is brought to the lunchroom for a project: students are to use their multiple intelligences to create a collage that depicts significant events of the Civil Rights movement. Pressure is put on the students as they are told the projects will be graded, and they are working under a time limit. Paper bags of supplies are passed out, and because there will be parent volunteers assisting, students are asked to put on the name tags found in their bags of supplies.

What the students do not realize is that the different colors of the name tags, randomly assigned, confer either privileged or underprivileged status to the named individuals. Students with gold name tags are privileged. Their bags contain plenty of supplies. They have ample markers, glue, scissors, paper, pages from magazines, and money to purchase even more supplies at the game store. Students with blue name tags receive most of the supplies that they need, while those with red name tags may have only scissors. As the students begin to work, the disparities surface. Parent helpers come in to discriminate against the students with red name tags. These students are taken to the judge, they are thrown into the "jail," they are sent to the end of the line at the store.

As you might imagine, the Poverty Game is a fascinating and sometimes emotional exercise. Some "wealthy" students become so absorbed in creating their own collage that they do not help their "impoverished" friends. It usually takes some time before the students really grasp what is happening. In some years the students begin sit-ins at the "jail," protests at the store, or hold hands in a circle singing "We Shall Overcome." Here, too, the Personal Intelligences play a key role in the students' interactions and learning.

There is an extensive debriefing session afterward in which the children reflect on their situation, feelings, and experiences and draw parallels to the Civil Rights movement and the discrimination issues that still remain today. Children gain true understanding from experiencing the real feelings and dilemmas that faced them during the simulation, and they apply their knowledge as they attempt solutions.

Children gain true understanding from experiencing the real feelings and dilemmas that faced them during the simulation, and they apply their knowledge as they attempt solutions. We believe that strength in the personal intelligences is the key to success, and our students use and refine them throughout the simulations.

We believe that strength in the personal intelligences is the key to success, and our students use and refine them throughout the simulations. Simulations help students experience events similar to those they are studying. They gain a clearer understanding of the situations, the feelings of those involved, and the decisions that have to be made. Simulations are more than an engaging and effective method of instruction; they help prepare our students for the real world.

11

Assessing Through PEPs (Projects, Exhibitions, Presentations)

BY JULIE STEVENS

When we think of assessment, we often equate it with standardized tests or quizzes and tests associated with classroom curricula. At New City School we use these forms of assessment, but we also complement them with a variety of projects, exhibitions, and presentations that allow students to draw on all eight of their multiple intelligences. Almost all of the projects that will be mentioned in this chapter are theme-based and relate to the year-long theme used at that particular grade. Here are some ideas about how to incorporate assessment activities that draw on all eight of the MI at every grade level.

PEPS AT ALL LEVELS

At the kindergarten level, the children study the human body, focusing especially on the brain, bones, and muscles; the circulatory, respiratory, and digestive systems; and overall well-being. Throughout the year, each child creates a "My Busy Body Book," which contains poetry, music, writing, and drawings connected with the human body. The culminating project is the creation of a three-dimensional, functional, life-size representation of their own body, which exhibits the systems they have studied. Not only is the body (made from construction paper, popsicle sticks, yarn, and pasta) accurate in its depiction, but the heart (juice box) inflates the lungs (plastic bags) when it is compressed. Finally, the children celebrate their accomplishments with their parents at a potluck "Busy Body Breakfast." At this time they share their book and life-sized body with their parents, while their teachers tape the presentations.

In the first and second grades, the students give "MI Shares"—presentations that require them to use multiple intelligences to show what they have learned. In the first grade these consist of a three- to five-minute presentation of a poem, biography, or fairy tale that the students have read, as well as a Naturalist Share. (The Naturalist Intelligence is singled out because the teachers feel this intelligence is particularly underrepresented and sometimes discouraged in our urban youngsters, which can lead to "nature deficit disorder.") In preparing for the MI Share, the teachers offer the students a choice of activities that reflect the various intelligences, such as a puppet show, a Venn diagram, a diorama, and so on. The second grade theme is "Westward Expansion," and their MI Shares center around pioneer homes (built by the students in teams), a pioneer how-to, and monuments that they have built. In creating a pioneer how-to, the students focus on the leisure activities and responsibilities of pioneer children as they teach their class how to complete or participate in one of the games or chores of the time. The culminating project for the year requires students to design and create their own original three-dimensional model to reflect some important event or person that has helped shape our country. Students also write a paper to describe their work, and they do a formal presentation for classmates and parents, which is videotaped.

The fourth grade theme is called "Citizens Who Have Made a Difference." The students research a person who has made a difference through the genre of biography. After the research and writing of the biography is complete, students construct a two- to three-minute mono-logue from the perspective of the individual they have chosen to research. The students then dress up as those individuals and do a three- to four-minute oral presentation in a Living Museum that is held in our library. Families and the school community are invited to discover the citizens who have made a difference.

In fifth grade, the students study American history. One of their projects, called "Living History," combines social studies and linguistics. The students choose a partner from an earlier generation for a letter exchange. These questions are asked: What was your fifth grade year like? What historical events have you lived through? How much did things cost during your fifth grade year? What were some of your childhood experiences? This exchange is kept in a binder along with photographs and other primary source materials and shared with parents on Portfolio Night.

The sixth grade project addresses the personal intelligences through autobiography. The book they create is set up as an "Alpha-Biography" with twenty-six chapters (one for each letter of the alphabet). Students write about becoming a member of their family, create a symbol of who they are as a person, and make a graph highlighting the positive and negative events of their life thus far, to name just a few chapters. The autobiography is then shared with parents and community during portfolio night at New City School. Here, too, students also use their Linguistic Intelligence as they write about what they are learning and presenting.

A CLOSER LOOK AT "KEEPERS OF THE EARTH"

Although your imagination is the only limit on PEPs you might develop and integrate into your curriculum, there are many details that must be considered for successful implementation of such an assessment strategy. A close look at the third grade's year-long theme will provide an example of how PEPs can enrich your classroom. The third grade's year-long theme is called "Keepers of the Earth," and through it we teach Native American history. This theme is divided into six units; within each unit, students work in MI centers that are related directly to that particular unit. The culminating project for the year is a research report on a particular Native American tribe, which is written at school, and a diorama, which is created at home.

In the fall, the students are given the opportunity to peruse a variety of books that describe Native American tribes. Students choose a tribe to research, and after the teachers model how to take research notes, the students find information about their tribe of choice, focusing especially on history, geography, shelter, food, clothing, celebrations and ceremonies, leaders, European contact, and the modern tribe today. Optional topics are tribal creation stories, tribal enemies, and tribal art. When the students have completed their note-taking, they compose their written reports. After several edits, pictures are added to illustrate the report.

> Although your imagination is the only limit on PEPs you might develop and integrate into your curriculum, there are many details that must be considered for successful implementation of such an assessment strategy.

Upon publication, the students create a decorative folder in which to place it.

At the same time, the students and their families work at home to create a diorama, approximately thirty by thirty inches, which is representative of their tribe. The diorama may include a village scene, a buffalo jump, a garden, and so on. A variety of materials can be used, such as Model Magic, clay, Sculpey, and papier-mâché. We encourage the students to use natural items like twigs, leaves, or seeds, which they can find in their own yards.

When both the reports and the dioramas are completed, a day in May is designated as Native American Day, during which the students display both their dioramas and reports. For this occasion, the students prepare an oral summary of their report and a description of their diorama to present to their families and school community who are invited to the display. For many students and their families, this day is the highlight of the year because it brings together much of what they have learned and showcases their MI and love for learning.

Assessment of both the report and diorama is completed by using separate rubrics for each. In the weeks following Native American Day, the dioramas are displayed in the front hall, during which time the students are videotaped doing an oral summary of their tribe and a description of their dioramas. The students take their videotape home for their parents to view, and the students are required to reflect on their presentation with an evaluation sheet. The teachers evaluate their presentations as well. The tape and reflections are then included in the student's portfolio.

Projects, exhibitions, and presentations enable students to use all of their intelligences and are central to each grade level theme at New City School. The multiple intelligences provide the opportunity to differentiate learning for each student to help them reach the goal of their full potential.

The multiple intelligences provide the opportunity to differentiate learning for each student to help them reach the goal of their full potential.

Assessment at New City School

BY PAT NUERNBERGER

Photograph: Patti Gabriel

To teach using the multiple intelligences requires a very different perspective on how to assess student performance. Paper and pencil activities simply cannot capture the depth of understanding that students acquire when they are involved in the variety of activities that complement an MI-based curriculum. Historically, most assessment has been directed towards the outcomes of instruction. Most testing is done at the end of a unit of study; unfortunately, by that time the instruction and learning phase is already over. The test score is generated after the fact, and the opportunity to change student understanding based on the results has passed.

Even when applied to classes of students, and not just individuals, summative measures of outcome tell us only *where* the achievement levels of a class lie. They do not tell us what brought about those levels, *how* those levels were obtained, or *why* the extremes in scores occurred. At this point, the teacher can only guess at what factors affected the final scores. To use the metaphor of a soccer game, you do not improve the play of a team by looking at the outcome. The coach must look closely at how the team is playing the game while they are playing, then use that information to change strategies or employ specific moves that can produce a better final score.

It is important to realize that assessment should never be an end in itself. Assessment should always be a tool to inform planning and allow the teacher to know how students are doing and what he or she can do to help them be better. That's true whether in an MI school or in a more traditional school where the scholastic intelligences are given higher value.

We know that we need to assess the *process* as well as the *product* of a child's learning and understanding, so there should be ways other than paper and pencil tests to assess the multiple intelligences. In addition to written work, assessment can take place through observations, inventories, checklists, dialogue, student reflection and self-assessment, presentations, videos, exhibitions, and projects. Regardless of how it is done, assessment must be ongoing and frequent, and the student must be provided with timely feedback about the performance. In addition, the criteria for assessing need to be clearly and explicitly articulated at the beginning of each evaluation.

The best assessment instruments are learning experiences incorporated into the daily activities of the classroom in natural and enjoyable ways. Designing such activities, however, is not as easy as creating more traditional paper and pencil methods, but it is well worth the extra time required, because exercises that allow students to draw on their multiple intelligences elicit information that is far more useful for instruction and planning. These types of activities also benefit students by providing opportunities to develop a deeper understanding of their own personal strengths and challenges.

ASSESSMENT APPROACHES AT NEW CITY SCHOOL

We believe any assessment should give students opportunities to demonstrate what they know and can do. Teachers at New City use a variety of assessment tools and techniques to determine how students are performing, to set goals for instruction, to monitor students' growth and development, and to give feedback to students so they can monitor their own development.

Checklists and anecdotal comments are useful tools to structure, direct, and record observations. These tools are usually supplemented by conversations, conferences, and interviews. Sometimes student activities may be audio-recorded or videotaped.

Observation of students is one of the most important components of assessment. Observation involves much more than teachers simply interacting with students or watching and listening to students in the classroom. It involves the systematic collection and analysis of observable data. This can—and should—be done regardless of the age of the child. Kindergarten teachers at New City School do this on a routine basis by using a series of learning centers (over twenty every two weeks) that incorporate all the intelligences. The teacher's major role during "Choice Time" is to observe his or her students. The centers are not just for exploration purposes; they are also used to teach specific Linguistic, Logical-Mathematical, or Science/Naturalist concepts. By observing the kids as they work, teachers gain information about their students' approaches to new tasks, their interactions with their peers, and how they solve problems.

> Observation of students is one of the most important components of assessment.

The video camera plays an important role in assessment because it can capture projects and presentations that cannot be easily recorded on paper. Beyond this, a visual record facilitates the Intrapersonal Intelligence. After each performance, the student takes home a flash drive with the file and watches the presentation with his or her family. During this review, the student participates in a self-reflection process, making notes of areas in which he or she excelled as well as areas in which he or she could have given more information, made better eye contact, spoken more loudly, used visual aids, and so on. This reflection plays an important role in helping students develop presentation skills as well as both their Intrapersonal and Interpersonal Intelligences. Plans are underway for a potential culminating project: the creation of a movie showing their own growth over their time at New City.

> Students learn to relish the process as well as the product, and they come to recognize the feeling of genuine success by accomplishing something they had originally thought was unsolvable. This is one of the ways in which we teach our students how to learn.

We have found the flip video camera to be an essential tool for student reflection. The ease with which this camera can be pulled out at a moment's notice—whether to be used by a single student wanting immediate feedback on his or her performance or by the teacher wanting to document each member's participation in group discussion—has opened up a plethora of assessment opportunities.

Projects, exhibitions and presentations (PEPs) are an important part of assessment at New City (see Chapter Eleven). Often teachers give choices of intelligences to be used in accomplishing a project. At other times, however, students may be directed to use the intelligence that they have identified as being most in need of strengthening. Going outside one's comfort zone is always a challenge, but such assignments are given in a way that makes the kids *want* to take on the challenge. In the end, students learn to relish the process as well as the product, and they come to recognize the feeling of genuine success by accomplishing something they had originally thought was unsolvable. This is one of the ways in which we teach our students how to learn.

Final assessment outcomes are clearly stated at the onset of an assignment, often in the form of a rubric. Rubrics delineate what must happen or be demonstrated to result in the best project; specific levels and examples of performance are presented. Assessment can be a particularly powerful learning strategy when students are involved in the process of developing the rubrics. Rubrics are even more valuable for us because we require students to show their knowledge by using many different intelligences in their culminating projects; for example, in the third graders' Native American diorama and presentation, the fifth graders' colonial village simulation, and the fourth graders' Living Museum of citizens who made a difference (all described in Chapter Eleven).

These kinds of projects allow the students to process and share information through their MI strengths, and to show a depth of understanding that could not be revealed by only writing a report. Not only do PEPs allow the students to show the factual information each has gained, but they also enable students to display a much deeper personal connection with the subject matter.

Self-assessment is an important tool that helps students develop higher-order metacognitive skills and identify individual learning goals. Because New City School puts a great deal of emphasis on the personal intelligences, students do much self-reflection during many phases of the learning process, on both their academic and social performance. Students participate in self-assessment to find out what they have learned so they will know on what to focus on next. To help them accomplish this, teachers use math journals, cooperative learning reflections, reading and writing surveys, research evaluations, field trip reflections, reflections on working with a substitute teacher, and responses to a report card.

Because we feel that the personal intelligences are the most important intelligences, and not something that can be captured in a small box on the last page of the report card (which typically reports on "effort" and "ability to get along with others"), the entire first page of our report card is devoted to the Interpersonal and Intrapersonal Intelligences. Children are assessed on such attributes as motivation, responsibility, confidence, problem solving, appreciation of diversity, and teamwork, both by a checklist and written narrative. Many teachers have the children assess themselves in these areas; they then use that information as part of the report (sometimes including student quotes in their narratives).

> Assessment can be a particularly powerful learning strategy when students are involved in the process of developing the rubrics.

A key component of self-reflection is the Student-Involved Conference, held every November with students in second through sixth grade. At that conference, each student sets both a scholastic and a personal goal, which they share with their parents along with the strategies they will use to achieve these goals. To prepare for these conferences, teachers spend time with the entire class modeling the goal-setting process and discussing goals to set for improvement in both scholastic and social areas. They then confer with individual students and help them decide on appropriate goals. Time is spent preparing an agenda for the conference, with the focus on deciding what's important to share and how to talk about their goals with their parents. Students then role play and practice with their peers. At the conference a contract is created delineating what each person will do to help the student reach his or her goals. Time is set aside throughout the year to assess progress in these goals, and, as needed, reframe the goal or set new ones. Subsequent report cards often refer to a student's observations about his or her progress toward these goals.

One of the most powerful progress reports is a portion of the final sixth grade report, which is partially written by the students themselves. Students write letters to the homeroom teacher describing the strengths they have developed while at New City, areas that still need work and how to address them in the future, as well as the most important things they have learned about themselves and the memories they will carry forward. The teachers respond in writing to these letters, and the full document is shared with students' parents. These letters are always enjoyable to read because they show how much a student has truly learned not just in reading, writing, and math, but also in ways that give a glimpse of who this young person will become.

Each child has a portfolio that reflects all intelligences, which is passed on from year to year. Our portfolios do not include only best work or routine papers and tests (though those are there). Our portfolios contain published stories as well as rough drafts, pieces of art work, self-assessment sheets, material made by sewing, physical fitness awards, or a student's musical compositions. Much of what happens in the classroom, and much of what needs to be assessed, cannot be confined to paper and fit conveniently into a portfolio, so each student also has a video file, an audiotape, and photographs capturing a myriad of accomplishments: role-plays, large projects, costumes they created, their finish time on the mile run, dances they performed, and interviews they conducted. All items have an accompanying Reflection Sheet on which the child tells why the piece is in the portfolio. The teacher also has the option of including an item, and the Reflection Sheet will indicate that the teacher, rather than the child, chose it.

To more easily see growth over time, some things are required to be in all students' portfolios. In addition to a videotape, there is an audiotape on which the student reads a book of his or her choice, or for the preprimary grades, the student talks; these are taped in September and again in May. The student reflects on the differences he or she notices.

An annual self-portrait is also required, as well as an annual autobiography. A Portfolio Night is held in the spring; parents are invited to come and view the portfolio and listen to their child discuss his or her own progress and explain why each piece was included. An important by-product of using portfolios is that the focus is squarely placed on what a student *can* do, not on what he or she *cannot* do. Parents come away from this evening with a solid understanding of the multiple ways in which their children are smart!

ASSESSMENTS SEND A POWERFUL MESSAGE

It is important to remember that whatever is assessed and reported on not only communicates to students and parents alike what is valued but also tells us what is important. If we only report on standardized test results, the message is that only the knowledge and skills that can be assessed with paper and pencil are important. That does a disservice to our students. Albert Einstein expressed it well: "Not everything that counts, can be counted, and not everything that can be counted, counts."

How do you shift your assessment focus? Start by answering the following:

- Do my methods of assessment empower my students?
- Do I learn about students' personal interests, goals, and academic needs?
- Do my methods have a direct connection to what is being taught, as well as what students are learning?
- Are the opportunities for evaluation embedded in my instructional activities?
- Do my assessment methods help students learn?

Just as children do not all learn in the same way, they cannot be assessed in a uniform fashion. Teachers must seek to assess their students' learning in ways that will give an accurate overview of the strengths and challenges of *each* individual child. The type of learning that is being focused on through the multiple intelligences cannot be assessed through traditional methods. It is true that many of the alternative forms of assessment just described are time-consuming and more difficult to evaluate; however, regardless of how we define intelligence, they are necessary if we are to truly capture the whole child.

> Just as children do not all learn in the same way, they cannot be assessed in a uniform fashion.

New City School Portfolio Reflection Sheet

Title of Work _____   Name _____

(or description) _____   Date _____

Teacher _____

This work exhibits the following of my multiple intelligences:

- ☐ Logical-Mathematical
- ☐ Linguistic
- ☐ Spatial
- ☐ Musical
- ☐ Bodily-Kinesthetic
- ☐ Naturalist
- ☐ Interpersonal
- ☐ Intrapersonal

REFLECTION

What I like about this piece is

_____

_____

_____

_____

If I could change or have done one thing differently with this piece, I would

_____

_____

_____

_____

PRODUCT

I worked on this project:

- ☐ Alone
- ☐ With the help of a teacher and/or friend
- ☐ In a group
- ☐ Other

I have chosen to include this piece in my portfolio because:

- ☐ It is work that I am proud of
- ☐ It shows my learning process
- ☐ I have done my personal best
- ☐ I feel that it is creative and/or original
- ☐ I was asked to put this piece in by _____

Comments

_____

_____

_____

_____

This work shows that I know about

_____

_____

_____

_____

New City School, 5209 Waterman Avenue, St. Louis, MO 63108
Progress Report

Name _____ Date _____

Attendance: Absent _____ Tardy _____

Teachers: Sally Boggeman/Susie Chasnoff/Carla Carroll/
Chris Wallach

Key: ED = Exceeding Developmental Expectations

DA = Developing Appropriately

AC = Area of Concern

= Needs Added Attention

Intrapersonal Development
Can self-access: understands and shares own feelings

Reporting period:	1	2	3

I. Confidence
- Is comfortable taking a position different from the peer group
- Engages in appropriate risk-taking behaviors
- Is comfortable in both leader and follower roles
- Copes with frustration and failures
- Demonstrates a positive and accurate self-concept

II. Motivation
- Demonstrates internal motivation
- Is actively involved in the learning process
- Shows curiosity
- Shows tenacity
- Exhibits creativity

III. Problem Solving
- Shows good judgment
- Asks for help when needed
- Can generate possible hypotheses and solutions
- Shows perseverance in solving problems
- Accepts and learns from feedback

IV. Responsibility
- Accepts responsibility for own actions
- Accepts responsibility for materials and belongings
- Handles transitions and changes well
- Accepts limits in work and play situations
- Uses an appropriate sense of humor

V. Effort and Work Habits
- Participates in activities and discussions ....
- Works through assignments and activities carefully and thoroughly ....
- Keeps notebook, desk, and locker/cubby organized ....
- Has age-appropriate attention span ....
- Works independently ....
- Follows written and oral directions ....
- Listens attentively ....
- Uses time effectively ....

Interpersonal Development
Can successfully interact with others

I. Appreciation for Diversity
- Makes decisions based on appropriate information, rather than stereotypes
- Understands the perspectives of others, including those of other races and cultures
- Shows concern and empathy for others
- Respects the individuality of others

II. Teamwork
- Cooperates with peers and adults
- Works at conflict resolution
- Behaves responsibly in groups
- Demonstrates an ability to compromise
- Expresses feelings and gives feedback constructively and appropriately

13

Learning Centers in the Kindergarten Classroom

BY MARY DALY

Photograph: Patti Gabriel

Is today "Free Choice Day" or "Partner Day"? Do I want to paint a picture of what I know or make up a song about it? Can I make a plan with some friends or work alone? Will I write a story or practice motor skills? Are there any centers I haven't tried yet, or can I go to my favorite one? All these questions and more can be answered during MI Choice Time in the kindergarten!

More than a few years ago, our kindergarten team looked at the use of learning centers as a way of integrating an MI approach to our curriculum. Our classroom had gone through a metamorphosis of sorts when we first began to look at Gardner's theory and how it related to our program. We had used the center approach for years and now were asking how we could make sure that it would give children the opportunity to use all of the intelligences to further learning. As a result, we have twenty-one learning centers in our shared, four-teacher space, which means there are twenty-one opportunities to develop all eight of the intelligences on a daily basis. Our challenge was to provide activities and lessons that incorporate the different intelligences in meaningful learning experiences while also allowing children to demonstrate genuine understanding of concepts.

USING LEARNING CENTERS TO ADDRESS MI

We use MI terminology in the naming of some of the centers to help children become familiar with the intelligences, and we group the centers under the headings of the different intelligences, using the Personal Intelligences (Interpersonal and Intrapersonal) as an "umbrella" over the other six. Important components in our center approach are the goal-setting and reflective pieces, which enable students to think about their own strengths, challenges, and choices. The following are some examples of the MI centers we offer:

- Linguistic: Alphabet Activities, Alphabet Board, Listening, Person of the Week, Library, and Computer Centers
- Logical-Mathematical: Games, Logical-Mathematical, and Puzzle Centers
- Spatial: Manipulatives, Wet Art, and Dry Art Centers
- Musical: Imagination Place and Musical Listening Centers
- Naturalist: Science and Naturalist Centers
- Bodily-Kinesthetic: B-K, Workbench, Filling Station, Blocks, and Writing Centers

Every other Monday the centers change, and we spend time introducing and modeling the activities in each center before children can set to work. Each center has a sign that shows the name of the center, the intelligence symbol (our school has devised a set of symbols for the intelligences that are used school-wide; they appear throughout these pages), and how many children can work at the center. We group the centers by intelligence, and we label different areas of the room with the names of one of the intelligences. These area signs hang from our ceiling with a brief explanation of how this intelligence may manifest itself in young children. For example: "I am SPATIAL. I like to paint, draw and work with clay. I enjoy looking at maps. I like to play with puzzles and complete mazes." Within this area are all the spatial centers. These signs also play an important role in educating our parents about the multiple intelligences.

We have nineteen centers that accommodate two or more students at a time, thus providing a more interpersonal focus. However, it is important to keep in mind that even when a child is working in an interpersonal situation, it does not mean the child is interacting with others. Each may be working completely as an individual, engaging in parallel play.

We also created two areas in our room that address the Personal Intelligences exclusively. These are not centers, but areas for children to relax or take a break from the busy atmosphere of "Choice Time." The "Social Table," a large round table in the center of our room, became a place for children to meet and just enjoy each other. This table can accommodate up to eight children, more than any other center in the room. We put out a variety of materials (pencils, paper, crayons, markers, tape, staplers, clay, puzzles, and so on) for the children to use creatively (no directions), or they can just visit with each other. The materials change throughout the year. During our study of world holidays, for example, we put out snacks, clothing, books, and decorations from other cultures for the children to play with at this table. We also use this table for children to do special projects with a parent helper. We have also created a "Me Place" in one of our "turrets," to support students' Intrapersonal Intelligence. (Yes, our classroom has a castle motif!) In this area can be found a big soft beanbag chair and a mirror on the wall; in this space we also rotate objects such as a book, a telephone, a doll, a stuffed animal, binoculars, or a puzzle. Neither of these spaces is ever assigned, and children are free to visit them at their own discretion.

RECORD KEEPING AND REFLECTION

Record keeping is a very important component in the success of our MI Centers. When considering what method to use, we asked ourselves: Will students always choose to use their strongest intelligences? Will they usually work with a partner or usually be alone? How can we keep track of the choices students make, and how can we help students be aware of their choices as well? Structuring the learning centers to be as child-oriented and self-managing as possible frees the teacher to do more observations and have more one-on-one interactions with the students.

Previously the teachers assigned all center work by the use of a "Job Board." When children finished their assigned jobs they were free to go to other centers. We completely reconfigured this by reducing it to a sheet of paper with a miniature center sign (an exact replica) for each center on it, thus giving children the words and a picture for each center. Each child gets her or his own "Job Sheet," which is laminated so that they can be used for several months. We give the children the

These signs also play an important role in educating our parents about the multiple intelligences.

However, it is important to keep in mind that even when a child is working in an interpersonal situation, it does not mean the child is interacting with others. Each may be working completely as an individual, engaging in parallel play.

Structuring the learning centers to be as child-oriented and self-managing as possible frees the teacher to do more observations and have more one-on-one interactions with the students.

task of choosing centers for some of our Choice Time each week, thus encouraging goal-setting.

On Mondays, students choose a job; teachers assign a job for Tuesday and Wednesday, and on Thursday the students are given "Partner Jobs." Sometimes the teacher chooses the partner and the job; sometimes students are allowed to choose. ("Partner Jobs" mean that the student and their partner go to the center, do the job, and check it with a teacher *together*.) Fridays are "free"—*if* you have completed all your assigned centers during the week. This becomes a self-motivating tool; the children love Free Friday! As students complete activities at the centers during this time, they tell/show a teacher what they have done, and the teacher marks the center on the sheet as completed. We have two choice times each day, and we begin the year with a scavenger hunt to familiarize the students with the names and locations of the centers. When the "real" work begins, teachers assign only one job a day. As the children become able to manage their time and complete assigned tasks, two, three or even four jobs are assigned. This enables us to individualize this time for each student. The time a student spends in each center varies with the activities and expectations for each individual child.

The teachers have developed a master sheet with each student's name and a grid of all the centers. It has columns that address the personal intelligences, with headings such as "works alone," "works with a partner," or "works in a group." There is also a space to note how students solve problems. On these sheets, teachers use their own method of noting progress, choices, challenges, and so on, and it has become a quick and easy checklist for tracking and noting observations about each student that fits easily on a clipboard to be carried around during Choice Time each day. Teachers also take random photographs of each student working in a center (about once a week) and use this collection of pictures to help students reflect on where they go and what choices they are making during this time. Children will look over these pictures and/or conference with the teacher during our "Quiet Time." At family conference times the teachers use these photos and notes as they share information gathered over time with the child's family.

MI has changed the way we view children, the way we teach, and the way we use learning centers.

Incorporating the eight intelligences into the learning centers has been an ongoing challenge for our team. We know that there will always be new ways to address the intelligences when creating activities to enhance learning. MI has changed the way we view children, the way we teach, and the way we use learning centers. Any of the kindergarten teachers will tell you that they would gladly give up any other part of the day rather than give up their choice times!

14

Photograph: Patti Gabriel

Genuine
Understanding

BY THOMAS R. HOERR

Assessment is the engine that drives curriculum and instruction. What is measured and how it is measured determines what is taught and how it is taught.

But too often when we assess, we merely focus on acquisition of information and mastery of skills. Students learn enough to parrot the answer or pass the test, but they do not truly understand what is taught. Ask someone to solve "What is 3/4 divided by 5/6?" for example. Although many won't know how to do this, a mathematically proficient teenager will know enough to invert and multiply. The computation is now 3/4 times 6/5 and can be readily solved. However, if you then ask why that process works, what was taking place when the numerator and denominator were inverted, it turns out that very few individuals can respond correctly. Similarly, ask why it is warmer in the summer than the winter, and chances are you'll hear that it's because the Earth is closer to the sun (rather than the correct answer, that the angle at which the sun's rays hit the Earth has changed). What these examples tell us is that the respondents no longer know—probably because they didn't truly learn—the concepts that they were taught in school, concepts that they and their teachers thought they understood. This lack of comprehension prevents other learning from taking place. Because assessment drives curriculum and instruction, the extensive use of multiple-choice tests and paper and pencil exams has limited what happens in the classroom to students working to master information, not to comprehend concepts.

A NEW WAY TO LOOK AT UNDERSTANDING

Howard Gardner and his colleagues at Harvard's Project Zero have developed a model for assessment called "Genuine Understanding" (sometimes referred to as "Teaching for Understanding"). While Genuine Understanding (GU) should be the goal whether or not MI is being used, pursuing GU works particularly well with the multiple entry points approach to learning that is the basis of MI. The two approaches, MI and GU, complement one another.

In his book *The Unschooled Mind*, Gardner says, "Such performances [of Genuine Understanding] occur when students are able to take information and skills that they have learned in school or other settings and apply them flexibly and appropriately in a new or at least somewhat unanticipated setting." David Perkins and Tina Blythe, in the February 1994 issue of *Education Leadership*, offer examples of GU: ". . . being able to do a variety of thought-demanding things with a topic—like explaining, finding evidence and examples, generalizing, applying, analogizing, and representing the topic in a new way." At New City, our concise definition of GU is "using skills or information in new and novel settings."

Rather than asking for the "right" (and often simple) answer, GU requires the student to synthesize his or her understanding and produce a conceptually complex response. Lower-order skills such as mastering math facts or dividing words into syllables, although important to a child's development and necessary, do not lend themselves to GU. Seeking GU in assessment, then, enriches the curriculum by ensuring that what is taught goes beyond the basics.

A PERFORMANCE PERSPECTIVE TO ASSESSMENT

It is perhaps easiest and most appropriate for a student to demonstrate that he or she possesses GU through a project, exhibition, or presentation (PEP). By definition, GU is a synthesis of skills and/or knowledge, not a specific skill or a particular piece of knowledge, so a PEP approach readily lends itself to this kind of evaluation. (A PEP approach also helps students develop their interpersonal intelligence, as it requires them to consider how they are perceived and received by others.)

GU is not limited to a PEP approach, however. GU can also be assessed by students responding orally or in writing to complex questions. For example, the question "How might the infrastructure and economy of the United States be different today if the initial settlements had taken place in San Diego, not Plymouth?" requires specific knowledge and GU about migration patterns, economic development, the effect of geography on migration and settlement, cultures, and even race relations. Although children's developmental levels vary, and a third grader's response to this question would be less sophisticated than that of a sixth grader, it is important for the teacher to go beyond the simple "The U.S. capital would be in California" answer and elicit a deeper level of analysis and understanding.

Another example of a GU problem that could elicit a written or oral response is, "Is it a better economic decision to lease or buy a car that costs $1,000 if you have $3,000 in the bank? How might that answer change if one started with only $1,500 in the bank?" As in the U.S. settlement example, the leasing question requires an understanding of many variables and how they interact. To respond correctly, the student will need to do more than simply compute the principal and interest payments of purchasing and compare them to leasing. At a minimum, she will also need to consider the effect of lost (or gained) potential earning from the savings in her bank, the cost of auto taxes and upkeep, the different effect of these payments on her income taxes, and the merits of leasing versus purchasing at the end of the lease.

Demonstrating GU for the settlement and leasing questions could be done orally or in writing, but the responses would be richer (and would be more likely to incorporate MI) if shown through a PEP approach. Answering the settlement question in narrative form requires strong linguistic skills; allowing the student to present her response through a project, exhibition, or presentation includes linguistics and capitalizes on her other MI strengths. Similarly, although formulas could be used to demonstrate GU of the leasing question, allowing a student to share her knowledge through a performance enables her to use her various abilities in MI. The PEP Approach is also more "intelligence-fair" (Krechevsky, Gardner, and Hoerr, 1994) by allowing students to use the relevant intelligence(s) to demonstrate understanding.

AN INTEGRAL PART OF CURRICULUM

Although the settlement and leasing examples are specific questions that address GU, it is far preferable to incorporate GU on an ongoing basis throughout the curriculum as part of an overall theme or generative issue. If, for example, a unit on transportation begins on Labor Day and continues to Thanksgiving, in addition to planning for the final PEP in which students would demonstrate their understanding of the entire unit, the teacher should be asking what could be done along the way, each day, to ensure that children are gaining GU. What are the smaller clusters of concepts, covered throughout the unit, for which GU can be shown? In their daily and unit planning, teachers should ask themselves how the curriculum could be designed differently to lead to GU; they should not be satisfied with their students' development ending with acquisition of knowledge or mastery of skills. Assessment of GU should be viewed as an integral, ongoing part of curriculum and instruction.

GENERATIVE TOPICS

For this kind of curriculum planning and instruction, GU is best seen as part of generative topics and overall themes. Generative topics are central to what is being taught and are amenable to students making connections among various subject matter areas. They are rich with possibilities and are interesting to both students and teachers. A generative topic for primary grade students might be, "How has technology helped and harmed us?" For intermediate grade students, asking, "How does geography shape culture?" is rife with possibilities. Creating semester-or year-long themes and topics and finding ways to integrate skills and content into these overall themes and topics makes learning more meaningful, integrated, and interesting. It also reflects the real world, in which disciplines meld together and are not separated artificially by a sound of a bell or by textbooks being put away. After generative issues are in place, specific goals for understanding ("students will understand . . .") can be developed.

An orientation to GU means that teachers design and evaluate their curriculum to determine learner outcomes; they do more than teach from a script. GU orientation also has implications for student behaviors. Students, rather than simply responding to the teacher's request for the right answer or filling in the appropriate small circles, must define the problem, choose the appropriate routes to the solution, and demonstrate their understanding. This process of teaching for understanding is not always easy, but it is always beneficial. If we want our students to learn, we must teach to and assess their genuine understanding. To do less does them a disservice.

> Generative topics are central to what is being taught and are amenable to students making connections among various subject matter areas. They are rich with possibilities and are interesing to both students and teachers.

> If we want our students to learn, we must teach to and assess their genuine understanding. To do less does them a disservice.

Part 3

Multiple Intelligences, Parents, and Teachers

15

Photograph: Patti Gabriel

Communicating About MI

BY BETSY BLANKENSHIP

For the theory of Multiple Intelligences to be fully implemented, all constituencies in the school need to understand and embrace the model. This means that not only the teachers and administrators but also young students, active parents, and busy board members—all need some knowledge of MI for the implementation to be as successful as possible. Sharing this information with all members of the school community is an important and critical step in the process of becoming a strong MI community.

BRINGING EVERYONE ON BOARD

Communication must be multifaceted; schools need to take every opportunity to instruct students' families and make MI come alive for them. That means finding ways to learn about MI beyond just reading about it. We want parents to also learn about MI by experiencing it—just as their children do.

> We want parents to also learn about MI by experiencing it—just as their children do.

As our teachers began to study MI, we began our communication with parents. Our first information came through the weekly newsletters sent by the head of school. Through these missives Tom Hoerr shared stories of our journey, gave information on the books we were reading, and recommended sources for the parents to explore as well.

As we opened the doors on the first day of school in our initial year of implementation, parents and students were greeted by a giant bulletin board proclaiming: "New City School—Where We Are Smart in Many Different Ways." The bulletin board had pictures and explanations representing each of the intelligences. It was eye-catching and succinct; it grabbed parents' and visitors' attention. A companion board had pictures of all the staff members using one of their strongest intelligences. These welcoming boards helped to set the tone for what was happening throughout the building.

We also asked teachers to use the parent bulletin boards near each of their classrooms to spread the MI message as well. They found many ways of doing this. Younger students made collages by cutting out pictures of people who were using their various intelligences; older children mind-mapped their personal strengths. Some classes posted graphs of students' preferred intelligences; others created and displayed symbols to represent the intelligences; and still others wrote stories, drew pictures, or posted photos of children acting out the intelligences. In addition, teachers made available articles and books that could be used as resources for the parents. One could get an education about MI and its use simply by walking down our halls!

To continue the education process for parents, we held parent evenings where we gave presentations on the various intelligences. To make these as relevant as possible for parents, we had examples of student work and even some student demonstrations and presentations. (We all know that engaging students in such events helps encourage parents to attend.) These events were another way to inform parents of what we were doing, and they provided a place where parents could ask MI questions.

KEEPING THE INFORMATION FLOWING

One of the important lessons we learned in our implementation and continued use of MI was that communicating with and educating parents, kids, and teachers was an ongoing process. To ensure their understanding about MI, we continued to use the walls as an instructional tool. Bulletin boards outside our classrooms were not only used to educate at the beginning of our MI work, but continue to do so twenty years later. These boards not only tell about upcoming events, daily schedules, and kids' work, but also have MI articles posted, list the intelligences, and present photos labeled with MI terms showing the children at work and play. A large section of wall in the main hall is covered with pocket folders with copies of *MI* magazine and journal articles written by our faculty members. Parents and visitors are encouraged to help themselves to these articles. Visitors are still greeted each year with a MI bulletin board when they enter the building, but we don't stop there.

The walls themselves can tell quite an MI story. We do not believe it is sufficient to just post student work—however attractive it may be (and it is attractive!). Rather, all work that is displayed is also accompanied by an explanation of the piece, telling why it was done, what intelligences were used in conjunction with the activity, and what grade level objective it addresses. If your school uses state standards as a benchmark, this is an ideal avenue for educating parents about how these projects directly relate to state requirements.

As teachers prepare for their annual fall Open House, they are encouraged to look for ways to actively involve the parents in some aspect of MI. Kindergarten parents receive a list of the centers in the classroom along with the explanation of how each one is related to an intelligence. Then at Open House, the parents actually have time to take part in a short Choice Time, allowing them to experience several of the activities. A fourth grade class has parents reflect on their own MI strengths by filling out a short questionnaire on likes and dislikes, while parents of second graders may learn about place value by using their Bodily-Kinesthetic intelligence. As the parents experience the connection between skill development and MI, they are better able to understand the importance of MI in their child's learning.

Just as we used school-wide weekly newsletters to begin the process of educating our parents when we began our MI quest, those newsletters remain an important component of the ongoing education as well. The head of school uses these weekly electronic letters to share resources, show examples of MI in action, explain curriculum, post photos of students using their various intelligences in activities throughout the school, or explain upcoming events related to MI at New City School. Recent parent letters have contained photos of students presenting puppet shows to show the causes of the Civil War, students using their Bodily-Kinesthetic Intelligence to make their bodies form a clock's minute and

One of the important lessons we learned in our implementation and continued use of MI was that communicating with and educating parents, kids, and teachers was an ongoing process.

As the parents experience the connection between skill development and MI, they are better able to understand the importance of MI in their child's learning.

hour hands to show their understanding of Spanish numbers, students performing in *Peter Pan*, and students using their Linguistic Intelligence to present monuments they created to depict westward expansion. (You can see recent weekly e-Parent Letters at www.newcityschool.org.) In addition, each grade level also sends home a weekly e-newsletter, and these too are filled with references to MI, photos, and explanations of activities completed in the preceding week or scheduled for the next week. Teachers are asked to make a concerted effort to use MI terminology and give concrete examples of MI in action.

STUDENT ASSESSMENT AND MI

Student assessment is an important tool not only in understanding how a child is developing academically and socially but also for furthering the understanding of teachers, parents, and students about a child's MI strengths and the areas needing additional focus. Student assessment and reporting take many forms at New City School and are informative for parents, students, and teachers alike.

Our report card (we title it our Progress Report) is a multipage document that is sent to parents three times a year. Regardless of the age of the child, the first page of the report deals solely with Interpersonal and Intrapersonal development. We believe that who you are is more important than what you know, so sharing this vitally important information is how we begin our written report to parents. Each portion of the report card (sections focus on the personal, Linguistic, and Logical-Mathematical intelligences) includes rubrics and narrative teacher comments. Often these comments highlight the student's strengths in the area of the multiple intelligences: "Barry did an excellent job on his mural piece, showcasing his Spatial Intelligence. His piece captured his commitment to diversity and the depth of his thinking." "Marley often uses her Bodily-Kinesthetic Intelligence to help herself problem-solve in math." "We have found that if Joe talks things out first, using his Interpersonal Intelligence, he can conceptualize his writing better." In addition, the reports have a page from each of the specialists whom the child sees, giving parents detailed information on progress in the Spatial, Bodily-Kinesthetic, Musical, and Naturalist intelligences. As students get older, teachers often weave student reflections and other Intrapersonal comments into their narrative on a child's report.

Parents also participate in four parent-teacher conferences each year. The last two of those are fairly typical, with the teachers and the parents engaging in dialogue about the contents of the report and student growth. However, the first two conferences of the year are different. During the first parent-teacher conference, held in the third week of the school year, we ask parents to do most of the talking. This "Intake Conference" is a wonderful way to open communication with the parents and to learn more about a child's life outside of school hours. We ask parents to share how they see their child's strengths and weaknesses, to talk about their child's activities, hobbies, special needs, and special talents. We ask if there are any intelligences the children might exhibit

We believe that who you are is more important than what you know.

or be involved in at home that we haven't seen at school. Not only does this conference give us wonderful information about the child early in the school year, but it also sets the tone for the parent-teacher communication throughout the year.

The second conference of the year, held in November, is special for students in grades two through six because during this conference the students are also involved. Prior to the conference, each child has worked with his or her teacher to set a personal goal and an academic goal. For the first fifteen minutes of the thirty-minute conference the student meets with his or her parents and teacher and shares the goals and strategies to achieve them. This personal reflection and discussion with the teacher and parents is an integral component in the development of the personal intelligences.

At the end of almost all units of study there is a culminating activity to which parents are invited. This allows the students to share their knowledge with others—peers, students from other grade levels, or parents. It has become a tradition that many parents come to school for these events. These projects, exhibitions, or presentations (PEPS) serve as a vehicle for assessing the students' knowledge base, their genuine understanding, and their ability to reflect on their own growth. In the year in which this book was written, for example, we saw a play presented by fifth graders that captured the history, music, poetry, and feeling of the Civil War era, and the fourth graders become the citizens who made a difference in the world in their Living Museum. We also saw third graders share their research papers, dioramas, and oral reports on the Native American tribes they studied, and kindergartners shared the life-sized bodies they created through the year. These special events are another way to educate parents and let them see the impact of students' learning in a variety of ways.

Another event that builds on reflection and sharing is Portfolio Night. On this May evening, the students share the contents of their portfolios with their parents. Each item that is placed in the portfolio has a reflection sheet attached. These sheets allow the students to reflect on why an item is placed in the portfolio, what the student might do differently if he or she were to do this activity again, and what intelligences were used in completing this project. By sharing their artifacts with their parents, they revisit the activities and have a chance to express their thoughts on the pieces in their portfolio. This evening allows parents to gain a deeper understanding of the work that has been done at school and to see the level at which their child is able to reflect and critique.

Communicating with parents and helping them understand the process of MI can only strengthen the program and the commitment to that program. Certainly, not all communication is MI-related, but communication is a critical key in involving parents in the school community. After all, children learn best when the school and parents work together!

This personal reflection and discussion with the teacher and parents is an integral component in the development of the personal intelligences.

Communicating with parents and helping them understand the process of MI can only strengthen the program and the commitment to that program.

16

Photograph: Patti Gabriel

Getting Started in the Classroom with MI

BY CHRISTINE WALLACH

It *is* possible to organize instruction to address the intelligences, follow state and district guidelines, and manage the logistics of students making choices.

The state and the district have a curriculum and guidelines that I am required to follow, and I have twenty-five children in my classroom. Some of them are discipline problems. How am I supposed to address all the intelligences, meet my district and state mandates, and manage students in that kind of setting?

Variations on this question are often asked at the end of any presentation on Multiple Intelligences, and it seems only logical that some readers may be asking similar questions right now. Take heart! It *is* possible to organize instruction to address the intelligences, follow state and district guidelines, and manage the logistics of students making choices.

GETTING STARTED

The easiest way to begin is to look carefully at your existing program to see what you are *already* doing that reflects MI. For example, Language Arts—the Linguistic Intelligence—is a part of every elementary school curriculum. Perhaps you already ask children to write in a journal as part of their language arts instruction. By asking students to reflect on topics and how they relate to those topics while writing in their journals, you begin to address the Intrapersonal Intelligence. By increasing the specificity of the writing prompt, the students will develop the ability to focus their reflection. Asking students whether they are aware of their own thinking is very different from asking them how they liked the assignment, as the former begins to address their Intrapersonal Intelligence.

By asking students to reflect on topics and how they relate to those topics while writing in their journals, you begin to address the Intrapersonal Intelligence.

Next, examine the way you present information to the students and how they share what they have learned with you and each other. For example, how often do students work with manipulatives or other hands-on activities? This is using the Bodily-Kinesthetic Intelligence. Do your students do projects? Often projects incorporate one or more of the intelligences. Are there Spatial components? Do your students make presentations to the class? These may involve the Interpersonal Intelligence if the students are reading to the audience, observing, and responding to feedback. Do the students listen to music during the day or learn songs? Both activities are starting points for the Musical Intelligence.

Good teachers have always used the principles of MI in their instruction.

Often MI is present in our classrooms—good teachers have always used the principles of MI in their instruction—and reflecting and focusing on the intelligences enables us to make them a more conscious and integral part of our classroom. With that foundation, you can push a bit further in enabling students to use all of their intelligences.

READING INSTRUCTION

Many components of the reading program lend themselves to the use of MI. Do your students discuss their reading in a Literature Circle? Students are using their Interpersonal Intelligence when they use active listening to give feedback to other members of the group and think about how to disagree on points in ways that others will listen. Of course, often teachers need to teach effective ways for this to take place, just as they teach effective ways to decode words or paragraphs. When students are asked to represent their visualization of a passage in the text, they are using their Spatial Intelligence. Book projects offer ways for students to make choices, especially when they are given the option of working within intelligences they consider to be their strengths to share their understanding of a book. Posters use the Spatial Intelligence, and during Reader's Theater students use their Bodily-Kinesthetic Intelligence. Puppet shows apply the Spatial and Bodily-Kinesthetic intelligences.

Learning Centers based on shared reading can be related to the intelligences. They are easy to create and facilitate, and they allow the teacher to differentiate instruction. Some are assigned to class members based on individual needs; other centers are given as a choice. To help develop students' sense of responsibility as well as Linguistic and Intrapersonal intelligences, write the instructions for the center on a piece of laminated construction paper, place all the supplies needed for a particular center in a plastic dish tub, and place it in a handy location in the room. It's then up to the students to get supplies from the tub and return to their desk or work in the area where the tub was placed. With older and younger children, identifying and beginning the task can be an important part of problem-solving. A Centers approach can help students develop their Intrapersonal Intelligence so that they know how they need to organize themselves and maintain their focus.

> A Centers approach can help students develop their Intrapersonal Intelligence so that they know how they need to organize themselves and maintain their focus.

Shared Reading Centers can be created for many books. As an example, one book that our fifth grade teachers have used is *Meet Addy* by Connie Porter. In *Meet Addy*, the main character, Addy, experiences the horror of life as a slave and the uncertainties of the escape to freedom. This is one of the books in the American Girls series and is a wonderful example of historical fiction. The teachers created MI centers to support the study of story elements, vocabulary, and comprehension skills; similar centers could be developed for almost any book that you would read with your class. For example:

- Students use the Intrapersonal Intelligence by comparing themselves to Addy. How would they feel if they were in her situation? One particularly good discussion starter is a statement made by Addy's father: "We're free on the inside." The Intrapersonal and Logical-Mathematical intelligences come together if students are asked to do this comparing and contrasting by creating a Venn diagram.

- To address the Musical Intelligence, the students can learn the song, "Follow the Drinking Gourd." An interpretation of its meaning helps children connect to the setting of the story. Students who are adept at the piano can use sheet music to play the notes. They can become teachers to the rest of the class in a quick lesson on how to read music. Other students sing the song with the accompaniment of the keyboard players.
- For the students who choose to work in the Logical-Mathematical Intelligence, offer the option of drawing a map of the route that Addy took to find freedom to reinforce the setting of the story. They can look at a real map of the area as a reference and draw a map that includes a key, compass, and scale of miles.
- To address the Spatial Intelligence, students can build a model of one of the forms of transportation that was used on the Underground Railroad.
- For the Bodily-Kinesthetic Intelligence, students can play a game of charades using vocabulary words from the story.
- Those who want to work within the Interpersonal Intelligence are instructed to work with a partner to conduct an interview. One student plays the part of Addy, the other student the part of the interviewer.
- To address the Naturalist Intelligence, students research cotton, including pulling apart a cotton boll to try to remove the seeds.

Students are given the opportunity to work within their strengths to share what they are learning from the book and to reinforce and strengthen intelligences through the choices they make. Students can work with teammates at many of these centers, and teachers can develop the Interpersonal Intelligence for all students by asking them to think about what their teammates want and how they should interact. These suggestions are provided simply as examples. Similar activities can be developed to accompany any story or book.

MATHEMATICS AND MI

There are many wonderful ways to begin bringing other intelligences into the mathematics curriculum. Again, begin by thinking of the ways in which you are already using the intelligences. During problem-based instruction, if students consult others, they are using the Interpersonal Intelligence. When they visualize and represent their thinking with a diagram, they are using the Spatial Intelligence. There are many children's picture story books available that allow students to use their Linguistic Intelligence to solve problems. For example, the book *Ten Little Rabbits* by Virginia Grossman and Sylvia Long can be used as an entry point for a lesson on consecutive number problems. Musical notation can help children understand fraction concepts. Math programs like *Box It and Bag It* or *Math Their Way* in the primary grades or *Connected Math* in the intermediate grades already address many of the intelligences. When math is experiential, students can pull from all of their intelligences and have opportunities to work from their strengths.

There are many wonderful ways to begin bringing other intelligences into the mathematics curriculum.

SCIENCE INSTRUCTION

Your science curriculum probably already addresses many of the intelligences too. Much of the scientific process uses the Logical-Mathematical and Naturalist intelligences. When students are involved in experimentation, they must think logically and use their mathematical skills to collect and organize data. Linguistic skills are used when student are reading text books to collect and report on information or when communicating findings. In addition, many schools require students to work in groups during labs. When students are analyzing and responding to their work within a team, the Interpersonal Intelligence can be developed.

To add MI to your lessons, begin by thinking about the concept or principle that you want the students to learn, then design activities or entry points into the lesson that allow the use of many intelligences. For example, during a unit on pollination and the adaptations of plants for pollination, students observe and classify flowers by shape, color, and size as an entry point; this uses the Naturalist Intelligence. They paint flower pictures that detail the structure of the flower and its adaptations for a pollinator, using their Spatial Intelligence. And they use Model Magic, sitting around big tables where they blend and share colors, to create a flower that shows these adaptations. During that activity they use many different intelligences, including the Bodily-Kinesthetic and Interpersonal. Consider what you are already doing and think about ways to expand on the strengths within your pedagogy.

> Begin by thinking about the concept or principle that you want the students to learn, then design activities or entry points into the lesson that allow the use of many intelligences.

> Consider what you are already doing and think about ways to expand on the strengths within your pedagogy.

SOCIAL STUDIES INSTRUCTION

The intelligences can easily be incorporated into an existing social studies curriculum. When studying other countries, use the intelligences to address cultural differences through art, music, dance, and tradition. Allow students to refine their knowledge of other countries by comparing and contrasting other cultures to their own. Add traditional dances or games to address the Bodily-Kinesthetic Intelligence. Listen to music as a starting point for the Musical Intelligence. Folk tales add a Linguistic component, and map study is an introduction to the Logical-Mathematical Intelligence. The study of climates and biomes within a country taps the Naturalist Intelligence.

If your social studies curriculum is based on American history, the intelligences work beautifully to expand students' thinking, using primary sources that come from others' use of their MI. The students gain historical perspective and become historians during the analysis. Colonial era portraiture gives a view of life during that period. Songs also share beliefs and views about historical events. The song *Jenny Jenkins*, which many children have heard since they were toddlers, tells about superstitions related to the color of clothing a woman might wear and comes from early immigrants; *The Trappan'd Maiden* tells of life as an indentured servant; and *The Rich Lady Over the Sea* creates a metaphor explaining the feelings of the colonial patriots before the Revolutionary War. Pictures, posters, charts, and other displays also allow children to use other intelligences to learn about history and draw their own conclusions. By examining their own thinking and the inferences they make, students learn something about themselves and develop their Intrapersonal Intelligence.

It is also important to create opportunities for students to be assessed using intelligences other than the Linguistic. Students might create a mind-map to show the causes of the Revolution, use a Venn diagram to assess a colonial-era portrait that illustrates their understanding of life within that period, or design a weighted timeline. These kinds of activities give the teacher much more information about a student's understanding of events and allows students to use their Logical-Mathematical Intelligence.

JUST GET STARTED

The most important thing is to just get started. It is neither necessary nor feasible to address all the intelligences in every lesson that you do or in every concept, skill, and fact that you teach. The more important consideration is to make sure that sometime during the day you have opportunities for those students who are strong in intelligences other than the Linguistic and Logical-Mathematical to be successful and use those intelligences. Start small and then build on your accomplishments. Work from your strengths as a teacher and within your own guidelines. Your reward will be the enthusiasm of your students and the growth you will witness as your students find a new love of learning.

The most important thing is to just get started.

Bibliography

Armstrong, Thomas. *In Their Own Way.* New York: St. Martin's Press, 1987.

———. *Multiple Intelligences in the Classroom.* Alexandria: ASCD Press, 2009.

Atwell, Nancie. *In the Middle: New Understandings About Writing, Reading, and Learning.* Portsmouth: Boynton/Cook, 1998.

Barth, Roland. *Improving Schools from Within.* San Francisco: Jossey-Bass, 1990.

Blythe, Tina, and Associates. *The Teaching for Understanding Guide.* San Francisco: Jossey-Bass, 1999.

Browne, Janet. *Voyaging.* New Jersey: Princeton University Press, 1995.

Burmark, Lynell. *Visual Literacy: Learn to See; See to Learn.* Alexandria: ASCD Press, 2002.

Campbell, Bruce, and Linda Campbell. *Multiple Intelligences and Student Achievement: Success Stories from Six Schools.* Alexandria: ASCD Press, 1999.

Cecil, Nancy, and Lauritzen, Phyllis. *Literacy and the Arts for the Integrated Classroom.* New York: Longman Press, 1994.

Collins, Jim. *Good to Great and the Social Sectors: A Monograph to Accompany Good to Great.* New York: Collins Business, 2006.

Csikszentmihalyi, Mihaly. *Flow: The Psychology of Optimal Experience.* New York: Harper & Row, 1990.

Dweck, Carol S. *Mindset: The New Psychology of Success.* New York: Random House, 2006.

Eisner, Elliot W. "Preparing for Today and Tomorrow." *Educational Leadership* 61, no. 4 (Dec. 2003–Jan. 2004): 6–10.

Fallows, James. *More Like Us.* Boston: Houghton Mifflin, 1990.

Fishman, Ted C. *China, Inc.: How the Rise of the Next Superpower Challenges America and the World.* New York: Scribner, 2005.

Florida, Richard. *The Rise of the Creative Class . . . and How It's Transforming Work, Leisure, Community, and Everyday Life.* New York: Basic Books, 2002.

Friedman, Thomas L. *The World Is Flat: A Brief History of the Twenty-First Century.* New York: Farrar, Straus & Giroux, 2005.

———. *Hot, Flat, and Crowded.* New York: Farrar, Straus & Giroux, 2008.

Gardner, Howard. *Frames of Mind.* New York: Basic Books, 1983.

———. *The Unschooled Mind.* New York: Basic Books, 1992.

———. *Creating Minds.* New York: Basic Books, 1993.

———. *Multiple Intelligences: The Theory in Practice.* New York: Basic Books, 1993.

———. *Leading Minds: Anatomy of Leadership.* New York: Basic Books, 1995.

———. *The Disciplined Mind: What All Students Should Understand.* New York: Simon & Schuster, 1999.

———. *Five Minds for the Future.* Boston: Harvard Business School Publishing, 2006.

Glock, Jenna, Wertz, Susan, and Meyer, Maggie. *Discovering the Naturalist Intelligence: Science in the Schoolyard.* Tucson: Zephyr Press, 1999.

Goleman, Daniel. *Emotional Intelligence: Why It Can Matter More Than IQ.* New York: Bantam Books, 1995.

———. *Social Intelligence: The New Science of Human Relationships.* New York: Bantam Books, 2006.

Griss, Susan. *Minds in Motion: A Kinesthetic Approach to Teaching Elementary Curriculum.* Portsmouth, NH: Heinemann, 1998.

Hoerr, Thomas R. *Becoming a Multiple Intelligences School.* Alexandria: ASCD Press, 2000.

———. *The Art of School Leadership.* Alexandria: Association for Supervision and Curriculum Development, 2005.

———. "The New City School Experience." In *Multiple Intelligences Theory Around the World,* edited by Jie-Qi Chen, Seana Moran, and Howard Gardner. San Francisco: Jossey-Bass, 2009.

Hyerle, David. *A Field Guide to Using Visual Tools.* Alexandria: ASCD Press, 2000.

Jensen, Eric. *Different Brains, Different Learners.* San Diego: The Brain Store, 2000.

———. *Music with the Brain in Mind.* San Diego: The Brain Store, 2000.

Krechevsky, M., Gardner, Howard, and Hoerr, Thomas R. "Complimentary Energies: Implementing MI Theory from the Lab and from the Field." A paper prepared for J. Oakes and K. H. Quarts (Eds.), Creating New Educational Communities: Schools and Classrooms Where All Children Are Smart. *National Society for the Study of Education Handbook,* 1994.

Kunstler, John Howard. *The Long Emergency: Surviving the Converging Catastrophes of the Twenty-First Century.* New York: Atlantic Monthly Press, 2005.

Levine, Mel. *A Mind at a Time.* New York: Simon & Schuster, 2002.

New City School. *Celebrating Multiple Intelligences.* St. Louis, MO: New City School, 1994.

———. *Succeeding with Multiple Intelligences.* St. Louis, MO: New City School, 1996.

Nisbett, Richard. *Intelligence and How to Get It.* New York: Norton, 2009.

O'Toole, James. *Leading Change: The Argument for Values-Based Leadership.* San Francisco: Jossey-Bass, 1995.

Pink, Daniel. *A Whole New Mind: Moving from the Information Age to the Conceptual Age.* New York: Riverhead Books, 2005.

Silverman, L. K. (2003, winter). "The Visual-Spatial Learner: An Introduction." *Soundview School Dolphin News*, pp. 6–7.

Sternberg, Robert. *Beyond IQ: The Triarchic Theory of Human Intelligence.* New York: Cambridge University Press, 1985.

Thomson, Barbara. *Words Can Hurt You.* New Jersey: Addison-Wesley, 1993.

Wagner, Tony. *The Global Achievement Gap: Why Even Our Best Schools Don't Teach the New Survival Skills Our Children Need—and What We Can Do About It.* New York: Basic Books, 2008.

Wiggins, Grant, and McTighe, Jay. *Understanding by Design.* Alexandria: ASCD Press, 1998.

About the Authors

BETSY BLANKENSHIP

has a B.S. in Education from the University of Missouri, Columbia, and an M.A. in early childhood education from Southern Illinois University, Edwardsville. She has been an educator for thirty-nine years, thirty-three of those at New City. "MI is just good teaching! It is the recognition that not all kids learn in the same way. We know they bring different strengths, talents, intelligences to the table. This theory gives a framework for using those strengths to help students succeed." Betsy taught kindergarten and is now the assistant head for admissions.

LISA BLUE

is a fourteen-year teaching veteran, with six of those years at New City School and currently teaches third grade. She earned her B.A. from Stillman College, and she feels that the single most important aspect of MI has been how it has continually stretched her learning and that of her students.

SALLY BOGGEMAN

says, "Using MI makes me think outside the box when planning. Students are actively learning as they use their strengths and strengthen their weaker areas. And I can differentiate instruction to the benefit of all." Sally is a veteran teacher of thirty-five years, twenty-five of them at New City. Her B.A. is from Hiram College and her M.A. from Maryville University. She teaches first grade and was one of the co-editors of our faculty's two other MI books.

SUSIE BURGE

has been a teacher for twenty years, nineteen of them at New City; she began as a science teacher and now teaches fifth grade. She has a B.A. in biology and her teacher certification from the University of Missouri, St. Louis. She says, "The single most important aspect of MI for me as a

teacher is to realize that we have a tendency to teach to our strengths. Students with different MI strengths would struggle in my classroom unless I stretch myself to include many opportunities for them to process information and demonstrate understanding using intelligences that are *not* my personal strengths."

SHANNAH BURTON

believes that "MI invites pathways of learning and discovery for every child." Shannon is completing her first year of teaching art—the Spatial Intelligence—at New City. She holds a B.S. in art education from Southern Illinois University in Edwardsville.

CARLA CARROL

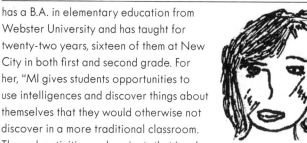

has a B.A. in elementary education from Webster University and has taught for twenty-two years, sixteen of them at New City in both first and second grade. For her, "MI gives students opportunities to use intelligences and discover things about themselves that they would otherwise not discover in a more traditional classroom. Through activities and projects that involve MI, students stretch their understanding of themselves and others. Plus, it makes learning fun!"

LINDA CHURCHWELL-VARGA

says, "MI encourages and fosters children's abilities to be their best selves, to see their strengths and areas of less competence. Searching for ways to reach students through MI allows for students to lead the process and for me to continually grow as a teacher in that search." She has taught for nineteen years and has been a fifth or sixth grade teacher at New City for ten of those years. She earned her B.A. in history from Spellman College and her M.A.T. from Wayne State University.

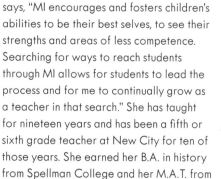

KRISTI CLONINGER

has been a preprimary teacher for seven years, five of those at New City. She has a B.S. in early childhood education from the University of Missouri, St. Louis. She says, "I have found that my focus on MI, and more specifically, the awareness and appreciation of the differences in students in my classroom has helped me know and understand my students better. It has also helped my students know and understand themselves better."

MARY CULLMAN

says, "As a pre-primary teacher, I find that the most important aspect of MI is the fun and excitement we have while learning." She has been teaching for twenty-five years, six of them at New City with our three and four year old students. She has a B.A. in psychology and elementary education from Saint Louis University.

JOE CORBETT

our librarian, has been teaching for twenty-one years, nineteen of those at New City (he previously taught second grade with us). He has a B.A. in history and political science from Webster University, an M.A.T. from Webster University, and a master's in library science from the University of Missouri, Columbia. He says, "The single most important aspect of MI is that it appreciates the strengths and talents of each individual child and allows him or her to shine in certain arenas, while stretching and learning in others. It is a form of diversity that is often overlooked and/or underappreciated."

MARY DALY

has been in education for twenty-three years and has spent twenty-two of them at New City School, where she taught kindergarten and is now the assistant head for student and family support. She has a B.A. in early childhood education from Fontbonne University. She says that MI "puts a value on all aspects of a child's development. They don't have to excel in only one or two traditional ways."

MELISSA DOLL

has been teaching for seventeen years, three at New City in the third grade. She earned her B.S. in elementary education and her M.A. in educational counseling from the University of Missouri, St. Louis. She believes the most important aspect of MI is that "it proves everyone has talents, abilities, and weaknesses; they are just in different areas. It is what makes the world go round!"

ERIC ESKELSEN

says, "MI makes learning more meaningful and fun." Eric is a thirteen-year teaching veteran, ten of those at New City, where he has been our science teacher. Eric has a B.A. from the University of Northern Iowa and an M.A.T. in science education from Webster University.

LAURIE FALK

has thirty-one years of experience in counseling, four at New City. She has her B.A. from Loyola University in Chicago and her M.S.W. from Washington University in St. Louis. For Laurie the most important aspect of MI is "the acknowledgement that both Interpersonal and Intrapersonal intelligences play a significant role in the education of the whole child."

MONETTE GOOCH-SMITH

says, "The most important aspect of MI is that it facilitates diversity—diversity of thought and style." Monette has been teaching for twenty-eight years, twenty-seven of them at New City, where she has taught preprimary and now teaches kindergarten. She has her A.A.S. from St. Louis Community College, her B.A. from Fontbonne University, and her master's in early childhood special education from the University of Southern Illinois, Edwardsville.

JOYCE GRAY

has been teaching preprimary for nineteen years, eighteen at New City, and has her B.A. in early childhood education from the University of Missouri, St. Louis. The most important aspect of MI to Joyce is "that it allows for teachers to differentiate in order to meet individual student needs."

EILEEN GRIFFITHS

says the importance of MI is the "ability to build a child's confidence by valuing an MI area of strength that might not be a traditionally recognized subject. It is also important to use the areas of strength to help develop another area of MI." Eileen has been a kindergarten and preprimary teacher for thirty years, twenty-four at New City. She earned her B.A. from Wilmington College and her M.A.T. from Webster University.

BEN GRIFFITHS

says, "MI addresses diversity within a group of learners; it is the answer for all those who wonder why they just didn't 'get it' when they were in school. When any given curriculum ignores the fact that we are not all mathematicians and linguists alone, an injustice has been done. With MI, there's a way in for every kid; every student can be successful." Ben has been at New City for all eight years of his teaching career, and he has a B.A. in elementary education from Maryville University. He began as a fourth grade teacher and is now our Performing Arts teacher (focusing on music, movement, drama).

THOMAS R. HOERR, PH.D.

says, "MI gives every child a way to learn and a chance to shine. It is also a great tool to help teachers succeed!" Tom has been an educator for forty-one years, eight years as a teacher, two as a research intern, three as a principal in University City, MO, and twenty-eight years as the head of New City School. His B.A. is from Harris Teachers College, his M.Ed. is from the University of Missouri, St. Louis, and his Ph.D. is from Washington University. Tom is also the author of *Becoming a Multiple Intelligences School* (ASCD Press, 2000), *The Art of School Leadership* (ASCD Press, 2005), and *School Leadership for the Future* (NAIS Press, 2009).

HEIDI KEHLE

believes that "by using MI in the classroom, all children feel valued as learners and as teachers." Heidi has been teaching for eighteen years, thirteen at New City. She has taught in many grades at New City

and is presently a preprimary teacher. She holds a B.A. in German language and literature from Lakeland College.

CHANAYA JACOBS

says, "For me as a teacher the single most important aspect of MI is giving children the chance to learn in different ways and find their own strengths and weaknesses." Chanaya is a sixteen-year teaching veteran, with twelve years of experience in the sixth grade at New City. She holds a B.A. in elementary education and an M.A. in educational administration from the University of Missouri, St. Louis.

LYNN JAMBORETZ

has twenty-two years of teaching experience, including five at New City School. She holds a B.A. from Missouri State University.

JENNIFER KASLOW

has been in education for ten years, two of those at New City. She has her undergraduate degree from the University of Colorado and her M.A.T. from Webster University. For Jen, the most important aspect of MI is that "it recognizes differences in learning styles and allows learners to capitalize on their natural strengths."

LEAH JOHNSON KUMAR

has taught for four years, one in the first grade at New City. Her B.A., as well as her M.A. in Education, are from Seattle University. She believes the personal intelligences—both Inter and Intra—are integral to student success.

KATIE LAMANTIA

says, "MI allows me to teach in a variety of ways while students are learning in a variety of ways." Katie has been teaching for seven years, five as the computer teacher at New City, and has her B.A. in elementary education from the University of Missouri, St. Louis.

HALLIE LINDEMANN

says, "The single most important aspect of MI for me as a teacher is that MI recognizes the fact that not everyone is book smart and that some people do better in nontraditional learning settings." Hallie has been in education for twelve years and has finished her first year at New City School, teaching fifth grade. Her B.S. is from Cornell College.

CARLA MASH-DUNCAN

believes "The Personal intelligences, Intra and Inter, are the most important aspect of MI. Reflection is needed for growth, and working together promotes problem solving, which is key." An educator for thirty-two years, with twenty-four at New City in the fourth grade, Carla has her B.S. in elementary education from Eastern Illinois University, and an M.A. in educational processes from Maryville University.

LAUREN McKENNA

says, "MI is a tool that allows me to present a lesson in many different ways and then build extensions of that lesson that can branch off in many different MI directions." Lauren has her B.A. in physical education from the University of Missouri, St. Louis, and has been teaching PE/B-K for twenty-eight years, twenty of those at New City.

SUSAN MATTHEWS

has spent her whole twenty-one-year teaching career as a kindergarten teacher at New City School. She has a B.A. in history from Indiana University and an M.A. in education from Maryville University. "MI has helped me look at my children in different ways, and to be able to meet their needs as learners. It has definitely helped me grow as a teacher!"

JESSICA BROD-MILLNER

has been teaching for eleven years, eight of them at New City. She has her B.A. in history, her teacher certification from the University of Colorado, and an M.A. in elementary education from Webster University. She began at New City as a fifth grade teacher and has been serving as our MI library coordinator.

PATRICE MURPHY

has been in education thirty-four years, ten of them at New City. She has a B.A. in psychology from Wheaton College and an M.A. in special education from the University of Connecticut. "The best thing about MI is it lets me be as creative (and crazy) as I want, and it is all for the good of the kids."

CHARLOTTE NAGY

has been teaching for fourteen years, three at New City in the fourth grade. She has her B.A. and M.A. from Loyola University in Chicago. To Charlotte the most important aspect of MI is that "it is fun! Using MI allows every child to successfully connect with a content area and what is being taught."

SHERNINA NICHOLS

says, "The most important aspect of MI for me is being able to reach each student where their strengths are, while challenging them to explore and develop in other areas." Nina has been teaching Spanish for seven years, four at New City, and has her B.A. in Spanish and marketing from Washington University in St. Louis.

M. PATRICIA NUERNBERGER, PH.D.

has been a teacher and administrator for thirty-seven years, thirteen at New City School, where she is the assistant head for academics. Pat has a B.S. in education from the University of Missouri, an M.Ed. in reading and learning disabilities from the University of Missouri, St. Louis, and a Ph.D. from Saint Louis University. "MI's greatest strength is its ability to allow *all* students to feel smart and to have their strengths equally valued."

JOY POOLE

has been teaching for thirty-two years and has taught in kindergarten at New City for seven of them. She has a B.A. from Spring Arbor University and an M.A. from Western Michigan University. She believes "identifying my own strengths as well as those of the children" is a crucial component of MI.

DEANN POMATTO

has spent five of her sixteen years of teaching in the first grade at New City. She has earned a B.A. from Knox College and believes the most important aspect of MI is that "children learn to appreciate and admire one another's strengths. Every child is recognized as unique."

CLAIRE REINBOLD

has been teaching for eight years, all of them in grades two and six at New City, and has a B.A. in elementary education from Saint Louis University. "MI allows me to see a side of my students that I could miss—often this missing piece is what connects you to a student, shows you an area where they shine, or just allows you to get to know something you wouldn't necessarily learn in a more traditional environment. It also pushes my own teaching so I can grow and learn with the kids."

SHERYL REARDON

believes the most important aspect of MI is the incorporation of music into daily life and learning. Sheryl has twelve years of teaching experience, ten at New City in the second grade. Her B.A. is from Saint Louis University, and her M.A. is from Fontbonne University. Sheryl is also our diversity coordinator.

TOMMI ROGERS

says, "Teaching with MI allows me to see a child's strengths, and when I see that I can only hope to expand on those strengths." Tommi has her associate's degree in early childhood education from St. Louis Community College. She has been teaching for twenty years, half of them at New City as our preprimary movement teacher.

MEGAN SANDERS

says, "MI makes the curriculum come alive for kids!" Megan has her B.A. in elementary education from the University of Missouri, St. Louis, and has five years in the teaching field, three as a second grade teacher at New City.

ANNE SIMMONS

is a first-year fourth grade teacher at New City, with a B.A. in educational studies as well as art history and archeology, both from Washington University in Saint Louis. Her M.Ed. is from the teacher training course at Shady Hill School (M.A.) in cooperation with Lesley University. She says, "I feel that multiple intelligence theory, when used as a tool, helps students access information in meaningful ways. By celebrating students' strengths and challenging their assumptions about themselves and their abilities, MI makes learning accessible and pushes students beyond their notions of what is possible."

JULIE STEVENS

is a veteran teacher with forty-four years of experience, twenty-two years at New City in the third grade. She has a B.A. in English literature from New Rochelle College and an M.A. in educational administration from Illinois State University. "The most important aspect of MI is the recognition of the differences of kids and how it serves to broaden their education."

ELIZABETH TOMASOVIC GAYDOS

"MI is proof that everyone can learn! MI is integral in education because, by connecting intelligences, it allows an area of weakness to be reached and mastered through an area of strength," says Liz who is our Substitute Coordinator. She is completing her first year of teaching at New City and has her B.A. in Elementary Education from Fontbonne University.

JACKLYN VOELKL

has been teaching for nine years, eight at New City in kindergarten and grade four. She has a B.A. in elementary education from Saint Louis University. For Jackie, the single most important aspect of MI "is that it allows each child to develop confidence in their unique abilities and talents. They are given the opportunity to push boundaries and express themselves creatively without the limitations and structure of a more traditional school model."

CHRISTINE WALLACH

says, "Helping children develop the habits of mind related to the personal intelligences is very important to me because they help children find success in life no matter how one defines success." Chris has been a teacher for thirty-three years, fourteen at New City School where she has taught fifth and first grades. She has a B.S. in secondary education and French from Southeast Missouri State University and an M.A. in curriculum and instruction from Southern Illinois University, Edwardsville. She was one of the co-editors of our faculty's two other MI books.

DENISE WILLIS

says, "The most important aspect of MI for me as a teacher is that it provides every child with the opportunity to excel in one or more areas, while providing a way to approach areas that may be more difficult." Denise has been teaching for twenty-six years, fifteen as a fourth and fifth grade teacher at New City. She has a B.S. in education from Shenandoah University, and an M.A. in educational processes from Maryville University.

The New City School

Because this is a book written by the faculty of the New City School, much of what we say is from and about the New City School. Thus it seems appropriate to offer readers some essential information about our school. Our mission statement captures both what we are and what we hope to become.

New City School Mission Statement

New City School prepares children age three through grade six to become joyful learners, to succeed academically, and to be confident and knowledgeable about themselves and others. As an international leader in elementary education, New City School offers outstanding academics, a nurturing ambience and a unique tradition of diversity. New City School students are insightful leaders and creative problem solvers who thrive in an ever-changing world.

The New City School is an independent school located in the City of St. Louis. We enroll 350 to 360 students, from preprimary through the sixth grade. Our school was founded in 1969 by neighbors who came together to create an urban school that focused on experiential learning and diversity. Our school has grown and evolved in its forty-year history, but those founding principles remain. In the 2009–2010 school year, for example, one-third of our students were students of color and over one-third of our students receive need-based financial aid. We also enrolled students from over fifty zip codes (but provided no transportation). Today "joyful learning" is referenced in our mission statement, and MI helps make that possible. Being an independent school offers some advantages: our pupil-teacher ratio is low, and we are able to create our own curriculum. The biggest advantage we have is that our school is framed around a mission. This allows us to focus our efforts and helps us be true to our values. Because we are an independent school, we must work diligently to attract and retain families who select us from among a myriad of options.

We began our pursuit of MI in 1988. Tom Hoerr read *Frames of Mind* and felt that it supported three educational beliefs embraced by our school: all children have strengths, the arts are important, and who you are is more important than what you know. Hoerr was confident that MI could be a powerful tool for reaching students, so he invited the faculty to join him in reading it as a summer book group. One-third of our teachers and administrators did so, and the group met every few weeks to discuss an intelligence and to talk about what implications this might have for our school. Learning experientially, we used each of the intelligences as we learned about them. We formed a faculty Talent Committee when school resumed in September. This group continued to talk about MI and look more specifically at what we should do with curriculum, pedagogy, and assessment to capitalize on and develop all of our students' intelligences.

Twenty years later, we are proud to consider ourselves an MI school. That doesn't mean that MI is found in every lesson; that's neither practical nor desirable. It does mean, though, that teachers consistently look for ways to weave MI into their lessons, that we give students ways to use MI in learning, and that MI plays an important role in assessment. In addition, MI has played a wonderfully powerful role in facilitating faculty collegiality, and it has been helpful with parent communication efforts. We believe that in an MI school, everyone must be familiar with MI and understand how it can be an important tool in learning.

We have hosted MI conferences, written MI books, and welcomed thousands of educators who come to see us to learn about how we use MI. But New City School is still a work in progress. We continue to work at finding the right balance between MI use and allocating time for traditional academic skills. We struggle with finding enough time to do all of the things that we want to do. And we continually work to educate parents, current and prospective, about the virtues of using MI. It has been a wonderful journey, and we look forward to the next steps!

More information, including a weekly parent letter from Tom Hoerr, our head of school, can be found at www.newcityschool.org. *(Tom Hoerr also facilitates the ASCD MI Newsletter, and readers who wish to be added to that subscription list can email him directly at* trhoerr@newcityschool.org.*)*

Index

plan, 120–121; and Living Museum lesson plan, 96–97; and Masai Jewelry lesson plan, 19–20; and Mathematical Masterpieces lesson plan, 150–153; and Mystery Photos lesson plan, 243–244; and Native American Storyteller Dolls lesson plan, 212–213; and Parts of a Letter lesson plan, 119; and Poetry in Sounds lesson plan, 183; and Prepositional Charades lesson plan, 90–91; and Rainforest Simulation lesson plan, 21–26; and Restaurant Project lesson plan, 160–161; and Self-Portrait lesson plan, 210–211; and Shadow Puppets lesson plan, 214–215; and Shrink Me lesson plan, 209; and Similes for Me lesson plan, 61–64; and Speed Demons lesson plan, 156–157; and Sun Shines Over Me lesson plan, 245–246; and Unfairness on Purpose lesson plan, 29–30; and Un-Natural Hike lesson plan, 240; and What I Believe lesson plan, 59–60

Interpersonal activities: to support Bodily-Kinesthetic Intelligence, 99; to support Intrapersonal Intelligence, 65; to support Linguistic Intelligence, 126; to support Logical-Mathematical Intelligence, 126; to support Musical Intelligence, 189; to support Naturalist Intelligence, 247; to support Spatial Intelligence, 218

Interpersonal Intelligence: activities to support, 31; children's resources for (books and recordings), 36–38; children's resources for (games), 38; Getting to Know You lesson plan for, 18; Gold Rush Inventions lesson plan for, 27–28; group assessment for, 34; group work self-assessment for, 35; House We Built lesson plan for, 15; identifying, in students, 32–33; Making Museums lesson plan for, 16–17; Masai Jewelry lesson plan for, 19–20; overview of, 9–11; Picture This! lesson plan for, 12–14; self-assessment for, 35; teachers' resources for, 39; Unfairness on Purpose lesson plan for, 29–30; web of, 8

Intrapersonal activities: to support Bodily-Kinesthetic Intelligence, 99; to support Interpersonal Intelligence, 31; to support Linguistic Intelligence, 126; to support Logical-Mathematical Intelligence, 162; to support Musical Intelligence, 189; to support Naturalist Intelligence, 247; to support Spatial Intelligence, 218

Intrapersonal intelligence: acting as result of, 45; activities to support, 65; assessment of, 67; Autobiography (My Story) lesson plan for, 55–56; children's resources for (books and recordings), 68–71; children's resources for (games), 71; Content of Their Character lesson plan for, 51–52; Goal Setting lesson plan for, 53–54; I Am lesson plan for, 50; identifying, in students, 66; improving, in classroom, 45–47; as key to success, 42–43; Letter to Myself lesson plan for, 57–58; and new way of looking at success, 44; Similes for Me lesson plan for, 61–64; teachers' resources for (games), 72–73; web of, 42; What I Believe lesson plan for, 59–60

J

James, L., 76
Jenga (game), 201
Job Sheet, 283–284
Johnny Jenkins (song), 301

K

Kahlo, F., 198
Katie's Picture Show (Mayhew), 16
Keats, J., 113
Keepers of the Earth (Bruchac and Caduto), 212
Kerwin, K., 107
Key Learning Community, xiii
Key School (Indianapolis, Indiana), xiii, 3
Kindergarten classroom, 281–284
King, M. L., Jr., 51, 106, 186, 264
King Bidgood's in the Bathtub (Wood and Wood), 83
Klee, P., 210
Kranowitz, C. S., 86
Krechevsky, M., 288
Krementz, J., 93, 94
Kriete, R., 86

L

Language Arts learning area: and Autobiography (My Story) lesson plan, 55–56; and Closer Look at Trees lesson plan, 236–237; and Everybody's Moving lesson plan, 81–82; and Express Yourself lesson plan, 83–84; and Extra, Extra, Read All about It lesson plan, 122–123; and Get It Done! lesson plan, 241–242; and Getting to Know You lesson plan, 18; and I Am lesson plan, 50; and Letter to Myself lesson plan, 56–57; and Literary Soundtrack lesson plan for, 184–185; and Literature Responses lesson plan, 124–125; and Poetry in Sounds lesson plan, 183; and Poetry lesson plan, 113–114; and Prepositional Charades lesson plan, 90–91; and Similes for Me lesson plan, 61–64; and Word Work lesson plan, 111–112

Learning Centers: in kindergarten classroom, 281–284; record keeping and reflection in, 283–284; and shared reading, 299; using, to address MI, 282–283

LEGOs, 65

Letter to Myself lesson plan, 57–58

Lewis, M., 226

Lindbergh, A. M., 41

Linguistic activities, 31; to support Bodily-Kinesthetic Intelligence, 99; to support Interpersonal Intelligence, 31; to support Intrapersonal Intelligence, 65; to support Logical-Mathematical Intelligence, 162; to support Musical Intelligence, 189; to support Naturalist Intelligence, 247; to support Spatial Intelligence, 218

Linguistic Intelligence: activities that support, 126; and Book reports the MI way, 117–118; children's resources for (books and recordings), 130–133; children's resources for (essay), 133; children's resources for (games), 133–134; children's